The Balancing Act

MW01277599

Enjoy Dubai &
the story of
Dubai Women's College

Mary Glen Sandelli

The Balancing Act

International Higher Education in the 21st Century

Foreword by Jennifer Rowsell

Mary Gene Saudelli
University of Calgary in Qatar

SENSE PUBLISHERS
ROTTERDAM / BOSTON / TAIPEI

A C.I.P. record for this book is available from the Library of Congress.

ISBN 978-94-6300-014-7 (paperback)
ISBN 978-94-6300-015-4 (hardback)
ISBN 978-94-6300-016-1 (e-book)

Published by: Sense Publishers,
P.O. Box 21858,
3001 AW Rotterdam,
The Netherlands
https://www.sensepublishers.com/

Printed on acid-free paper

This book is dedicated to my wonderful husband, Rob Saudelli.
You mean everything to me.

This book is also dedicated to my stepchildren,
Eric and Erin Saudelli.

TABLE OF CONTENTS

FOREWORD

A Place to Call Home

Reading Mary Gene Saudelli's book made me think deeply about the concept of home and what home means. That is, home is at once a simple and complicated idea. Simple, in that home should be a place of belonging and comfort; it is a visceral feeling. Complicated in that home is also varied, idiosyncratic and a composite of larger ideologies that have to do with language, religion, culture, race, and social class. In *The Balancing Act: International Higher Education in the 21st Century*, Saudelli depicts a world where home is paradoxically hybrid and inclusive. With candour and thoughtfulness, Saudelli gives readers an entangled sense of home and how home changes when people move across different landscapes to settle, at least for a while, in a new place.

In the book, the notion of home is informed by the stories of nineteen international educators who work in higher education in the Middle East. Home is Dubai with all of its cosmopolitan and transcultural associations. Home is Dubai Women's College as a gender-segregated university with its own culture. Home is Islam as a religion, but also as a way of life. Home signals the original nationality of each international educator from contexts that range from Japan, North Korea, Tunisia, and Canada, just to name a few. Home is seen in the lives of Islamic female students attending the college. Finally, home can be seen in a 21st century way, in virtual homes that we create within social media to exist globally in local worlds. As a reader, I reflected again and again on how rich it is to move to very different realities and to pick up and put on varied parts of self the sum of which is a place that we call home.

There are multiple interpretations of home across Saudelli's rich research from Izzy's unmoored sense of 'homeland' to Kelsey's desire for multiple 'homes' and for homelessness to Taylor's eschewing of home for the sake of his wanderlust. In chapter four alone, there are 70 references to home and the complex relationships that participants feel in relation to home. Of particular note, Saudelli's international educators frequently think about what it is like 'back home.' At times, for many of the participants, 'back home' seemed like less of a home as years went by. What came out strongly for me in reading about individuals like Morgan, Shane or Ellis is how they approached their new home with acceptance, without judgement, and how they adapted to new practices, rites and habits of mind. Having spent years living and working in a variety of places, the participants' optics on home were as I said earlier, entangled with histories, cultures, epistemologies, and of course lived experiences.

A host of theorists came to mind as I contemplated Saudelli's conceptual strands such as Dorothy Holland (Holland et al., 1998) and the idea of figured worlds or 'as if' realms that we create to put on certain kinds of identities. As well, I found myself thinking about the work of Alessandro Duranti and Elinor Ochs (1996) and their writings on Samoan American families and their use of syncretic literacies as 'an intermingling or merging of culturally diverse traditions that informs and organizes literacy activities' (Duranti & Ochs, 1996, p. 2). Reading about Saudelli's international educators recalls the work of Brian Street (1984) and his extensive field work in Iran when he forged the notions of autonomous and ideological models of literacy. Street showed how literacy is shaped by local practices and belief systems and not by top-down versions of what literacy is or should be within specific, non-Western contexts. Indeed, Saudelli offers a similar picture of educators who shape their teaching around the religion, practices and beliefs of students attending Dubai Women's College. Theoretically, I am even reminded of the work of Henry Jenkins (2006) and his writings on the convergence culture in that Saudelli's international educators' lives converge in their teaching and pedagogy and this is a key piece in the efficacy of their higher education work. The international educators in Saudelli's book unify their entangled selves into teaching methods that adapt to the very particular needs of the student body at Dubai Women's College.

With the ubiquity of social media and the web, being a local who exists globally is relatively easy nowadays. However, to my mind, what is much less easy is living globally while maintaining and respecting local roots. When I think about the stories and reflections of Saudelli and her nineteen higher education professionals, I marvel at the ways that they listen to the nuances of culture, language, and class stratification and quietly reshape their pedagogies and principles in respectful, even gentle ways. To conclude the foreword, I offer a quote from the T. S. Eliot poem *Four Quartets*, "Home is where you start from" and to me this refrain certainly connects with Saudelli's underlying message in the book about teaching from a listening, respectful pedagogy.

Jennifer Rowsell
Brock University

REFERENCES

Duranti, A., & Ochs, E. (1996). *Syncretic literacy: Multiculturalism in Samoan American families.* Santa Cruz, CA: National Center for Research on Cultural Diversity and Second Language Learning.
Eliot, T. S. (1943). *Four quartets.* New York: Harcourt.
Holland, D., Lachiocotte, W., Skinner, D., & Cain, C. (1998). *Identity and agency in cultural worlds.* Cambridge, MA: Harvard University Press.
Jenkins, H. (2006). *Convergence culture: Where old and new media collide.* New York: New York University Press.
Street, B. (1984). *Literacy in theory and practice.* Cambridge: Cambridge University Press.

MODULE 1

EXPLORING THE CONTEXT AND THE THEORIES

SETTING THE STAGE

Introducing Dubai Women's College and the United Arab Emirates

Future generations will be living in a world that is very different from that to which we are accustomed. It is essential that we prepare ourselves and our children for that new world. (HRH Sheikh Zayed, 2005, cited in 2007)

We will strive to develop in our students the values, the qualities, and capacities to be leaders in their communities" (HRH Sheikh Nahayan Mabarak Al Nahayan, 2007)

INTRODUCTION

Consider the following scenario: I am a Canadian, postsecondary educator who walks into my classroom at Dubai Women's College (DWC), in Dubai, United Arab Emirates (UAE) enthusiastic to teach academic English to first-year, gender-segregated, Muslim, female Business and Information Technology students. I encounter a cluster of women, covered from head to toe in long, elegant, black robes (*abbayahs)* and beautiful, black scarves (*shaylahs*), which not only cover the hair but for some also veil the entire face from sight. Observation and consideration of each other is reciprocal: As much as I am engaged in an appraisal of them, they too are engaged in an appraisal of me. I imagine they wonder: What kind of "Western" woman am I? As I gazed at the figures cloaked in black, I thought about the curriculum I was about to implement, the team of international educators with whom these learners were about to interact on a daily basis, and the interesting interplay of culture, curriculum, and constructivism that would be part of our lives for the next year as students and educators in the Higher Diploma Year One (HD1) of the Business and Information Technology (IT) program at DWC.

Interestingly, in this age of globalization and mass flow of human movement, from my experience with people in Canada and overseas, knowledge is somewhat limited of people in other lands, especially the Middle East, except for information extrapolated from various media sources or brief tourist visits. I make this observation about interactions occurring in my Canadian homeland about "over there in the Middle East," and also in relation to my role as an international educator and researcher, in various countries throughout the world.

Particularly relevant is this lack of understanding about the Middle East, which is a complex location that seems mired with mystique, misinformation, and misunderstanding. This location often conjures a multitude of visions that may or may not have a basis in reality for a context as diverse and dynamic as the Middle

East. Further, for inhabitants of the Middle East, mention of the word "Western," a term that commonly refers to cultures and nationalities typically associated with countries such as Canada, the United States, United Kingdom, Australia, and some European countries, equally conjures a multitude of visions that may or may not have a basis in reality. Understandings about each other appear to be veiled.

This book is designed to chronicle the experiences of international educators, working, teaching and living in Dubai, United Arab Emirates. They taught or were supervisors at Dubai Women's College and designed and implemented one of the most interesting curricula I have ever seen or had the pleasure and the pain to deliver.

The student body was unique as it comprised exclusively Emirati, female students. The team of international educators was unique as its members are from all over the globe who had taught in many contexts for most of their professional careers. The curriculum was unique as it was highly attuned to who these students were and their specific needs in this fast-paced, globalizing and rapidly changing society.

My Role as an International Educator and Researcher

For 5 years, I was employed as an educator in the UAE: first in a private, tertiary institute, and from 2005-2009 at DWC. Although I am a Canadian citizen, born, bred, and educated, most of my teaching experience has transpired in international contexts, in Istanbul Turkey, Hong Kong, Afghanistan, and the UAE. After my experience in Dubai, I returned to Canada for five years at taught in a university in Ontario. Currently, I am an Assistant Professor and Director of Teaching and Learning at the University of Calgary in Doha Qatar, the Middle East.

My educational background provides a strong influence on the philosophy of education that I embrace. My educational background depicts an overwhelming interest in sociology, psychology, religious and cultural studies, and educational philosophy, particularly in relation to curricular emphases. This fascination with these disciplines provided the catalyst for my decision to experience other cultures, not as a tourist, but as a contributing member of society in an international context. Hence, I enrolled and graduated from a TESL Canada program as an English as a Subsequent Language (ESL) teacher. Years of living an international life have not quelled the fascination for me; in fact, I continue to embrace this adventure of living, learning and loving life as an educator in international contexts.

After several years, my identity evolved from being a Canadian English teacher, working overseas, to being a Canadian international educator. This evolution in identity represents a function of how my worldview has evolved due to my international experiences and through the amelioration of both Western and Eastern life circumstances. When I first went overseas, I believed I was "bringing" education in the form of English to "the other." Now, I, like many of my colleagues, see myself as an amelioration of influences from both my Western identity and as a part of an international, educational community. In essence, I have become an "other" of myself, a concept identified as Third Space Theory

(Bhabha, 1990, 1994), which occasionally results in tensions related to national affinity, cultural dissonance, and conflicting allegiances.

I have a close affiliation, a carefully maintained bridge, with my Canadian life while concurrently deeply valuing and maintaining a very different life formerly in the UAE and now in Qatar, collectivist, Islamic Arab nations where, I live, teach, and learn. Frequently, I find myself occupying a space in between two very diverse, often conflicting, polarities of ideas related to my two worlds, the "others" within my lived experiences, and the "other" I encounter in me when I experience dissonance. When I am in Canada, I often feel that I must explain or defend misunderstandings regarding my life in the Arab world, even amongst the most educated, worldly, and respectable peers, colleagues, or acquaintances. In Dubai, I felt that I must explain or defend misunderstandings regarding my Western life, again, even amongst some of the highest, most educated and respectable members of society.

Misinformation, misunderstanding, and the ease with which others are spoken of in a manner that implies fact but is actually merely biased opinion based on ignorance results in tensions that exist amongst those of us who choose to learn about and live amongst the "other," whoever that other may be. This is a tension I encounter regardless of the country where I am. However, this is also a challenge that provides intellectual stimulation, and confers a sense of responsibility to engage in research that will contribute to knowledge globally that has the potential to challenge assumptions in both of my current worlds. With time, experience, and growth, I have learned how to adjust to this space, and accommodate my worlds, as many international educators do.

My educational background, my professional international experiences, and my own philosophy of education contribute a very definable theme, a wariness of strict allegiance to extremes in thought, behaviour, depictions, theories or ideals. In fact, I reject the notion of strict allegiance to extremes or universal dogmas: Western or Eastern, religious or atheist, intelligent or dim-witted, dominant or passive, constructivist or objectivist. There are far too many variables in relation to our human condition and contextual circumstances for me to ascribe to these kinds of universal labels, particularly in relation to educational issues.

In terms of my educational philosophy, I believe that understanding the context of the educational event is crucial to any discussions of theory and practice. I attribute my success as an international educator and scholar to my willingness to learn. In my years in the Arab world, I have attempted to develop insight through reading the Holy Qur'an, the *Hadith* (reporting of the life and sayings of the Prophet Mohammed, peace be upon him), Arab folk stories, and regional, historical texts. I also participate in religious and social celebrations, such as *Ramadan, Eid al Fetr, Eid al Adha,* and *Iftar.* Ramadan requires waking before dawn for *Sahoor* (food and water) followed by *Fajr* prayer (first prayer of the day) after which complete and total abstinence from food or water is required until *Maghrib*, the fourth prayer of the day. After *Maghrib*, the fast is broken by *Iftar* (feast in gratitude to Allah). During the fast, individuals are expected to consider the plight of those less fortunate and be grateful for whatever prosperity one enjoys, no matter how humble.

My participation in these events has been beneficial in a number ways. First, I understand and appreciate the self-discipline required of learners during Ramadan. As well, I highly respect and value the message that underlies this particular religious event in addition to other religious events. My participation in the religious experience, although I am not a Muslim, has been a consciousness-raising experience regarding the beauty of Islam as a faith and a way of life. As an international educator, I believe these experiences provide social, cultural, and religious insight, which aids in honouring diversity and promotes positive cross-cultural contact. As many of my international educator colleagues have discussed, insight and contemplation regarding the nuances of culture and religion impact educational events and have an effect on the classroom dynamic the educator initiates. Further, I believe that awareness of context provides insight into curricular content and instructional methods that facilitate relevance and the meaning-making process for students.

The Context: Dubai, United Arab Emirates

Geographically, the UAE is located at the littoral of the Arabian Peninsula, commonly referred to in the West as the Persian Gulf, but usually referred to as the Arabian Gulf by society in this Gulf region. Prior to 1971, the UAE functioned as a British colonial protectorate known as the Trucial States (Al Fahim, 1995). The Trucial States consisted of seven core gulf tribal regions which were often feuding over territory and resources. Although politically they were a British protectorate, the people of the Trucial States received little support from Britain, or any other international region, to intervene politically for peace or to provide the people of the Trucial States with basic health care, education, food, or clean water (Al Fahim, 1995; Davidson, 2008). In fact, as recently as the 1960s, the Gulf region was "one of Britain's poorest and least developed protectorates" (Davidson, 2008, p. 31).

On December 2, 1971, the tribal regions of the Trucial States federated and became the seven Sheikhdoms of the UAE: Abu Dhabi, Dubai, Fujarah, Ajman, Ras al Khaimah, Sharjah, and Umm Al-Qaiwain (Al Fahim, 1995; Kazim, 2000). Complete transformation of society occurred within the next 20 years; the UAE went from existing as an impoverished Bedouin society under British control to becoming an independent country with the world's highest per capita income (Gardner, 1995). In fact, the UAE is the second-richest country in the Islamic world (Patai, 2002). Dubai is the commercial and economic centre of the UAE and, arguably, is the most developed Emirate (Davidson, 2008; Gardner, 1995; Patai, 2002). In turn, this development has led to a complete social transformation affecting every aspect of the lives of Emirati people, but particularly education for women.

Contrary to common perceptions regarding women's status and role in Islamic nations, education for women in Dubai is publicly promoted, government supported, (Salloum, 2003; UNESCO, 2003; Whiteoak, Crawford, & Mapstone, 2006) and socially desired (Al Fahim, 1995; Salloum, 2003). Today, a highly educated woman is considered to be a national symbol of social strength, prestige, and family honour (Salloum, 2003; Nashif, 2000; Whiteoak et al., 2006). However, this philosophical stance is not represented historically in the UAE, nor is it widely accepted throughout the UAE in general (Godwin, 2006; Salloum, 2003; Whiteoak et al., 2006). Rather, it is a cultural repositioning emanating from rapid transformation that has particularly affected the larger Emirates, such as Dubai.

To a degree, this social prestige afforded an educated woman is cosmetic because undercurrents of traditional thinking persist. To illustrate, young Emirati women are expected to attain higher education, but accept the norm of cultural restrictions and conform to traditional roles after graduation (Godwin, 2006). These are roles that many Emirati women are questioning as modern thought and traditional thought suddenly and forcefully collide in an andragogical extreme that they encounter. This is but one of the challenges that arose from the UAE's fast-paced social and economic transformation, inherently caused by the rapid influx of financial wealth from oil and development. This wealth rapidly transformed this society from a tribal nation to one that desires a cultural identity that maintains its Islamic religious beliefs and Emirati cultural norms within a modern framework (Gardner, 1995). All of this affects higher education for women, particularly in relation to curriculum at DWC because the HCT Learning Model (HCTAS, 2007) and DWC's curriculum explicitly encourage a participatory role for women in society and in the workforce after graduation, and include discussions of Emirati female empowerment and identity, while also acknowledging cultural expectations and restrictions on women's behaviour and activities.

For example, two curricular events for HD1 curriculum are publically open; however, entrance is restricted to Emirati learners' families, the ruling members of society, and some media. Strict rules regarding student behaviour and appearances are in place regarding the events. Every year, the president of DWC and the supervisors hold an assembly wherein behaviour rules and appearance rules are reiterated to students; for example, students are specifically reminded to ensure they wear their *abbayahs* and *shaylahs*, not be overly made up with cosmetics, wear their hair too high on their head, no "boyish" behaviour, and no music or dancing is allowed anywhere on campus.

As well, the campus is not open for students to arrive or leave at their will. In fact, our female students are barred from leaving campus at all unless they are chaperoned by a teacher, are picked up by a parent or guardian, or have special written permission granted by their legal guardian and the president of DWC. Thus, the curricular focus is on women's participation in the work force and Emirati female leadership and empowerment, while simultaneously restricting their movement due to cultural expectations and restrictions on women, which adhere as stridently as in years past and with veracity that belies challenge or change (Godwin, 2006).

Dubai Women's College, Higher Colleges of Technology

The government-funded Higher Colleges of Technology (HCT) opened in 1988. These exist as English-language medium, vocational institutions and function to prepare Emiratis for three purposes: (a) to work in technological, technical, and professional occupations (Diploma program); (b) to build skills to enter university (Higher Diploma program); or, (c) assume leadership and supervisory positions (Higher Diploma program) (HCTAS, 2007). There are 16 gender-segregated campuses in the seven Emirates, with DWC widely regarded in the UAE as a premier educational institution (Macpherson, Kachelhoffer, & El Nemr, 2007).

At its inception as a higher educational facility, HCT operated with no formal, federal, quality model of educational standards or quality assurance (Burden-Leahy, 2005). Each educational facility developed its own framework and policy regarding institutionalized standards and quality assurance, which led to significant variation throughout colleges and educational programs. In 2002, the introduction of the HCT Learning Model (HCTAS, 2002) articulated a framework for measuring student performance across the college system and incorporated International English Language Testing System (IELTS) as a graduation requirement.

The HCT Learning Model was later updated; all of the graduate outcomes articulated in the updated HCT Learning Model (HCTAS, 2007) demonstrate a profound conceptual shift from traditional orientations of education (rote learning, passive learning) toward a constructivist ideology that endorses a task-based, experiential curriculum. The updated HCT Learning Model identifies the following eight Graduate Outcomes (GOs) as essential to students' holistic development:

> Communication and information literacy (GO1); Critical and creative thinking (GO2); Global awareness and citizenship (GO3); Technological literacy (GO4); Self-management and independent learning (GO5); Teamwork and leadership (GO6); Vocational competencies (GO7); and Mathematical literacy (GO8). (HCTAS, 2007, p. 8)

Higher Diploma Year 1 (HD1) is actually most students' third year or fourth year of college at DWC. Due to the fact that most students seek entrance to higher education, but fail to meet the minimum entrance requirements (Nowais, 2004, 2005), the first 2 years are referred to as Foundations and the focus is for students to achieve passing grades on the Common English Proficiency Test (CEPA English) and CEPA Maths tests created by the National Admissions and Placement Office of the Ministry of Education, UAE. The CEPA English test is not an internationally recognized test of English proficiency, nor is it geared for academic English proficiency. It is not designed as an Arab equal to Test of English as a Foreign Language (TOEFL) or IELTS Academic. Its purpose is to determine placement of low level, Arab users of English in governmental higher educational facilities in the UAE and is a required standardized test administered during the last year of secondary schooling.

Upon successful completion of Foundations, students can enter the Higher Diploma program with their first year being HD. Upon successful completion of HD, students may proceed to HD1, the year that is the focus for this study. HD1 is comprised of an integrated approach to the four core curricular subject areas of: Business, Information Technology, Maths, and English. All instruction is exclusively taught in English.

Defining Terms

For the purposes of this body of work, given the unique context, definitions of culture, society, and religion are necessary as these aspects permeate every facet of 21st curriculum, teaching and learning in this context. The discipline of educational sociology distinguishes culture and society.

According to Hofstede (1997), culture and tradition refer to collectively learned habits, norms, values, aspects of life, and meanings attributed to these concepts that "distinguishes the members of one group or category of people from another" (p. 7). DWC is a higher-educational facility, which at the time of this study was exclusive to Emirati, female students. Any reference to culture in this study specifically refers to either aspects of life or circumstances that pertain to Emirati people, or issues and observations affecting Emirati people specifically as they are the indigenous peoples who trace their ancestry to Arab regional tribes of the former Trucial States (Kazim, 2000).

The sociological conception of society refers to a grouping of people who "occupy a particular territorial area. ... Loosely, it refers to human association or interaction" (Scott & Marshall, 2009, p. 715). Society in Dubai demographically is constructed of a multitude of people from diverse cultures, nationalities, and political affiliations, who interact on a daily basis and through many different facets of behaviours and relationships. For the purposes of this study, any reference to society refers to the multicultural, multipolitical, and multireligious peoples who reside in Dubai, including Emiraties (Davidson, 2008).

Religion is defined as "a set of beliefs, symbols, and practices which is based on the idea of the sacred, and which unites believers into a socio-religious community" (Scott & Marshall, 2009, p. 643). In this study, any reference to religion, unless otherwise specifically stated otherwise, refers to the religion of Islam, which is the religion of the UAE.

Limitations of This Book

It is important to consider limitations in any body of work and this research is no different. There are three specific limitations to this research that I acknowledge: transferability of information, limitations to data sources, and my role as researcher and educator at DWC.

This study is subject to the typical limitations inherent with case study research such as generalizations. This study was designed for the purpose of understanding the design and implementation of HD1 curriculum, in depth for this geographical context. According to Stake (2005), case study researchers "seek out both what is common and what is particular about the case, but the end product of the research regularly portrays more of the uncommon" (p. 447). Thus, the intention of this case study is not to generalize results or apply to them to another situation. The purpose is to conceptualize and illustrate a thick description of this particular educational context and during this specific moment in time, the 2008–2009 academic year.

As the context of my study was Dubai, UAE, this research is limited in terms of those with whom I could recruit as data sources. The President of DWC and my supervisor in HD1 granted me access to all textual materials related to curriculum including syllabi, assessments, lesson plans, objectives, strategic plans, and I was granted permission to recruit participation from educators and supervisors within HD1. Although students' voices would add significantly to this case study, I requested but was not granted permission to access student information or recruit participation from the HD1 student body.

A further limitation arises from my dual role in this study as both researcher and educator at DWC. The dependability of responses at the interviews was member checked through provision of transcripts to each participant for their addition, deletion, revision, clarification, and further contribution. As well, a copy of preliminary findings, which provided a basis for conclusions, was provided to participants for comments. This research study endeavoured to balance and respect the relationship of participants' roles as colleagues, and me in my role as both researcher and educator at DWC. Through member checking, we revisited and clarified interpretations drawn from patterns in the data in order to assess significance of events, instead of merely relying of isolated interpretations from me in my dual role of teacher and researcher.

Outline of the Book

This book has been organized into three modules. The first module is entitled "Exploring the Context and the Theories" and contains three chapters. Chapter 1, entitled "Setting the Stage: Introducing Dubai Women's College and the United Arab Emirates" is designed to provide the background information that a reader will need to understand the locus of the research that guided this body of work. The research that guided this book emanates from my doctoral dissertation entitled *Beyond the Veil: A Case Study of Context, Culture, Curriculum, and Constructivism at Dubai Women's College* (Lovering, 2012). This introductory chapter outlines how I came to Dubai, introduces a brief history of Dubai and the United Arab Emirates, and provides a framework for understanding the Higher Colleges of Technology and Dubai Women's College. Chapter 2, entitled "Constructivist Learning Theory and Contemporary Debates" presents an historical overview of the constructivist learning theory and includes a discussion of what is colloquially referred to as the 'Paradigm Debates.' Constructivist learning theory and experiential learning are the guiding premises for how DWC envisions teaching and learning. Chapter 3, entitled "Adult Learners and Change Theories" presents adult learning and transformative learning theories. As the UAE is a country and a society experiencing profound change, sociological and change theories contribute to the theoretical frameworks guiding this book. This module is intended to present the background and the theoretical framework to guide the later modules which disclose details related to decisions made by international educators in relation to the design and implementation of the 21st century curriculum at DWC.

The second module is entitled "Presenting the Educators, Learners and Curriculum." I believe that this particular study centred on a very unique situation. It involved a unique group of international educators, teaching to a unique group of learners, in a unique place, and a unique 21st century curriculum that was designed specifically to meet these learners where they were and take them forward to envisioning their future as they define it and on their terms. Chapter 4, "Introducing the International Educators" presents the 19 international educators that were involved in this body of work. Chapter 5, "21st Century Curriculum Design and Emirati Learners" outlines the nature of 21st century curriculum and introduces readers to the nature of Emirati learners. Chapter 6, "Making Learning Meaningful: Trans-Disciplinary 21st Century Curriculum" presents the details of the trans-disciplinary curriculum and assessment including a description of the teaching and learning tasks. Aspects of this chapter have been published in "Making it real: The role of authenticity in interdisciplinary curriculum" (Saudelli, 2014).

The third module is entitled "Delving in the Learning Context, Religion, Culture, Society, and Language." This module explores in depth the international educators experience teaching the 21st century curriculum and becoming engaged with aspects related to Islam, Emirati culture, Dubai as a rapidly changing society, and English as a global language. Chapter 7, "Encountering Islam in the Classroom" shares how the international educators understood the role of religious faith and the implications for teaching and learning. Chapter 8, "Balancing Issues and Exploring Boundaries: Emirati Culture and 21st Century Curriculum" presents the international educators' experiences with teaching for cultural relevance at DWC. Chapter 9, "Globalization on Steroids: 21st Century Curriculum and Societal Change in Dubai" shares how these educators incorporated globalization, multiculturalism, and societal change into their teaching and learning practices. Chapter 10, "English – A Global Language" presents educators' perceptions regarding the role of English as the medium of instruction, international English proficiency tests and making teaching English relevant for Arab learners. The final chapter, Chapter 11 "Capturing 21st Century Curriculum Design in Practice: What Can Be Learned from Higher Education at DWC" revisits the theories and contextualizes educational theories and practice in relation to international 21st teaching and learning at DWC. The chapter concludes with the author's final thoughts.

How to Think about and Use This Book

This book should be used as a way to think about how we approach internationalization in education. Currently, internationalization efforts form part of many universities' and colleges' strategic plans. New international branch campuses are opening throughout the world. Recruitment efforts to bring international students to a host country and educational institution are pursued and international students are taking advantage of opportunities across the globe. But, how well thought out are these internationalization efforts? How well do internationalization efforts balance the needs of learners and educational mandates? How is 21st century educational approaches integrated in these internationalization efforts? How will educational theories evolve as a result of internationalization efforts and new understandings? Do educators recognize how their teaching practices can and should change to embody consideration of 21st century knowledge and skills while recognizing the impact of religion, culture, society, and language needs in relation to contexts and changing learner demographics?

Anecdotally, from teaching in higher education in Canada and various other countries across the globe, I have personally witnessed international branch campuses close due to unrealized tensions and unrealistic expectations. I have heard conversations among faculty in Canada about international students such as: "they can't reflect," "they plagiarize," "they can't critically engage" and I often wonder how these faculty would survive and thrive if they were moved from their comfort zone to attend a learning facility in a different country, taught in a different language, with different styles of teaching, different understandings of successful achievement, and different religious, cultural and social understandings?

As you read through this book, I ask you to think about the content from your own personal lens of beliefs, philosophies, understandings, values and judgments. I ask you reflect on your own educational background and how that contributes to your personal belief systems and ways of being and knowing. Then, I ask you to try and think of how different you may be, how you might change, if you went international for an extended period of time. You will encounter many aspects in this book that may challenge your belief systems but I ask you to think about this not only from your own personal lens, but to try and embrace an international lens. How do you think you might change if you went international? What would compel change and why? What would cause tension and what would you appreciate? How would you accommodate or not?

This book is intended to explore difficult questions in this age of internationalization. How much of international education merely represents educational colonization? Are educational learning theories meant to be applicable across geographical, cultural, religious boundaries? Do we need to begin considering theory differently in this 21st century time of increasing internationalization of education? I do not presume to provide a definitive answer, but I do wish to present a detailed study that has elements of all three of these complex questions embedded within and will contribute to this important discussion.

CONCLUSION

This chapter sets the stage for the rest of this book. I began with a discussion of how I came to be interested in the field of international education and shared my background as an international educator. As it is crucial to understand the context of this body of work, I also provided information about Dubai, the United Arab Emirates, and Dubai Women's College as one campus of the Higher Colleges of Technology educational system. Subsequent to this is an outline of the modules and chapters of the rest of the book and a discussion of how this book should be read were presented. All of this sets the stage for the rest of this book. Enjoy the journey ahead.

CONSTRUCTIVIST LEARNING THEORY AND CONTEMPORARY DEBATES

INTRODUCTION

Educational theory into practice is a crucial factor to consider in the teaching and learning process. Theories of teaching and learning guide decision making processes in relation to teaching practices and, in turn, practices that embrace educational theories impact conceptualizations and re/conceptualizations of education theories. Hence, the process is cyclical. The advent of globalization of education as a contributing factor to 21st century teaching and learning has added a new area of inquiry in relation to educational theory and practice – the voices of international educators in international contexts, currently an under-explored area of knowledge. This chapter will introduce constructivist learning theory, the dominating teaching and learning theory that guided the design and implementation of 21st century curriculum at DWC. Subsequent chapters will revisit discussions of constructivist learning theory and situate the conceptions of this learning theory in practice.

Constructivist Learning Theory

Historically, the dominating classifications prominent in discussions about constructivist learning theory are: cognitive constructivist theory based on Dewey's (1934/1980) assertions and social constructivist theory based on Vygotsky's (1978, 1986) assertions. These theories have largely been discussed in relation to children's learning processes, but in the past few decades connections between constructivist learning theory and adult learning theories (Chapter 3) have gained in prominence. Generally, the essence of constructivist learning theory is that "individuals learn best when they actively construct knowledge and understanding in light of their own experiences" (Santrock, Woloshyn, Gallagher, Di Petta, & Marini, 2007, p. 282). The actual mechanisms of how construction of knowledge occurs has been debated among lines of cognition, social interaction, or a combination of both.

Cognitive Constructivist Learning Theory. Constructivist theory of learning, based on individuals' constructions of knowledge through experience, has an historical context that von Glasersfeld (1990, 1996) attributes to Jean Piaget (1952). However, earlier, James (1890) discussed learning as the acquisition of "Habits" and "Will." James believes that daily existence results in habitual activity: "All our life, so far as it has definite form, is but a mass of habits – practical, emotional, and intellectual – systematically organized for our weal or woe" (James, 1992, p. 750). James considers systemizing of habits a virtue and exhorts educators to inculcate habit as an educational ideal. Will is the student's enactment of strategies and effort expended to complete a task despite difficulty or distractions: the internal fortitude to press on. Thus, according to James, thought and action are linked through a sequence of events. An action, or habit, must first be triggered from an idea in the mind which is the catalyst for firing an activity. Thus, with "the firing of action A (the first action of a habitual activity) action B is triggered, and so forth until the entire sequence has been activated and implemented" (Fox & Riconscente, 2008, p. 377). James's discussion regarding Habit and Will provide a backdrop for Piaget's (1952) later discussion regarding children's use of schema as a framework for learning.

Piaget (1952) is considered a cognitive constructivist because he emphasized the importance of cognition in the construction of knowledge. Another influential, cognitive constructivist assertion by Piaget (1952) concerns his belief that learning proceeds via restructuring mental concepts to understand and interpret information. Schema, or the plural schemata, refers to these mental concepts or frameworks as existing "in an individual's mind to organize and interpret information" (Santrock et al., 2007, p. 41). Thus, a student's construction of knowledge involves linking new information with prior learning experiences, or schemata.

Piaget (1952) argues that two schematic processes are involved in the construction of new information: assimilation and accommodation. According to Illeris (2002), assimilation is learning by addition. Students learn when new information "is linked to a scheme or pattern already established in such a manner that it is relatively easy to recall and apply" (p. 84) when called upon to do so. Sternberg and Williams (2010) describe assimilation as a process of incorporation of new information or knowledge into existing schemas. Accommodation refers to information that is "difficult to immediately relate to any existing scheme or pattern" (Illeris, 2002, p. 84) and the learner must either adjust the new information or adjust the schemas to suit the knowledge environment (Santrock, 2007) or "create new schemas to organize the information that he or she cannot assimilate into existing schemas" (Sternberg & Williams, 2010, p. 42). During the accommodation process, also known as "transcendent learning" (Illeris, 2002, p. 84) construction of new knowledge occurs. The educator's role is to provide a forum and the opportunity for individuals to discover knowledge. Both learning processes clearly incorporate the concept of individuals' active construction of knowledge through their previous and existing experiences as the mechanism for learning acquisition. But, what is the nature of experiences and how can educators in the 21st century use experience pedagogically?

Experiential Learning. Prominent educational philosopher John Dewey (1934/1980) contends that knowledge and learning, by their very nature, are experiential. Knowledge gleaned through every day experience provides the basis through which to understand new knowledge and new learning. Dewey (1938/1997) critiques the polarity in philosophy in education: traditionalists who emphasize curricular content over content and process, and progressivists who endorse freedom in education as the oppositional response to traditionalists. Dewey's opposition to this polarity is well before its time and certainly has credence today. According to Neill (2003a, 2003b) and Guisbond and Neill (2004), this debate continues to wage in educational philosophy to this very day: structured, disciplined, and didactic orientations to education against student-directed, free exploration, and progressive education. This debate is also manifest in educational emphases of "standards" vs. "relevance" (Drake, 2012) that is well known among curricular specialists, policy makers, and educators. This debate is commonly linked to curricular tensions between accountability measures in teaching and learning often in the form of large scale mandated assessment standards and the construction of curriculum supportive of a 21st century and constructivist approach (Drake, Reid, & Kolohon, 2014).

Dewey (1929) believes that it is necessary to link the constructivist theory of education with the nature of human experience. He argues that we must understand how experience occurs in order to design and conduct education for the benefit of individuals in society both in the present and the future. He believes that educators are responsible for providing students with experiences that are immediately valuable and enable their contribution to society. In order to do so, educators must endeavour to understand students' characteristics, and behaviour, in addition to their environment in order to understand existing experiences.

Dewey believes that experience appears as a result of continuity and interaction. Continuity refers to the premise that any experience an individual has will have a positive or negative impact on that person's future. Interaction refers to awareness of situational influence on one's experience. Therefore, according to Dewey, a current experience is understood in light of past experience and the current situational context and has both internal and social components. The educator's role in this is to understand experience and then engage in organizing content in a manner that incorporates students' past experiences while providing them with new experiences which will aid their intellectual growth and promote their ability to contribute to society. Dewey claims that students should be given control over their experiences, which will increase their perceived value of those experiences, and ultimately nourish learning. Dewey (1916) claims that the "intelligent element of our experience" (p. 146) is actively cultivated through intentional efforts to realize specific connections between actions and effects, or experiences and outcomes. It is important to understand that Dewey emphasized the need for educators to understand the subjective quality of students' experience, which depends on social interaction between students and educators.

In order to achieve deep learning from experience, reflection is crucial (Dewey, 1934/1980). Joplin (1995) states that "Experience alone is insufficient to be called experiential education, it is the reflection process which turns experience into experiential education" (p. 15). Reflection on experience is the process through which personal and social meaning can be extrapolated to interact and become unified into experiential learning. According to Bell (1997), "Experience 'exists' through interpretation. It is produced through the meanings given it. Interpretations of lived experiences are always contextual and specific" (p. 10). These premises are supported by Zhenhuan (2010) and by Bergsteiner, Avery, and Neumann (2010), who state: "Learning is a cognitive process involving constant adaptation to, and engagement with, one's environment. Individuals create knowledge from experience. … Conflicts, disagreements and differences drive the learning process as learners move between modes of action, reflection, feeling and thinking" (p. 30). Therefore, in the discussion of experiential learning, reflection, context, sentiment, and interpretation are salient considerations in understanding the potential for learning and learners' constructions of knowledge.

The influential scholar David Kolb developed a prominent model of experiential learning that draws from Piaget, Jung, and others. His seminal book *Experiential Learning: Experience as the Source of Learning and Development* (1984) provided a framework that describes four definite learning styles (accommodating, diverging, assimilating, converging), which are connected to a four-phase progressive learning cycle. Kolb believed that all learners have a learning style preference from among these four. The "accommodating" style prefers hands-on engagement (often connected to tactile or kinesthetic learning). With the "diverging" style learners are sensitive and appreciate considering things from various perspectives. In the "assimilating" style learners appreciate logical and concise, systematic approaches to learning. Lastly, with the "converging" learning style is pragmatic. Converging learners prefer problem-solving types of learning approaches. His framework provides a way to think about different learners' individual learning preferences in addition to an explanation of the cyclical nature of learning from experience.

Kolb's model works on two levels: a four-stage cycle and the above described four-type definition of learning styles. Kolb's "Experiential Learning Cycle" consists of: (1) 'immediate or concrete experiences' (CE) which are the foundational experiential moments. For learning to occur, these experiences provide a basis for (2) 'observations and reflections' (OR). These observations and reflections are then assimilated and refined to form (3) 'abstract concepts' (AC). Ultimately, abstract concepts develop to form new implications which can involve (4) 'active experimentation' (AE) – thus creating new experiences. Ideally, an educator can create teaching and learning moments where the learners engage at each point in the cycle, thereby experiencing, reflecting, thinking and acting in an ongoing cycle of learning.

Kolb's work, while influential, has been critiqued. For example, Rogers (1996) highlights that "learning includes goals, purposes, intentions, choice and decision-making, and it is not at all clear where these elements fit into the learning cycle" (p. 108). Other scholars question the role of informal learning (Bergsteiner, Avery, & Neumann, 2010), negative experiences, and cultural and languages differences in relation to experience (Kelly, 1997), from a feminist perspective (Michelson, 1996) and from an ecological/environmental perspective (Seaman, 2008).

Regarding the model, Kolb (2007a, 2007b) himself indicated what he sees as a poignant limitation, which is that the learning output is solely based on the way learners perceive for themselves. Ratings by virtue of standards of behaviours, skills or knowledge, are not incorporated into the framework or in his learning style inventories. However, Kolb's contribution to exploring experience as the basis for learning and presenting a framework to explore the nature of experience in a "scientific form" (Kelly, 1997) has "helped move educational thought from the locus of the instructor back to the learner." This influence has ensured that the nature of experience as a construct of learning is a viable topic of discussion and reconceptualization for educational theorists such as Brookfield, (2006), Jarvis (2012, 2010), Merriam (2007) Merriam and Bierema (2013) and many others. For this purposes of this book, learning through experience is defined as:

> a combination of processes throughout a lifetime whereby the whole person – body (genetic, physical and biological) and mind (knowledge, skills, attitudes, values, emotions, beliefs and senses) – experiences social situations, the perceived content of which is then transformed cognitively, emotively or practically (or through any combination) and integrated into the individual person's biography resulting in a continually changing (or more experienced) person. (Jarvis, 2012, p. 4)

Social Constructivist Learning Theory. An influential theorist in the history of constructivist learning theory is Vygotsky (1978) who also believed in the individual's active construction of knowledge as the mechanism for learning. Vygotsky viewed learning and development as "historically situated and culturally determined" (Fox & Riconscente, 2008, p. 383), emphasizing the impact of both experience and social interaction in the learning process. Vygotsky believes that knowledge, and the tools for constructing knowledge such as language, have a social historical context at the core (Vygotsky, 1978). Vygotsky's argument suggests that an educational context and particular culture hold conceptualized beliefs which are passed forward generationally. These beliefs represent a social historical conception of knowledge and acquisition – learning. Vygotsky (1986) believes that this social historical conception impacts the social customs and discourses of the community through the language of communication:

> Any function in the child's cultural development appears twice, or on two planes. First it appears on the social plane, and then on the psychological plane. First it appears between people as an interpsychological category, and then within the child as an intrapsychological category. (p. 163)

According to Vygotsky, the acquisition of knowledge and the development of intellectual capacity are "socially and culturally defined," as opposed to "individually constructed" (p. 163). The educator's role is to generate opportunities for students to learn from interaction "with teachers and more-skilled peers" (Santrock et al., 2007, p. 52). Accordingly, Vygotsky's sociocultural learning theory epitomizes a paradigm of learning where social interactions and social cultural history are essential in knowledge construction.

Rogoff (1998, 2003) expanded Vygotsky's discussion regarding social cultural theory to argue that knowledge construction transpires on three planes: the individual; others within the community with whom the individual interrelates; and the social cultural context that defines how this community engages in the processes of knowledge construction and communication. Development, then, "is a process of people's changing participation in the sociocultural activities of their communities" (Rogoff, 2003, p. 52). Therefore, knowledge construction is characterized and determined by social cultural history, culture, and context of the place where the knowledge originated, and in accordance with particularized goals and values in relation to the cultural context from where this knowledge originated. Foundationally, social constructivist curriculum builds on the importance of students' social interactions, social cultural histories, and social cultural contexts in the processes of learning (Altun & Büyükduman, 2007). However, if social constructivism is premised on the recognition of social interactions, social cultural histories, and social cultural contexts, what are the implications for globalization in teaching and learning in the 21st century?

Constructivism – A Western Learning Theory? Higher educational facilities across the globe are internationalizing: new campuses are opening across geographical borders, new ideas are being shared with a wider audience, and educational theories and practices are being promoted in new contexts. The driving force of internationalization efforts in education predominantly consists of Western higher education institutions promoting their programs in international contexts. This results in either international students enrolling in Western degree or diploma programs in Western countries, or with whole campuses opening in various localities across the globe for form an International Branch Campus (IBC). For example, in the United Arab Emirates, campuses from New York University, the Sorbonne, George Mason University (now closed), University of Waterloo (the Engineering program – now closed) and Wollengong universities exist.

With the advent of educational internationalization, there is a corresponding concern regarding the transference of "Western" theories (Bleakley, Brice, & Bligh, 2008; Garson, 2005; Halbach, 2002; Hoppers, 2009; Richardson, 2004) and practices with "embedded Western values into foreign countries" (Garson, 2005, p. 322). This debate extends across educational disciplines, methodological approaches, and geographical boundaries. According to Halbach (2002), "exporting methodologies" (p. 243) is problematic because this "ignores the importance of personal and cultural factors in learning" (p. 243). Due to recognition of different belief and value systems, this is a valid concern. However, several theorists (Grange, 2004; Kalupahana, 1986; Kamis & Muhammad, 2007; Merriam, 2007; Sim, 2009; Sun, 2008) have made connections between elements of constructivist learning theory and various international philosophies and religious tenets related to learning.

The term "Western" describes Constructivist Learning Theory and related curriculum (Clarke & Otaky, 2006; Grange, 2004; Richardson, 2004), but concepts such as lifelong learning, reflection, critical thinking, and experiential learning inherent in the constructivist curricular model, connect to other, non-Western philosophies, ways of knowing, and religious traditions. Kalupahana (1986) has written about the comparisons between Buddhism and the epistemology of William

James, and Ames (2003), Cheng (2005), Chinn (2006), Grange (2004), Kee (2007), Sim (2009), and Sun (2008) have written comparing the ideas of Dewey and Confucius. These comparisons have been critiqued in terms of the theories and ideas being absolutely interconnected, divergences between the theorists, faiths and philosophies exist. For example, Sim (2009) discusses Dewey's and Confucius's philosophies:

> There are definite affinities between these thinkers' emphasis on the social ... but there are also drastic differences that surround their visions. ... These differences pose a challenge to the wholesale appropriation of Dewey's democracy and his education for democracy for Confucius and Confucian societies. (p. 98)

Thus, caution in this regard is warranted. It is not wise to advocate that these thinkers, believers and faith systems, and philosophers offer an absolute comparison in terms of ideas and belief systems. But, thinking about their visions of knowledge opens the door for exploring commonalities as well as differences in discussions regarding construction of knowledge, educational theories, and the educational context, which is relevant for balanced discussions of teaching and learning in our globalized and interconnected world.

Dewey and Vygotsky believe that individuals are social beings and schooling is integral to our learning processes. "Dewey holds that multiple social relations are prerequisite to human development" (Sim, 2009, p. 85). Confucius as well emphasized the salience of social relations. "Human life is never simply individual, in the Confucian view" (Sim, 2009, p. 85). In Confucianism, a being is always a member in a complex web of social relations and defined roles within those relations (Cheng, 2005; Sim, 2009). Dewey believes that learning, thinking, and believing are inherent in experiencing and all are the product and process of interacting with the world. As Dewey (1938) states,

> Experience ... includes what men do and suffer, what they strive for, love, believe and endure, and also how men act and are acted upon, the ways in which they do and suffer, desire and enjoy, see, believe, imagine – the processes of experiencing. (p. 18)

For Dewey, a learning experience is a continual interaction with humanity, and the elements of our environment. He believed that there was no conscious experience devoid of inference. Inference is the process of guiding behaviour within the experience itself.

Dominant faiths such as Confucianism, Buddhism, and Islam support respect for education. Confucianism endorses the belief that all in society should be educated and supports a learner-centred epistemology (Kee, 2007; Sim, 2009). Kee (2007) states that in Confucianism, learning "cannot be separated from one's daily experience. True learning is being constructed by learners through the inner self interacting with nature" (p. 156). Chinn (2006) notes that adult learning must entail both experience and reflection, concepts that also are inherent in the religious faith of Buddhism (Chinn, 2006). The ancient learning philosophy described by Al

Ghazzali in *Kitab* (translated by Faris & Ashraf, 2003) speaks of both of these concepts in addition to endorsing respect for teachers because they have acquired vast knowledge through varied experiences.

Islam and Islamic philosophy have learning virtues that connect to constructivist learning theory, particularly the concept of lifelong learning and learning through experience (Albertini, 2003, 2005; Cook, 1999; Hague, 2004; Kamis & Muhammad, 2007). The Holy Qur'an is the holy book of Islam and is believed by Muslims to be the word of Allah (Kamis & Muhammad, 2007). The *Sahih Al-Bukhari* is a collection of compilations in the *Hadith*, a book of sayings and deeds of the prophet Muhammad, Allah's earthly messenger (peace be upon him). Both texts exhort the high status of knowledge and the duty of every individual to learn "all there is to know" (Albertini, 2003, p. 457). According to Kamis and Muhammad (2007), "In Islam, a person is never too unintelligent to seek knowledge nor too old to embark on the journey of learning" (p. 24). As well, knowledge is meant to be shared; thus, an obligation in Islam is to share knowledge (Cook, 1999; Holy Qur'an, 3:184).

Al Ghazzali is a prolific Islamic thinker who wrote the *Kitab al-Ilm* (Book of Knowledge) in the 11th century. According to a translation by Faris and Ashraf (2003), the quest for knowledge and learning "should be a lifelong endeavour as well as humanities truest accomplishment" (p. 33). According to the Kitab al-Ilm, as translated by Faris and Ashraf (2003), three principles exhorted in the Book of Knowledge exemplify this ideal: a cradle to grave ethos, borderless learning, and acquisition of knowledge for both genders. This means that according to this early Islamic philosopher, learning should be a lifelong quest for knowledge that is shared and to the benefit of all in society. The quest for learning should continue regardless of war or crisis. One should seek learning opportunities from wherever they may be. As well, both women and men are obligated to seek learning and knowledge. It appears that the religion and philosophy of the Islamic world connect to some principles of constructivist learning, Dewey's and Confucius's discussion of the experiential and social nature of learning, and learning for all.

Although Constructivist Learning Theory has specific theorists (e.g., Dewey, Piaget, Vygotsky), some of the concepts of this learning theory relate to non-Western theories, philosophies and religions. Perhaps, the concern about "Western" theory and embedded "Western" values" (Garson, 2005, Richardson, 2004) being implemented in international contexts can be better understood as exploring balance between and among theories, and connections between theory, Western or non-Western, and understanding the specific context where multiple theories, beliefs, and philosophies are transformed into teaching and learning practices.

Paradigm Debates in Constructivism. Contemporary discussions regarding constructivism often focus on a paradigm war: instructional design is either objectivist or constructivist (Cronje, 2006). According to Jonassen (1991), "The two theories are generally described as polar extremes on a continuum from externally mediated reality (objectivism) to internally mediated reality (constructivism)" (p. 8). Further, "constructivism is completely incompatible with objectivism" (Bednar, Cunningham, Duffy, & Perry, 1992, p. 91). This opinion, and the classification that underscores the opinion, is problematic because it requires educators and curriculum designers to decide between the two extremes (Cook, 1993; Lebow, 1993; Phillips, 1995; von Glaserfeld, 1996), negating regard for learning contexts and programs that contain features of both approaches.

Cronje (2006) argues that this paradigm war has been protracted partially because the terms "objectivist epistemology" and "constructivist epistemology" are vaguely defined, a position mirrored by Terhart (2003) and by Jonassen (1991). For the purposes of this research, reference to objectivist epistemology incorporates the following set of world views as discussed by Cronje (2006). Objectivism epistemology views the world as a collection of entities that can be categorized on the basis of commonality: Reality is a construct that can be "modelled and shared with others" (p. 390); symbols are representations of learning that are only meaningful "to the degree that they correspond to reality" (p. 390). The brain processes these symbols and human thought is a process of "symbol-manipulation [that] is independent of the human organism" (p. 390). Thus, meaning has an external, objective and independent existence from the human being. Constructivism epistemology views the world as constructed, cognitively and socially, from our interactions, and this construction forms a collection of multiple realities modelled upon the way human beings construct their reality. Thus, symbols are "products of culture" (p. 390) that the human mind perceives, interprets and ultimately results in a construction of reality dependent "on the experience and understanding of the knower" (p. 390).

According to educational theorists (Cronje, 2006; Reeves & Harmon, 1994), differences between these two philosophies in terms of instruction and curriculum can be noted. Objectivism is an epistemology that endorses a standardized form of instruction to meet specific, sharply focused goals. The role of the educator is directive and didactic. Educational content is highly structured with minimal learner control. Student motivation is usually external (often in the form of standardized measures on testing instruments and grades), and the educational concern is focused on errorless learning. Constructivism is an epistemology that endorses a form of instruction geared toward students' construction of meaning from experience. The role of the educator is facilitative, with an emphasis on learning from the experience. Educational content is flexible, with an emphasis on experiential and collaborative approaches. Cultural sensitivity is necessary and student motivation is intrinsic.

Further, complicating the discussion of constructivism are the multiple forms of constructivist models: radical constructivism, moderate or trivial constructivism, and pseudo-constructivism, all of which operate on a continuum with radical constructivism representing one end of the spectrum, pseudo-constructivism representing another, and moderate constructivism, also known as trivial constructivism, falling somewhere in the middle (Cronje, 2006). According to von Glasersfeld (1996), radical constructivism claims that knowledge emanates from internal, cognitive processes of the brain. This discussion appears to be influenced by Piaget's (1952) cognitive constructivist learning theory. Von Glasersfeld further argues that the process of learning is self-regulatory, and, because knowledge is a construct rather than a collection of acquired information, the degree that knowledge reflects reality of a specific individual is hard to understand. Moderate constructivism (von Glasersfeld, 1990) refers to the meaning-making process undertaken by the student through experiences generated and facilitated by the educator. For the purposes of this research, any reference to the constructivist curriculum as taught at DWC will refer to moderate constructivism as the theory that underpins the curriculum and curricular outcomes.

Moderate constructivism is a theory of learning (Unal & Akpinar, 2006) and, therefore, teaching. Inherent in moderate constructivism are claims that knowledge acquisition is an active, developmental process involving physical growth and social interaction (Altun & Büyükduman, 2007); thus, learners construct and interpret their own reality filtered through the lens of their consciousness and experience within the social existence. Inherent in constructivism is the belief that students' knowledge is a direct manifestation of their prior experiences, schemata (Piaget, 1952), and the mechanisms employed to decipher those experiences, assimilation, and accommodation (Piaget, 1952). Fox (2001) claimed that, "conceptual growth comes from the negotiation of meaning, the sharing of multiple perspectives and the changing of our internal representations through collaborative learning" (as cited in Altun & Büyükduman, 2007, p. 31).

CONCLUSION

This chapter presents Constructivist Learning Theory as an educational philosophy of learning and therefore teaching. The historical legacy of constructivist learning theory has been presented including cognitive constructivist, social constructivist, and contemporary debates particularly in relation to constructivism as a "western" theory and paradigm debates related to conceptions of constructivist learning theory. As a movement in educational philosophy, this learning theory generally dominates with connections to what many curricular scholars refer to as "relevance" in curriculum design. A consistent theme in discussions of constructivist learning theory emphasizes polarities of thinking: Cognitive constructivist, social constructivist; Western or Eastern; objectivist or constructivist. It is important as we continue through this book to think less in terms of polarities, and more in terms of balancing ideas and contextualizing theories and approaches into curriculum, teaching and learning processes.

Regardless of the philosophical debates, many educators, curriculum designers, higher education administrators, and scholars regard their approaches to their instructional design as constructivist in orientation. Twenty-first century orientations to teaching and learning support the role of constructivist orientations regardless of whether the locus of instruction is elementary, secondary or post-secondary education. Thus, elucidating how constructivist learning in an international, post-secondary context is designed and implemented gives another lens for which to consider this learning theory. The following chapter explores adult and transformative learning and curriculum theory and sociological theories of education. These theories are integral to understanding teaching and learning in higher education in a rapidly transforming and globalizing country such as the UAE.

ADULT LEARNERS, SOCIOLOGY OF EDUCATION AND CHANGE THEORIES

INTRODUCTION

In years past, many of the long standing theories of adult learning, sociology of education and change theories have privileged Western orientations. While these theories provide a framework for thinking about higher education, with the advent of the 21st century, globalization and cross-national migration, we need to explore theories from an international lens inclusive the voices of international educators in international contexts. This chapter will lay the groundwork for subsequent chapters by presenting current conceptions of adult learning theory, transformative learning and curriculum theory, sociology of education and change theories and incorporates controversies and questions of these theories from a 21st century and international perspective. Subsequent chapters will integrate re-conceptualizations and nuances of these theories relative to education at DWC.

Adult Learning Theory

Discussions of adult learning theory began with Malcolm Knowles. His early work focused on the factors that distinguish pedagogy, principles of teaching children, from "andragogy," the "art and science of helping adults learn" (Knowles, 1970, p. 39). In this endeavour, Knowles (1984) identifies five assumptions about the characteristics of adult learners that differ from child learners: self-concept, experience, readiness to learn, orientation to learning, and motivation to learn.

Self Concept. Knowles argues that as people mature, their self-concept shifts from being dependent to being self-directed, an assumption Mezirow (1981) endorsed in his redefinition of andragogy: "An organized and sustained effort to assist adults to learn in a way that enhances their capability to function as self-directed learners" (p. 137). This assumption is highly dependent upon cultural understandings of "dependence" and "independence," as well as differing perspectives of what constitutes learning and knowledge. Merriam (2001) argues that "Some adults are highly dependent on a teacher for structure, while some children are independent, self-directed learners" (p. 5) a premise supported by Brookfield (1995). As degrees of self-directedness can vary among learners, and for some may be difficult if the learner lacks confidence, motivation or resources for learning, it is an assumption about adult learners that needs to be nuanced as part of the mosaic of adult learning theory. Exploring learner self-concept is particularly relevant in the 21st century given the nature of change, globalization and cross cultural migration, consideration of cultural, religious and social diversity, and the influence of media and technology that characterizes our learning and social experience in the 21st century.

Experience. Knowles' (1984) work in adult learning characterizes the role of adult experiences and the accumulation of experiences throughout a lifetime as integral to understanding adult learning. Knowles believes the wealth of experience an adult brings to the learning endeavour as a profound difference between child learning and adult learning. Ultimately, Knowles envisions adult experiences as a reservoir of knowledge and a resource for learning. Mezirow (2000), taking more of a critically reflective stance, argues this reservoir of experience is a space for deep reflection with the potential to lead to prominent change for the adult learner. Thus, Mezirow believes critical reflection should be an integral component of adult learning approaches.

This assumption, while valid, is a matter of degree, kind, and nature. The amount, form, exposure, character, and nature of the constellation of experiences an adult learner accumulates throughout life are inherently tied to the cultural background of the learner and the learning context (Ahmad & Majid, 2010; Alfred, 2003; Antikainen & Kauppila, 2002; Garson, 2005; Hazadiah & Majid, 2007). The reservoir of experience of a typical, female Arab learner in an international context is quite different from the reservoir of experience of a typical, female learning in Canada; this is particularly in relation to educational and social experiences (Gardner 1995; Garson, 2005; Godwin, 2006; Harb & El-Shaarawi, 2007; Lovering, 2012; Richardson, 2004). While this difference in experience does not negate the assumption of experience, it does add a layer of complexity to understanding this assumption particularly in relation to international 21st century teaching and learning with adults in higher education.

Readiness, Orientation, and Motivation to Learn. In my view, these last three assumptions that Knowles articulated are interwoven in adult learning and are inherently connected to personal aspects of each individual learner. Initially, Knowles' assumptions indicate that adults are ready to learn when they assert new social or life roles. Knowles further claims that adults are oriented toward problem-centred, task-focussed learning approaches that allow them to apply their learning immediately. Motivation to learn for an adult learner differs from that of children. Children attend school because parents are legally required to provide education for their children. While some children may also experience more or less internal motivation to learn, the assumption with pedagogy is that motivation is external (Brown, 2006). Adults who enter an educational facility do so because their "motivation to learn is internal" (Knowles, 1984, p. 12). Knowles (1980) described the classroom climate as one of "adultness," meaning that the classroom is a space where adults "feel accepted, respected, and supported" in addition to feeling "a spirit of mutuality between teachers and students as joint inquirers" (p. 47).

Again, readiness, orientation and motivation to learn are inherently tied to personal factors of an individual as well as culture and context. While, there is little literature available that explores the role of adult learning theory or readiness, orientation and motivation to learn from international contexts, there are some studies that explore components of readiness, orientation and motivation to engage in critical reflection and active learning principles in international contexts. Richardson's (2004) study of incorporating critical reflection activities in higher education in the UAE indicated that Arab students were disadvantaged in their abilities to engage in critically reflective learning tasks by virtue of their cultural and religious beliefs. Richardson argues that because these students are not encouraged to question religious tenets or cultural understandings, they were unable and unwilling to engage in critical reflection activities. However, Clarke and Otaky (2006) challenged Richardson's assertions, and explored female Bachelor of Education learners' readiness and orientation to learning using adult learning theory's approaches including critical reflection and active learning. They state that Emirati students are "wholeheartedly embracing" (p. 111) of adult learning theory teaching and learning approaches, particularly reflection, but they indicate that students' outputs may be characteristically different, a premise supported by Lovering (2012). Stapleton (2002) studied Japanese undergraduate students in an ESL writing class. Contrary to stereotypical constructions which characterize Asian students as passive learners, "lacking individual voice" (Littlewood, 2000, p. 250), both Stapleton (2002) and Littlewood (2002) reported that the participating students attitudinally desired education that conforms to adult learning theory principles and were ready willing and able to engage. "Asian students do not, in fact, wish to be spoonfed with facts from an all-knowing 'fount of knowledge.' They want to explore knowledge [for] themselves and find their own answers" (Littlewood, 2000, p. 34). These studies demonstrate the role of readiness, orientation and motivation related to the incorporation of an adult learning theory approaches with international students in three different geographical contexts: the UAE, Japan, and South Korea.

A great deal of discussion of adult learning theory in the last few decades has centred on characteristics of learners, motivation of learning and assumptions related to adult learning. With a 21st century approach, this is incomplete as this negates the role of context and sociological aspects (discussed later in this chapter) impacting adult learning. In addition, consideration has to be given to the role of curriculum and teaching and learning in relation to adult learning. Brown (2006) argued that there are three aspects forming cornerstones of consideration in relation to adult learning: the learner, the learning process, and the learning context. Thus, in framing this study pertaining to 21st century teaching and learning in an Arab context, I reiterate Jarvis's (2012) conception of adult learning which I feel embodies a more holistic dimension to discussions of adult learning. Learning involves:

> the combination of processes throughout a lifetime whereby the whole person
> – body (genetic, physical and biological) and mind (knowledge, skills,
> attitudes, values, emotions, beliefs and senses) – experiences social
> situations, the perceived content of which is then transformed cognitively,
> emotively or practically (or through any combination) and integrated into the

individual person's biography resulting in a continually changing (or more experienced) person. (Jarvis, 2012, p. 4)

This definition provides a more balanced and holistic understanding of adult learning embodying humanist, sociological, genetic and biological dispositions with the recognition of experience, context, and change integrated as part of the person's history. This leads to a question: If our world is constantly changing particularly with globalization, how can educators support the nature of change through curriculum, teaching and learning particularly in international contexts?

Transformative Learning Theory

During the last few decades, discussions of adult learning have emphasized the role of transformation as a manifestation of learning. Thus, transformative learning theory was born as a theory focussing on learning to empower transformation and change in some fashion within the learner. The essence of transformative learning theory is the facilitation and creation of learning opportunities that transform a learner's core values, patterns of thought, frames of reference, or beliefs when they are found to be inappropriate or unacceptable, with the ultimate goal being autonomy of thought (Mezirow, 2000). In transformative learning theory, change is integral; change in the manner with which people perceive themselves, and change in the attempts people make in order to explain, develop, or understand their assumptions, expectations, ideas, beliefs, frames of reference, and habits of mind (Mezirow, 2000). Mezirow (1998) notes that transformative learning theory contains two key aspects of transformation of a person's frame of reference: individually held perspectives and habits of mind. The educators' role is to design learning moments that will assist the learners to identify and challenge their individually held perspectives and habits of mind freeing learners from socialized influences for autonomy of thought. Further, integral to challenging frames of reference is to explore: how they form, inform, and influence an individual; how they are socialized and maintained; and, how they may or may not be appropriate in given situations.

Kegan (2000) expanded transformations in frame of reference to describe transformations in the Socialized Mind, Self-Authoring Mind, and Self-Transforming mind as these are the three core adult meaning-making systems. Kegan described the Socialized Mind as the level of consciousness wherein a person's identity is connected to relationships with others, their roles in relation to that individual's life, and the cultural systems that inform understandings and worldviews. "Socialized Mind is drawn to seeking alignment between itself and its surroundings" (Pruyn, 2010). According to Kegan, the Self-Authoring Mind is independent; it recognizes the influences of others and is capable of extricating others' opinions from personally held opinions, formulating a person's "seat of judgment" (Kegan & Lahey, 2009, p. 17). Ultimately, the Self-Authoring Mind is capable of authoring an individual identity that is independent from the person's environmental influences. Kegan identifies the Self-Transforming Mind as the highest level of consciousness. The Self Transforming Mind can explicate the Self-Authoring mind, incorporate multiple ideologies in the meaning-making process, and engage in simultaneous comparison of all thereby embracing the potential for change and transformation.

Recently, Knud Illeris (2014) provides an historical overview of transformative learning and asserts that the theory, from inception, has privileged "the cognitive dimension at the expense of the emotional and social dimensions and the situatedness of learning processes" (p. 149). He indicates that this imbalance in understandings of transformative learning has begun to be addressed by scholars such as Patricia Cranton (2012, 2005), John Dirkx (2006), and Edward Taylor (2009). Scholars such as Sharon Merriam (2008) and Saudelli (2012) are examining the imbalance not only from an emotional, spiritual and contextual perspective, but are considering the questions remaining about transformative learning theory from international perspectives. Ultimately, Kegan (2000) asks a very important question: what transforms? I extend this question to ask: Who and how does one decide if a transformation has occurred? Illeris (2014) asserts that "Mezirow's concepts of meaning perspectives, frames of reference and habits of mind are insufficient to capture the full range of the area in which transformative learning can take place" (p. 152).

Illeris (2014) seeks new definition of transformative learning theory and to this end asserts a connection of transformation to "identity" (p. 151). Drawing from Tennant (2012) who described the target for transformation as the self, Illeris (2014) preferred the term "identity" (pp. 151–152). He states that identity "has been understood not just as a psychological but specifically as a psychosocial concept" (pp. 151–152), thereby explicitly encompassing the individual and the "interaction between the individual and the social environment and how this influences the development of the individual" (p. 152). Illeris's discussion of transformation of identity connects to Dirkx (1997, 2012) beliefs that transformative learning involves transformations of both the learner's conscious understandings but also the deeper layers of unconscious understandings inherent in the individual.

From a teaching and learning perspective, a further logical question is: How do adult educators facilitate these transformative changes through curriculum and teaching? Transformative curriculum, as defined by Henderson and Gornik (2007), refers to curriculum with the following foci: students' active involvement and immersion in the meaning-making process and engagement of critical thinking and critical reflection during the meaning-making process. Thus, in a transformative curriculum, the facilitator is designing opportunities for learners to engage in task-based, problem focussed experiential learning opportunities that embed critical thinking components together with the expectation for critical reflection related to their learning through the experience.

According to Brown, (2006), Cranton (2002) Cranton and Taylor (2012), Brookfield (2008), and Henderson and Gornik (2007), critical reflection on the part of the adult learner should be an aspect of all curriculum in adult education. Critical reflection, according to Brookfield (1995), focuses on three interrelated

---

processes. First, the adult learner engages in a process of questioning and reframing an assumption that has been personally accepted as representing "commonsense wisdom" (p. 2). Second, the adult learner then examines alternative perspectives and applies these alternative perspectives to personally held ideas, actions, and ideologies. Third, the adult reflects and comes to realize "the hegemonic aspects of dominant cultural values" (p. 2). Mezirow (2000, 2003) explains that this is a process of transformation that the adult learner goes through via critical reflection with the result being a transformation in individually held perspectives and in habits of mind. It is important to note, teaching for transformation means taking learners out of their comfort zones to explore new and potentially uncomfortable or even frightening aspects of personally held beliefs and values. Teaching for transformation has the potential to expose a learner to an entirely new way of thinking, believing, and behaving.

Brown (2006) found in her andragogical study of 40 graduate students in education that the implementation of the transformative instructional strategy of critical reflection resulted in increased students' perceived "awareness of self" (p. 720). Quantitative methods were employed to ascertain the effects of transformative strategies on graduate students' attitudes regarding issues of diversity in education. Qualitative methods were employed to uncover the effects of transformative strategies on participants' personal beliefs and discussions of educational practices. These students in this mixed-methods study perceived the value of this strategy as "perspective shifting and life changing" (pp. 720–721). In addition to the process being considered life-changing, it was also found to be "physically and emotionally" (p. 721) exhausting because it forced students out of their comfort zones and into difficult, thought-provoking, and frightening terrain. Findings also indicated that students grew in awareness of who they were, and who they wanted to be in the future, particularly in relation to their professional aspirations. Brown reported that "through reflection many of the participants became more critically conscious of oppressive practices and their responsibilities [as educators] to change them" (p. 722). These findings on the use of transformative strategies are consistent with those by other theorists (Asgharzadeh, 2008; Clarke & Otaky, 2006; Lovering, 2012) in the field of international education.

However, some theorists (Cranton, 1994, 2000; Taylor, 2007) believe that critical reflection is granted too much prominence in the facilitation of transformative learning. Yorks and Kasl (2002) note that transformative learning is an intuitive and emotional process. Gunnlaugson (2007) acknowledges the intuitive and emotional roles in transformative learning, but also queries how to "advance modes of discourse that draw on a broader spectrum of multiple ways of knowing, including critical reflection" (p. 138). Gunnlaugson advocates for "generative dialogue as a method and practice of conversation that can support and serve as a catalyst" (p. 139) for transformative learning recognizing the power of interactive discourse as a means for transformation. Generative dialogue is a process that frames the movement of discussion through phases: conventional dialogue (talking nice); debate (talking tough); reflective inquiry (reflective dialogue); "toward the cocreative engagement in the final field of generative dialogue" (p. 138). Generative dialogue involves slowing down the discussion, collapsing closely held boundaries, and, importantly, "listening from one's Future Self" (p. 140). This involves contemplation to move beyond reflection. Listening to one's Future Self involves thinking of past experiences, embracing the concept of listening to the '*who you want to be voice*' and embracing this perspective of the future. This is both challenging and personally empowering.

Merriam and Ntseane (2008) describe transformative learning theory's use in international contexts, with different cultural values. They question the description of transformation as privileging Western values of individualism and autonomy. Mezirow (2000) asserts that "frames of reference often represent cultural paradigms – collectively held frames of reference – learning that is unintentionally assimilated from culture" (p. 19). Merriam and Ntseane believe that current studies of transformation learning theory conducted in Western contexts have focused on delineating the process of how transformation happens and the nature of the change. Merriam and Ntseane and also Taylor (2003, 2007) identify that many questions remain to be answered with transformative learning theory, particularly in relation to "the role of context; the nature of catalysts of transformative learning; the importance of emotion and spirituality, and relationships in the process" (Merriam & Ntseane, 2008, p. 184). While Merriam and Ntseane and Taylor (2003, 2007) do not dismiss transformative learning theory in an international context, they believe that "the role of culture … and transformative learning continues to be poorly understood" (Taylor, 2007, p. 178).

Specifically, Merriam and Ntseane's (2008) study of transformative learning theory in Botswana sought to explore how the cultural context shaped the process and outputs of transformational learning moments for participants. Their findings reveal three culturally relevant factors specific to Botswana as salient to the process of transformation: spirituality and the metaphysical world; community responsibilities and relationships; and gender roles. They assert that

> Cultural values shape the choice of assumptions to examine and the new perspectives and subsequent behaviours to engage in calls into question some aspects of Mezirow's theory. For example, the outcome of transformational learning is assumed to be increased autonomy and individual empowerment … greater self-directedness, assertiveness, self-confidence … found in Mezirow's (2000) interpretation of transformative learning. (Merriam & Ntseane, 2008, p. 196)

However, participants in this study reveal that they are more aware of their "interdependent positionality rather than [becoming] more discriminating and autonomous" (p. 196). Ultimately, Merriam and Ntseane assert that more research is needed that questions these assumed cultural values of individualism and autonomy as goals of transformative learning. I agree with Taylor (2003, 2007) and with Merriam and Ntseane (2008) and Merriam (2007) that exploring the nature of spiritual and intellectual meaning making through transformative learning theory will inform our understanding of the roles of culture, religion, society and curriculum in practice, which is particularly essential in 21st century international higher education. I further agree that Gunnlaugson's discussion of generative dialogue emphasizing the Future Self, in addition to generative dialogue and critical reflection are mechanisms that provide opportunities for transformation from learning. These elements will be explored in subsequent chapters.

SOCIOLOGY OF EDUCATION AND CHANGE THEORIES

Sociology of education is a discipline concerned with schooling as a function of society (Angell, 1928). Sociological theories in education debate issues pertaining to power, access, the form and nature of knowledge constructs in relation to education and society at large. Questions regarding "whose knowledge, for whom" (Ballantine & Hammack, 2009, p. 35) are inherently connected to school as a function of society.

The father of sociology of education, and the theorist who pioneered the functional approach to education movement is Emile Durkheim. Durkheim (1956) was concerned with societies' institutions, such as schools, and social cohesion, particularly as societies move from tradition to modernity. This led Durkheim to consider: "With the transition from traditional to modern societies, what provides for the social regularity of modern life?" (as cited in Davies & Guppy. 2010, p. 20). Durkheim (1956, 1977) believes education provides the mechanism for moral and socialized regularity of modern life: changes in society mirror corresponding changes in education, which then reciprocates. Schools, then, play an active role in the process of social change through socialization of students. Durkheim (1956, 1977) believes that important areas of sociological research are: the social functions of education and the nature of empowerment and social change. In addition to these areas of sociology of education research, in the 21st century, it is crucial to consider how schooling as a function of society and change feature in international contexts of higher education.

Structural Functionalist Theory

As stated, Durkheim (1956, 1977) pioneered discussions related to the structural functionalist theory of education. Contemporary discussions of functionalist theory declare that each part of a society's system – education, religion, economics, and politics – has a vital, interdependent and contributing role in a functioning society (Ballantine & Hammack, 2009). According to Parsons (1937, 2007) the central function of education is to impart the knowledge and the behaviourial norms necessary to maintain order in society. The socialization process of education functions to unify groups to work toward common goals, which keeps society from "disintegrating" (Cookson & Sadovnik, 2002, p. 267). In schools, learners develop their social skills, learn appropriate social behaviour, and socially acceptable values for the larger society. Thus, "schools are an important training ground ... for the transmission of moral and occupational education, discipline and the values as necessary for the survival of society" (Ballantine & Hammack, 2009, p. 16).

Structural functionalist theory posits that schooling reinforces the desired norms and behaviours determined as valued by those social groups that are dominant and/or privileged socially in society. It is important to note, international contexts may conceptualize the function of schooling to be disparate from that of Western contexts (which is the locus for most current research); thus it's important to consider the differences and the commonalities in relation to how the function of schooling is enacted in international contexts for an informed and balanced perspective in relation to discussions of 21st century education.

In addition, many scholars critique the role of the functional theory of education in society. One criticism is that this approach does not "deal with content" in the educational system (Karabel & Halsey, 1977, p. 11): What is taught, how, and by whom, for what defined outcome? Ballantine and Hammack (2009) edify this critique: "Individuals do not perform roles only within the structure; they create and modify the roles and dynamics not focused on by functional studies" (p. 16). Ballantine and Hammack assert that functionalist theory assumes that change occurs as a slow, deliberate, and nondisruptive evolution. This assertion depends on the circumstances and is hardly absolute. This assumption is certainly not representative of change in all societies (Lovering, 2012). As well, functionalist theory views schools as supporting the interest of dominant groups, which is not necessarily equitable (Ballantine & Hammack, 2009; Davies & Guppy, 2010; Hurn, 1993; Lovering, 2012).

Arguably, the most salient criticism of structural functionalist theory of education relate to notions of reproduction of social status and a person's 'place' in the education system, which has an impact on their roles in society and maintenance of a system of socialized status quo. Apple (1979, 2004, 2008), Bourdieu (1974, 1977, 1986), Giroux (1981, 1983, 2010), Liston (1986), McLaren (1989, 1994), Robbins (2009), Stevens (2007), Stuber (2009), and Stevens, Armstrong, and Arum (2008) assert that school as a political entity, and particularly curriculum, functions to reproduce the class structure and hegemony features which figure prominently in workplaces. The essence of the critique is that schooling operates to stream learners by virtue of place and social status into representative educational programs that will guide their future prospects. In this way, society reproduces itself by streaming desirable educational prospects and opportunities toward those who hold privileged status in society.

Bourdieu began the examination of status quo with his theory of social reproduction. In essence, a person's cultural capital refers to non-financial social assets bestowed on children by their family circumstances and social place in society. These social assets may be educational, relational (powerful family friends or relations that may have influence) or intellectual. Bourdieu (1974) termed this as a person's *habitus*. *Habitus* is thus a "cultural inheritance" (p. 204) that represents a person's class or social position in relation to the social structures dominant in society. It is important to note that Bourdieu believed a person's habitus is legitimated through institutions such as schooling which then reaffirms a person's place in society, thereby reproducing social inequalities. Scholars of cultural, social and class reproduction as a function of schooling are focused on how the education system intentionally or unintentionally operates to ensure the dominant in society maintain their dominant positions (Myrberg & Rosen, 2006).

Social reproduction works like this: Teachers, being quite highly educated, are often from the dominant social and cultural group in society. Children, from a very early age, are exposed to and socialized in the cultural capital of their families. Children socialized by elite cultures at home are often advantaged in schools as the cultural capital they present is the cultural capital the teachers recognize and reward often through assessment and evaluation strategies, but also through overt and covert in-class behaviours supporting the advantaged students. This advantage also may be as simple as having parents who value educational attainment, have a computer in the house, or are able to provide extra-curricular support for educational or social interests (Brinton & Yamamoto 2005; Loehlin 2004). These are advantages that translate into student actions, which are perceived as valued within the schools systems and embraced as "meritocratic and legitimate" (Tzanakis, 2011, p. 77) – thus fair and equitable. In fact, social reproduction theory argues that teachers are introducing "bias in their grading of student educational performance by actually rewarding elite culture-related competences rather than scholastic performance. Thus, schools reproduce particular forms of intergenerational social mobility and stratified outcomes" (p. 77) privileged by the elite, dominant, social group.

McLaren drew scholars' attention to the hidden curriculum – that knowledge which is not formally part of curricular content or objectives, but is present in every educational institution as it pertains to socializing and streaming of students and other practices of hegemony. He described:

> The hidden curriculum deals with the tacit ways in which knowledge and behaviour get constructed, outside the usual course materials and formally scheduled lessons. It is part of the bureaucratic and managerial "press" of the school – the combined forces by which students are induced to comply with the dominant ideologies and social practices related to authority, behaviour and morality. (McLaren, 1994, p. 191)

Ultimately, while these critiques of structural functionalism of education have merit, they first gained prominence in the age of modernity and post-modern discussions pertaining to education, and are especially prominent in contemporary discussions related to critical theories such as critical literacies, critical feminist theory, critical race theory, queer theory and so forth. Does structural functionalist theory of education have any place in today's 21st century discussions of international education? Do the critiques still have merit today? Or, is it possible to understand structural functionalism differently given our globalized and interconnected world? Can, the social functional role of education be used as a mechanism of empowerment and promotion of societal change (Freire, 1970)?

Empowerment Theory and Emancipatory Education

Can curriculum, teaching and learning empower students in their learning process? It is generally accepted among theorists that empowerment theory places an emphasis on the perception of power (Zimmerman, 1995) as held by and within the individual. For the purposes of this research, the definition presented by Gutierrez (1995) which refers to empowerment as "the process of increasing personal, interpersonal, or political power so that individuals, families, and communities can take action to improve their situations" (p. 29). However, this question of power and empowerment is complex for education in international contexts. Who is empowered, how, and to what ends? Who is entitled to say if someone is empowered or needs empowerment? How does education as a function of society contribute or not to power and empowerment?

It all began with Paolo Freire and the English translation of his seminal text "Pedagogy of the Oppressed" (1970). Freire based this book and his theories of emancipatory education on his experiences in Brazil assisting adults to read and write. His theory of pedagogy proposes a new relationship among the teacher, the learner, and the larger society. Freire refers to traditional pedagogy as the "banking model" of learning because it views the learner as an empty bank to be filled with knowledge by the all-knowing teacher. Freire asserts that the banking model is dehumanizing for all involved in the learning process: teachers and learners. Freire believes that pedagogy should envision the learner as a co-creator of knowledge and active contributor to meaning-making.

Freire (1970) claims that education does not rest solely with teaching vocabulary in the same way that "literacy is not about syllabification" (Freire, 1970, as cited in Shor & Freire, 1987, p. 66). By this, Freire means that teaching literacy means more than merely teaching students about syllabi or word choice; teaching literacy should be about "discussing the national realities with all its difficulties ... of raising the issue of the people's political participation in the reinvention of society" (p. 66). Freire endorsed the use of real-world experiences in curricula as a means of extending or challenging currencies of thought beyond acceptance of the status quo.

Freire (1970, 1994) believed that education is a political institution designed to create and share knowledge. Freire believed that people acquire knowledge from different experiences, particularly adult learners. As well, Freire endorses a change in the teacher's "role" in the classroom from one of presenting "expert" knowledge into the vacuous minds of the "ignorant" learner called "banking" (1970, p. 72), to a paradigm presenting educational opportunities requiring dialogue and problem-posing exercises. Further, Freire's concept of critical consciousness involves a mode of thought that is marked by analysis and interpretation of issues, self-confidence to articulate ideas in discussion, receptiveness toward alternative ideas, and a refusal to shirk or transfer responsibility (Freire, 1994). According to Freire (1970, 1973), critical consciousness marks the ideal outcome of a critical, liberatory education that is emancipatory and empowering.

The important question of how to mediate between respect for culture and support for transformation and empowerment becomes an issue in this discussion. Bell (1997) discusses how hegemonic practice is maintained through "discourse, which includes ideas, texts, theories, and language" (p. 11) embedded in networks of control. Foucault (1980) referred to these networks as "regimes of truth."

Regimes of truth that may be embedded in culture legitimates discourse to authorize the voices of some in a position of power, and also sanctions what discourse is true and valued (Egbo, 2009; Kreisberg, 1992) in society. However, how can education facilitate for students' empowerment and legitimize their voice in international contexts if prevailing regimes of truth are embedded in culture? According to Adams and Marchesani (1997) it is important for education to raise awareness though helping learners "identify their own social identities and experiences" (p. 263) and the relationship between how these differences are regarded in mainstream culture. They believe that awareness leads to recognition which allows students to view their social world differently, as a form of Freire's (1970) critical consciousness. Kubota (2004) suggests that multicultural education involves more than "simple respect for cultural difference, appreciation of ethnic traditions or artifacts, or promotion of cultural sensitivity" (p. 31). Kubota further promotes the ideal of education for social transformation through:

> Seeking social justice and equality among all people rather than merely celebrating differences. … [Multicultural education] has an intellectual alliance with critical pedagogy that aims to raise students' critical consciousness about various forms of domination and oppression and to help students become active agents for social change. (p. 37)

I agree with these statements, but all of these theorists are speaking of Western educational contexts. In an Arab context, how does the design and implementation of an international curriculum encapsulate the concepts of empowerment and employment/participation in the workforce and civil society? What does this mean to a 21st century international curriculum as delivered to Emirati women in a rapidly changing, globalizing and developing country? According to Ghosh (2009), globalization has an impact on discussions of "women, human rights, and citizenship" (p. 81). Petras and Veltmeyer (2001) discuss the complex changes in society from technological advancements and blurring of national borders as leading to changes that diffuse values and restructure cultural practices and belief systems. There is little practical research that speaks to curriculum teaching and learning in relation to any of these aspects in an Arab context. In addition, there is little practical research that speaks to female empowerment in an Arab context, or the role of globalization and international education as inherent constructs of change in education.

DWC supports empowerment of women as part of its mission statement, but within particular culturally and religiously mediated constraints. DWC also supports task-based and problem-focused strategies in the curriculum. Accordingly, Freire's discussion in this regard provides a relevant theoretical basis to think about the nature of empowerment in this context. As part of their way of knowing, women in Dubai encounter and internalize certain religious and cultural restrictions that serve to limit their contributions in society (Nashif, 2000; Richardson, 2004). In fact, every aspect of life and higher education for female Emiraties must be measured against the boundaries of these social, cultural, and religious understandings of role and place in society. Restrictions not based on religious ideals are open for dialogue, which is an aspect that HD1 initiates in the curriculum. In essence, Dubai is a transforming society and women's role in this society is transforming as well. Therefore, sociological functionalist educational theories and empowerment theories are core theoretical conceptions that lie at the heart of discussions related to social change and higher education for women in Dubai in the 21st century.

Change Theory

In consideration of the rapid transformation that that characterizes Dubai, and how it has affected every aspect of the lives of Emiraties including education, change theory provides a framework for analyzing the transformation. Punctuated Equilibrium, a term originally coined by paleobiologists Eldredge and Gould (1972) and later adopted for sociological discussions (Gersick, 1991; Tushman & Romanelli, 1985), analyzes social periods and social change as successive periods of relative stability, the equilibrium period, interspersed by punctuated moments of profound change, or the "revolutionary period" (Parsons & Fidler, 2005, p. 447). The revolutionary period of punctuated equilibrium occurs through complete upheaval that dismantles the deep structure of the system affected by change. According to Parsons and Fidler (2005), deep structure of a society involves core values and beliefs, basic priorities and structures, distribution of power, organizational structure, and control systems.

Currently, Dubai is in a state of equilibrium; Gersick (1991) describes equilibrium periods as time periods when "the system's basic organization and activity patterns stay the same" (p. 16). This is not to state that change does not occur; rather change occurs as "incremental adjustments to compensate for internal or external perturbations without changing their deep structures" (p. 16). While Dubai is a modern, technologically advanced Emirate, it is also a monarchy that is ruled and controlled in all respects through the precepts of the Islamic religion, patriarchy, and monarchical rule. Additionally, much of the stability and modernization afforded to the region is the result of the global demand for oil, formerly Dubai's main industrial export (Gardner, 1995).

While revolutionary transformations have occurred in Dubai in the past, during the data collection period a significant revolutionary period occurred, which has a salient effect on higher education, particularly for Emirati women. The global financial crisis of 2008 began in October and extended over a period of several years in Dubai. The fallout was significant. Some Emirati families lost a great deal of their wealth, businesses closed, companies defaulted on loans, several construction projects and other corporate projects ground to a halt, and hiring froze. In April 2009, Emirates Airlines reported over 20,000 abandoned cars –

people who could no longer afford to live in Dubai, lost their jobs, or had too much personal debt in a country that does not recognize bankruptcy protection meant that many people abandoned their lives in Dubai. The lasting effects of the global financial crisis appear to be mediated and Dubai is now a thriving economy, having worked its way back into a state of financial and developmental equilibrium.

However, and directly impacting education for women, there are concerns in the region about the stark imbalance between the relatively inexpensive foreign workforce recruited to work in Dubai and the Emirati people employed or seeking employment in Dubai. This concern is not limited to Dubai, or the UAE – several countries in the Middle East are encountering this very same issue. In its effort to create a global marketplace, professionals in industries such as medicine, technology, engineering, and education were and continue to be recruited internationally. According to the Government of Dubai, Dubai Statistics Centre, the total population in Dubai in 2014 is 2.269 million people. Out of this statistic, 1.997 million are foreign born "expatriates" and this number is continually increasing due to rapid development and available employment opportunities. Therefore, 88% of the total population of residents in Dubai are foreigners, comprised largely of neighbouring Arab nations such as Pakistan, Lebanon, Afghanistan, and Egypt. The result of this mass influx of expatriates is that Emirati citizens constitute an extremely small proportion, merely 7%, of the employment sector. In addition, this 7% figure primarily refers to the male gender as the figures for Emirati women in the workforce were not statistically reported.

The result of this imbalance in relation to foreign presence in employment in comparison to Emirati nationals' presence is an extreme overreliance on expatriates in all sectors of the economy; a domination that has the potential to threaten internal control of the nation's future unless alternative measures are implemented. In an effort to redress this domination of the foreign labour force and economy, the ruling Sheikhs of all Emirates implemented a reform policy, "Emiratization" (United Nations, 2006). This mandate represents a catalyst for a moment of revolution in the equilibrium because it is both a federal law and a guiding educational, philosophical mandate for higher education, particularly women's higher education.

Emiratization refers to the governmental mandate that all businesses in the UAE, by the year 2009 would be required to employ at least one Emirati citizen in some capacity (Godwin, 2006). The sanction further stipulated that beginning in 2010, Human Resources departments of all industries would need to employ an Emirati citizen in a supervisory position. Banking and financial sectors, also by 2010, would be required to provide evidence that 6% of their workforce is comprised of Emirati citizens. Thus, a strong educational force is in motion to educate and employ Emirati citizens in Dubai, especially the female gender, with a particular interest in human resources, high finance, information technology, engineering, and business industry related programs. The governmental mandate for Emiratization had a profound impact on the nature of curriculum design and implementation in higher education at DWC.

CONCLUSION

Crucial to any discussion of a specific educational context is an inherent need to conceptualize the theories that guide thinking in the context. In addition to educational theories, such as constructivist (discussed in Chapter 2), are also theories related to the learners and the learning context. Thus, setting the stage to explore the design of the integrated, 21st century curriculum and implementation at DWC, it is important to consider adult learning theories, transformational learning and curriculum theory and sociology of education and change theories including the critiques and related debates. In later chapters, I shall contribute to current debates regarding these theories particularly in relation to international education, globalization, and 21st century thinking.

MODULE 2

PRESENTING THE EDUCATORS, LEARNERS AND CURRICULUM

INTRODUCING THE INTERNATIONAL EDUCATORS

INTRODUCTION

It is challenging to think about this unique educational context without understanding those who choose to live an international life and become international educators. This chapter introduces the international educators and explores third space theory (Bhabha, 1990, 1994) as a way to explore their ways of being and ways of knowing from their international experiences. The chapter finishes with a re-examination of third space theory to include concepts such as their thoughts, their learning, spirit of community, their motivation, and their sense of "home" in their perceived "homelessness."[1] Tensions encountered by international educators are also explored.

The International Educators

So, who are these educators who designed and implemented this 21st century curriculum? How do they describe themselves and what are their tensions? It is important to understand the educators involved in the process of design and implementation of a 21st century curriculum. These international educators mediate a balancing act of third space (Bhabha, 1990, 1994) as they embrace a culturally responsive approach to their educational lives, and encounter tensions relating to beliefs and understandings that can be challenging for even those most embracing of cultural difference.

All of the educators teaching at DWC are foreign to the UAE, and many have worked internationally for extensive periods of time, in many diverse locations. Third space theory underpins the nature of the educators' approach to their work. Wang (2007) discusses third space as a space wherein a person discovers a sense of symmetry between what may be seemingly oppositional forces, ideologies, or thought processes. She argues that the underlying principle or purpose of third space is not to infer consensus but to move "between, beyond, and with the dual forces simultaneously" (p. 30). Wang's conception of third space clearly emphasizes an internal process of negotiating between oppositional forces or beliefs and implies the existence of tension. International educators as an aspect of their professional lives constantly move between, beyond, and within contexts, cultures, and learning environments.

Third space theory, according to Bhabha (1994), is a place of hybridity emanating from cross-cultural interaction. Spring (2007) describes hybridity as the "cultural changes resulting from the intersection of two differing cultures" (p. 14). Bhabha (1990, 1994) speaks of third space as an internal and external state of being where opposing or diverse beliefs, thought processes, lifestyles, ways of knowing, and experiences interact, find symmetry, and develop into learning experiences. Bhabha (1994) argues that "hybridity" is the third space: "the importance of hybridity is not to be able to trace two original moments from which the third emerges, rather hybridity … is the 'third space' which enables other positions to emerge" (p. 211) and new knowledge to grow. In Bhabha's (1994) discussion of working in the third space, he argues for the conception of an "*inter*national culture," identifying the *inter* as the "cutting edge of translation and negotiation, the *in-between* space – that carries the burden of meaning of culture" (p. 38). Understanding this third space, Bhabha argues, may allow us to "elude the politics of polarity" (p. 39) for improved international, social and cultural understandings.

Accordingly, discussion regarding third space theory directly relates to international educators, particularly those who consider themselves "global workers" (English, 2003, p. 68). International educators move from one geographical location to another, living amongst their new communities as active members of society. With this movement, international educators bring with them a wealth of experiences, knowledge, ways of knowing, and thought patterns, which become shared. According to Vadeboncoeur, Hirst, and Kostogriz (2006), through this global flow of human movement, "our memories and experiences, identities and identifications, discourses and social languages" (p. 163) are situated within diverse and shared discourses, which are inherently tied to context. This results in "identifications with particular spatial-discursive locations" (p. 163). Essentially, this means that with international movement among educators, the essence of our self and our experiences are shared with others in the new context. This shared discourse builds a bridge among experiences, culture, time, space, and geography to form a third space (Bhabha, 1994). Third space functions through social interaction, shared discourse, and new experiences; hence, "there is no dominant correct meaning prevalent" (Knain, 2006, p. 657) to the exchange – rather, a new construction of meaning is negotiated.

English (2003) claims that international educators experience a hybridization of their identity. In one respect, international educators identify with their home nationality. Concurrently, they develop a sincere appreciation through coexistence within a new cultural and geographical context. This evolves into the development of a third space identity, with inherent cross-cultural and cross-national connections as they learn from diverse people. English argues, "International educators practice in different geographical locations, inhabiting an in between 'third space,' which is neither northern or southern, global or local, left or right, liberatory or colonized, [Eastern or Western]" (p. 68). International educators are "in between" (p. 68): nationally, socioculturally, and professionally. They utilize third space in their daily lives and interactions, and negotiate an identity that forms a hybridity of diverse experiences (Bhabha, 1990).

This study sought to understand the perceptions of international educators at DWC, who may be experiencing third space, as they design and implement the HD1 curriculum, and the tacit wisdom, or tensions they have encountered as international educators and occupiers of third space. If the work of international educators is better understood for the complexity, sensitivity, and embrace for diversity requisite in their international roles, we may be better prepared to engage in education that crosses boundaries of cultural, linguistic, educational, religious, and political differences. As Gee (1994) states, it is the international English language educators, due to the growth of English as an international language, "who stand at the very heart of the most crucial educational, cultural, and political issues of our time" (p. 190).

By virtue of introduction to the international educators who contributed to this study, all of the pseudonyms below are for reference only. All of the names are gender neutral; thus no assumptions should be made regarding identity or gender of these international educators. All educators have worked at DWC for over 4 years, and some since the college opened in 1989. Although all teaching faculty is foreign to Dubai, there are some Emirati supervisors and many Emirati staff employed with DWC. Many of the foreign faculty have lived in Dubai for several years on their second, third, or fourth contracts. In fact, none of the educators in this study were on their first contract; all have worked in Dubai for at least 4 years.

An Introduction to the Educators. All educators report having taught in geographical contexts other than their homeland including: Japan, South Korea, Lebanon, Jordan, Europe, Africa, Bahrain, Kuwait, Hong Kong, Egypt, Singapore, China, Canada, the United States, Tunisia, Saudi Arabia, and many other locations. Below is a delineation of the educators by a gender-neutral pseudonym. All of the 19 educators, including the Emirati educator, report living, working, and studying in some international context other than Dubai during their careers. The educators are as follows:

- Nat – Faculty, a strong believer in quality. Quality in resources, in teaching practices, in content, in curriculum, assessments and marking. Nat has been teaching internationally for over 15 years in Asia and the Middle East.
- Morgan – Faculty, interest in creating positive group interactions and dynamics as integral to andragogy. Morgan has been teaching in the Middle East for over 10 years and appreciates the freedom to change teaching practices that is afforded educators in the Middle East.
- Izzy – Faculty, feels most comfortable in an expatriate community rather than homeland. Izzy has been international most of his/her professional life.
- Kelsey – Faculty, discusses the concept of "home and homelessness" of being an international educator. Multiple "homes" around the globe and reports a feeling of comfort wherever one finds oneself. Kelsey has been international for over 8 years.
- Drew – Supervisor, strong belief in supporting students' learning and supporting educators' excellence in teaching. Having taught in Asia, the Middle East, and Australia, Drew is a firm believer in reflective educational practice. Drew has been in Dubai for 4 years.

- Bailey – Faculty, believes that everything in international education and international relations must first consider culture and religious beliefs of those involved in the relationships. Bailey believes that being international allows a person to grow. Bailey has taught and been educated in several different countries and has been in the Middle East for over 8 years.
- Jordan – Supervisor, enthusiastic regarding the opportunities for future research at DWC, especially in relation to advanced technologies and cross-cultural interactions through technology. Jordan has been in the Middle East for over 14 years.
- Spencer – Faculty, enthusiastic regarding the opportunities for creating learning opportunities that demonstrate students' capabilities in the public sphere. Spencer holds a firm belief in authentic tasks as vehicles for relevant teaching and learning opportunities. Spencer never intended to spend most of his/her professional career in an international context, but this is what has happened. Spencer has been international for over 20 years.
- Perry – Faculty, believes in allowing students to engage in activities that mirror the competitive workplace, such as organizing events and engaging in the decision making process. Perry thrives on travel and visits many countries during holidays. Perry has been international for over 15 years.
- Taylor – Faculty, loves the adventure in international education. Finds "home" boring. Taylor loves the unexpected nature of Dubai and the constant change. Taylor has been international over 15 years and has been in the Middle East for over 10 years.
- Sam – Faculty, passionate about "giving back" and community-mindedness with the UAE. Sam has been educated around the world and has taught in many diverse countries but feels a strong sense of connection to the UAE. Sam grew up in Dubai when his/her parents fled a war torn country.
- Jaden – Faculty, believes that working internationally has provided rich experiences from which to draw, should he/she ever feel a desire to return "home." Jaden has taught in Asia, Africa, and the Middle East. Jaden has been international over 20 years.
- Shane – Faculty, believes in using humour and stories to make information comprehensible for students. Shane values reflection on the teaching practices and strategies to make learning enjoyable and interesting. Shane has been international for over 20 years and feels that learning from being outside your own culture and exploring these connections is important to teaching regardless of the location of the educational event.
- Parker – Faculty, belief in experiential learning and takes pride in the real-world practicality of DWC's curriculum. Parker loves to ponder different conceptions of knowledge. Parker loves debates and ideas about philosophy, knowledge, thinking and learning. Parker has been international for over 15 years.
- Ellis – Faculty, believes a sense of humour is crucial to success as an international educator. Personally, Ellis has an amazing sense of humour, and uses it to support teaching practice. Ellis describes the life of an international

educator as one filled with adventure. Ellis has taught in Asia, Europe, and the Middle East for over 15 years.

- Addison – Supervisor with a strong concern for positive international relations and emphasis on Emirati female empowerment. Addison is very concerned about ensuring exceptional learning opportunities for students and feels a great commitment to being a positive role model. Addison has taught and studied in other contexts. Addison is an Emirati supervisor.
- Alex – Supervisor, Alex has a well-developed sense of awareness regarding the complexities of social and cultural relations in education. Alex emphasizes innovation in teaching and technological approaches. Alex has a strong belief in Emirati students' successes and believes Emirati women will guide the future of the UAE. Alex feels proud of the work at DWC and takes pride in all of the accomplishments of students, current or graduated. Alex has been in the Middle East for over 15 years.
- Corey – Faculty, Corey is fascinated by world history, both ancient and contemporary. Corey is concerned that educational strategies should facilitate to the needs and the context of students in their current reality. Corey is very intellectual and very philosophical in discussions regarding what the educational team at HD1 accomplish and the changes witnessed in society. Corey has been international for over 15 years.
- Cassidy – Faculty, Cassidy is interested in understanding diverse world cultures and the effect on andragogy. Cassidy has a strong belief in critical andragogy and human rights education. Cassidy has taught in several war torn countries and feels passionate about teaching for social justice and empowerment. Cassidy has been international for over 20 years and has taught in Africa, Palestine, Asia, and the Middle East.

As all educators except one Emirati national, are from various international nationalities, and all have taught across the globe for the majority of their careers. Their perceptions regarding what it means to be an international educator provides a critical dimension to understanding 21st century curriculum design and implementation. One educator was born into slavery, one was born in a war torn country, and one educator had lived for many years in a country that encountered conflict as a result of religious differences. All educators had backgrounds that feature prominently in how they characterize international education and 21st century teaching and learning. These educators characterize international educators as embodying: call to adventure – growth and learning; cultural curiosity; learning to see beyond the veil; heading home; "home" in "homelessness"; spirit of community.

Call to Adventure – Growth and Learning. What is it that motivates someone to teach internationally, and why do they stay away from their homeland for extensive periods of time? This is a significant question because third space theory has not yet explored why a person would choose or seek this kind of lifestyle. Third space theory addresses how an individual accommodates when international experiences occur (Bhabba, 1994; English 2003; Spring, 2007; Wang, 2007), rather than why these international experiences are sought.

Significantly, all but three educators reported their love of the adventure of moving to a different country, learning a different language, and experiencing different cultures and faiths as active members of society as the prime motivating factor in their decision to go abroad and stay abroad. Shane commented, "The whole package appealed to me – it is exciting from a cultural and a teaching point of view." Alex indicated "I became a better leader and educator from going abroad. I was thirsty to experience something totally new. I did not want to live a life where I knew how to function. I wanted to live a life where I would learn new ways of living, educating, being." Parker feels that it is "healthy to live outside your comfort zone. Everyone should experience this kind of adventure at least once in his/her life."

For many people, the idea of living an international life is appealing as it is an opportunity to be an intimate voyeur of a culture. In reality, many people who are mere travelling teachers only stay for short periods of time, and/or only superficially learn about the culture of residence. In addition, occasionally educators may consider short excursions to different places for research. These opportunities do offer a taste of what it means to consider the role of culture in context. They do not, however, allow immersion in the community of residence, where international educators as "the other" and must operate within third space, which is where the in depth learning begins. Addison commented "you have to come and you have to stay. Short term visits, or one or two year contracts offer a taste but the real learning comes when you are fully immersed in the community."

In addition, some people cannot adjust to an international life and do a "midnight run" ("ESL Glossary," n.d.). This is a colloquial term common among ESL teachers internationally to refer to teachers who suddenly and without notice return to their homeland. Often they leave due to anxiety, culture shock, home-sickness, or just an inability to live an international life (Austin, Gregory, & Martin, 2007; Brettingham, 2007a, 2007b, 2007c; Cohen, 2001). Occasionally, some teachers are forced to return home, deported, due to cross-cultural blunders, which could occur with any international educator in any context. The life of a professional international educator who is dedicated to the adventure of his or her lifestyle and functions in third space is not one of superficial understanding of context. Rather, this is a life pursuing knowledge that emanates from living within a community as "the other" (Bhabba, 1994): making mistakes, apologizing and correcting them, reflecting on the growth that occurs, and thriving from the adventure.

It is significant that none of these educators had taught only in one country; all had lived in various geographical places for most of their professional careers and for extended periods of time. These educators explicitly desired international experiences of diverse cultures, and diverse religious beliefs. They wanted to be part of the experience – not superficially as a tourist, or as a short-term visiting teacher/lecturer, or even in one international community. This motivation, this curiosity appears to form an ontological state of mind for these international educators.

All educators acknowledged that "going international" changed them in deep and meaningful ways. Predominantly, these educators suggested that expatriate educators must release a neocolonialist hold on "their knowledge" to embrace new and alternate "knowledges." This discussion emanated from my question to educators: "What have you learned from being an International Educator?" Instead of commenting about specific cultural elements, or teaching elements, as I had anticipated, all educators spoke of reciprocity of their learning from students and colleagues in addition to commenting on their personal growth. Educators stated their real learning was to let go of their hold on knowledge to learn from others' knowledge. All educators warned against the danger of fostering a colonialist agenda or fostering an "internal colonialism" (Scott & Marshall, 2009, p. 367). This premise was elicited from educators, regardless of their homeland. They posited that international educators should not approach their position with predetermined, rigid, idealized, and universalized educational objectives. All stated the danger in thinking that they are the *purveyors* of knowledge and internalizing a belief that rationalizes a heightened level of self-importance. All educators identified that "the ones who don't make it have expectations about how grateful everyone else will be [the students and society] that they have deigned to go to the country of residence to teach. Not realistic and highly egotistical" (Bailey).

Among all educators, I sensed a level of humility for themselves and a sense of awe for the potential to learn from colleagues and students alike. Eleven educators specifically identified the necessity for international educators to be sincere in their will to learn from the context and all educators acknowledged that it is essential to "go deep" in learning "here" about the context in order to teach effectively. All educators identified that they get involved in the national holidays, have read the Qur'an, visit families of the students, and are part of social events involving Emiraties. Third space theory does not support fostering a colonialist agenda. Third space is about releasing a colonialist hold as purveyors of knowledge and with sincerity embracing the potential for learning from every experience and every person. This is a significant contribution to third space theory: sincere, eager anticipation and embrace of cultural learning as a motivation for becoming and remaining an international educator.

However, this ontological position and perspective has the potential to be misinterpreted by those who cannot imagine the life of an international educator, and those who respond negatively to musings of international educators (Getty, 2011). This might explain, in part, why these international educators in this study appeared resistant to return to their homelands; many of these educators encountered negative reactions to their observations regarding their lives in third space.

Learning from the rich experiences that international educators have is not always easy, and an open mind and welcoming nature is imperative to the process. According to Spencer, Perry, Addison, Morgan, Sam, Jordan, Kelsey, Bailey, Cassidy, Shane, and Jaden an open-minded world view comes through willingness on the part of the educator to learn from, and sincerely embrace the context with all of its distinctiveness. For example, Kelsey explained

> You have to come with an open mind and you have to stay long enough to drink in the culture. That changes what you do and what your expectations are. That's how one grows and that's part of the kickback from going abroad.

Similarly, Spencer stated, "You have to pay attention to their feelings and put yourself in their place, as a foreigner wanting to avoid causing offense. It does make you aware." Corey noted that regardless of the sensitivities required to live an international life in the UAE, "There is a huge amount of forgiveness here."

These educators were driven by the adventure of cultural learning through immersion as participating members of a new cultural group. This involved a willingness to embrace the new, stay long enough to understand what is new, and awareness that regardless of the will to forgive potential blunders, educators attempt to place their mindset in the heart of the culture in order to sincerely understand: who their learners are; what their lives are like; what they value; and, what they need in their learning.

Cultural Curiosity. International experience provides valuable growth and personal development. However, living as a participating member of a new culture is something for which few have the capacity to adjust as this requires a sincere curiosity and willingness to embrace, adapt, and learn. Some people cannot live and adjust to an international life. Jordan discussed recruitment considerations of future potential faculty: "We call it 'cultural curiosity.' Do they really want to experience it? Do they expect it to be like the current place where they live." Addison commented "People come with presupposed notions. They have to understand that they should learn about this culture, and do it sincerely. It is important."

Cultural curiosity is sincere and passionate; it involves a devotion to learning about culture that allows a person to live, appreciate, and be sensitive to the tenets and nuances of that culture so active participation in society for which the international educator is the "other" can evolve. Based on the comments from these international educators, I define "cultural curiosity" as the heartfelt curiosity and passion to learn about a specific culture that leads to the desire to intimately know about a culture through direct immersion for extended periods of time. Having this sense of cultural curiosity can support a person's passion for his or her role in society even during moments of tension due to divergent belief systems or values. All participations spoke with devotion to these Emirati students and their learning as being the primary reason why they worked so hard to create optimal learning experiences for them; this same devotion provides the grounding they need when tensions inevitably surface. These educators want the best for their learners for their today and for their tomorrows. Addison said it best:

> I am passionate about my position. I [want to] contribute positively to our students' learning, to make them active educators in their own country. Using

their culture and language gives them strength to function in their world out there. They are half of the present but all of the future.

This cultural curiosity can be in relation to one specific cultural community, or the curiosity can foster a desire to learn more about other cultural communities. Kelsey commented "This moment in time only fuels my curiosity for more. I cannot stop – so much more to experience." Thus, as the adventure continues, it becomes a lifestyle.

The devotion to an international life and the cultural curiosity that is part of being an international educator is not necessarily pervasive among all who teach internationally. Within the international education realm, several colloquial terms are used to describe the industry that I have purposely refrained from using: the terms "teacher tourists" and "travelling teachers" (Meddings & Thornbury, 2009, p. 72). These terms refer to those who choose an international life mainly as an opportunity to travel for a few years and then return to their homeland. For teacher tourists, the adventure does not become a lifestyle. They may visit the tourist sites, try some new food items, teach for a while, and then move on or go home. They may or may not be qualified teachers, and in some cases they may be teaching illegally on tourist visas. This is an aspect of international education, particularly in relation to ESL "teachers" in this (Al Sweidi, 2006; Harb & El-Shaarawi, 2007) and other regions of the world (Griffith, 2005; Meddings & Thornbury, 2009).

The international educators who were involved in this research are excited about the contribution they make from their work to the growth and development of these students and this country. They embody cultural curiosity and have a thirst for adventure and learning from international experiences. They want to know, they want to learn, they want to be full participating members of the new societies for which they immerse themselves.

Learning to See beyond the Veil. All educators identified that going and staying international changed their worldview. All educators report that a crucial aspect was to learn to see beyond the veil of their own belief systems. Kelsey noted the importance of learning "To not colonize. To not take an attitude that 'my way' is the right way." Perry stated, "I have learned the importance of not using your own culture as a measuring stick. The perceptions that well educated people have about this place. The reactions when you advise otherwise! Living abroad broadens your perspectives." Addison commented "when you live according to a different subset of epistemologies, religions, cultures, and you have to understand how they impact your way of living, you become a well-rounded educator. Many people teach how they were taught. Here, that is not an option."

Interestingly, a theme that emerged related to how people "back home" wherever that place may be geographically, were not willing or able to comprehend the educators' lives in the Middle East. It is significant to note that every educator articulated that life, learning, and living do not conform to assumptions or ideas others at home hold. For example, Morgan commented

Educators back home can be narrow in their willingness to open themselves to other ways of seeing the world. Part of their job is to be willing to see the world through others' eyes; but I am shocked by how narrow people in developed countries are.

These comments were mirrored by 11 educators as well. Cassidy reported "They want to hear about veiling and nothing else. They are actually affronted when I talk about all the amazing things our students do through curriculum, and how students want to be strong participating members in their country's growth." "There is a much stronger sense of civic mindedness here. These ladies want to be a part of change and the future" (Sam). Parker and Shane were affronted by the emphasis on veiling by others from their homeland. "Our students are incredible. But, all anyone else can see is a piece of cloth... so what if our students veil. So what if they don't. They have amazing understandings of knowledge and talents and gifts to bring to the world" (Shane). Corey discussed some of these false perceptions:

> This part of the world is developing its own style. People say, "it will be years before they catch up." They don't want to "catch up." There are far too many ideas about the developing world wanting to "catch up" with the first world.

Interestingly, both Corey and Cassidy identified that people "back home" do not understand their changed perceptions. Cassidy mentioned "I am often accused of 'going Arab' because I defend their values." Corey noted "I am aware of visible flesh back home; you don't see flesh here. I also realized how much of our social life back home revolves around visible flesh and alcohol. It is interesting because the interpretation [back home] is that I have been 'Islamicized.'"

International educators embody an ability to see beyond the veil: they do see beyond using their own cultural values as the means to interpret their new experiences. This ability is problematic for international educators when they described their experiences upon their return home as this ability does not extend vicariously to others. When stories of information are relayed by international educators that belie the expected or challenge assumptions, these educators have encountered negative attitudes. Seeing beyond the veil as international educators broadens their perspectives, which proved to be distasteful for some who are not capable of this same ability.

Heading Home? None of the educators reported an inclination to return to their homeland in the foreseeable future. In fact, during discussions it was clear many were not sure what to say as they had not considered the idea. Ellis stated, "There used to be a time when I thought about [my nationality] as home. When you have lived overseas, there comes a time when you just don't feel it anymore. The boundaries disappear." Taylor relayed a prolific story to explain:

> I can't go back, the horrendous culture shock. The other day, a friend was driving into the car park area, she looks up and she sees one of the workers up in a tree. Babu is that you up in the tree? "Yes madam. I am collecting

leaves. My friend said "Babu why are you collecting leaves?" and he says, "My wife says if I collect these leaves and put them in a bath my [chicken pox] spots will go." Where would you find that back home? Back home is too cleansed for me.

Four educators (Kelsey, Taylor, Cassidy, & Izzy) acknowledged no intention to return to their homeland, but rather moving on to the next homeland. Kelsey stated "I'm not going back, I'm going on. I will be taking on whole new experiences there as well so I won't get so dispirited and down hearted as we do when we go home." These educators have a sense of the nomad in them. They feel that being international is such an integral part of their existence and identity that the adventure must continue.

"Home" in "Homelessness." Current discussions of third space theory (Bhabha, 1994; Wang, 2007) do not consider an aspect that dominated educators' responses in this study: A sense of being at "home" in "homelessness." A sense of the nomad appeared to be present in all these educators who had lived in international settings for many years. When I questioned the educators about their intentions about returning home, surprise was the most frequent reaction. Seven educators were clearly taken aback and returned the question to me: What is home, and also why? For some educators, going home may mean returning to political turmoil, or difficulty in obtaining employment, which are relevant and valid concerns. However, these issues do not explain the reactions of other educators entirely.

"Homelessness" was not discussed with discomfort by educators in this study. Rather, it was seen as an element describing who they are, the life they lead, the learning they continue to acquire, the beliefs they hold from their international experiences, and their identity in third space. In speculating about this, I consider two elements that may contribute to international educators in third space sense of being "home" in "homelessness."

First, several educators observed that people from their homelands do not understand their lifestyle, and, in some cases, distrust the nature of their new global perspectives. International experiences have become part of these educators' sense of identity with an internalized desire to continue the adventure. Educators seemed to have developed a sense of "home" as being the global landscape. Thus, the globe may be these educators' perceived home. Second, it appears that few people can understand the real life of an international educator. Educators stated many people express desire for an international life, but cannot envision or thrive in one. As well, many who try it cannot adjust or adapt and they often return home especially if the expectations or the fantasy of going abroad does not meet the reality of the experiences. Some people do manage to live internationally for brief periods and then return home after a few years. Rarely, does "going international" become a lifestyle unless the person is capable of thriving in third space.

The accommodation process involved with an international life aligns with Wang's (2007) discussion of third space as the discovery of a sense of symmetry between seemingly oppositional forces, ideologies, or thought processes. However, based on this study, current discussions of third space are incomplete and must be reconceived to include the sense of "home" in the "homelessness" as part of an international educator's life, identity, and values. This sense of "home" in their experience goes beyond accommodation, adaptation, symmetry, or hybridity to a sense of being at "home" regardless of where they reside or what comes next. Indeed, it appears that the globe is an international educator's home.

Spirit of Community. A dominating theme educators discussed relates to the spirit of community among these educators. Parsons (2007) describes "community" as a relationship of solidarity within a social relationship, based on a common set of circumstances. All educators in this study acknowledged that the most valuable aspect of working on the HD1 team emanates from the opportunity to work with this highly devoted, knowledgeable team of faculty and staff. All educators acknowledge the strong team spirit, the international diversity, the opportunity to learn from the diversity represented among the team, and the spirit of professional and personal support present among the HD1 team. In fact, three educators and one supervisor educator referred to the HD1 team as the "Dream Team" of international educators. Alex and Addison were the supervisors who articulated their respect for this team of educators in the strongest terms. Addison stated "Our students hold their heads higher because they are learning from these teachers." Alex indicated "We have assembled a very strong team of educators and curriculum team leaders. We know what we are doing is incredible. This team does not always agree, they debate, they consider, they respect each other. This is not an easy curriculum to teach but this group of educators do it, do it well, and all are working together for the benefit of students, for whom they are devoted. Great team spirit." This team appeared collegial, innovative, supportive, and genuine.

It appears reasonable that the multinational nature of these professionals operating in third space, and the collaboration required from the nature of the integrated curriculum are factors that coalesce and nurture this spirit of community in a manner that aligns with Parson's (2007) description of "community." They are involved in this experience together and in order to make this form of curriculum work to the benefit of students they must foster this spirit of community. All educators specifically identified the pleasure they experience from working together, sharing ideas, debating merits, and arriving at consensus and potential strategies for continual improvement. Ellis commented "We know that these women will be the future of this country. They are going to define it in the manner that they believe is best for them and for their future generations. That is exciting to be a part of." Educators believed they are contributing to shape the education and future with these female students in a way that values the students' beliefs, empowers them in their decision-making process, and gives them voice in this rapidly changing developing country. All educators indicated a sense of pride at what is accomplished in HD1 and a sense of homage toward each other and the students. There existed among this team of international educators a very strong spirit of community that sustains them in third space.

Tensions for International Educators

The life of an international educator is rife with internal tensions. As a participating member of a different cultural group, the space between divergent beliefs and values can cause great anxiety. This is certainly the case for the most experienced international educators regardless of whom they are and where they have lived. The primary tensions these educators reveal are: (a) social justice, equity, and human rights; (b) fear; (c) public pressure and media backlash; (d) controversial issues.

Social Justice, Equity and Human Rights. Sometimes educators experienced internal tension due to different beliefs in relation to equity, social justice, and human rights. This was discussed by Morgan, Nat, Izzy, Kelsey, Alex, and Cassidy. Alex commented "In the community you have supporters and detractors – people who think there shouldn't be men in a Women's College for instance. Many other equity issues. Consequently, we are always walking on a tightrope."

According to Nat and Cassidy, as international educators, there are times when you just have to "zero out" (Cassidy) particularly in relation to human rights issues, social justice, and racism: "You have to switch off. There are zero human rights in this country, and I can't do anything. You have to be able to take your personal politics out of the equation. Otherwise, you will suffer" (Nat). Cassidy related a recent incident:

> A student came to me, she was 17 and her family was demanding that she marry her cousin. She was beaten terribly when she refused and, in a few weeks, she will be married. I have another student who was upset about her family's maid being mistreated. I am thrilled that these students are questioning these occurrences, but it kills me because I can't do anything but listen, offer soothing words and allow them to express themselves and their emotions.

Addison related "Although I am committed to human rights, especially given my history, but changing cultural perceptions must begin with allowing the culture to question within itself." Shane indicated "the fine line between what is 'selling out' in terms of my beliefs and 'colonialism' is constantly blurred. I see myself as a role model. I mirror my beliefs, I raise the questions in the classroom, but I don't impose. Instead, I offer and encourage alternative perspectives. Best I can do."A very challenging aspect for international educators relates to social justice and equity issues. Dubai is an emirate in a developing country and some issues arise that caused intense feelings of tension, particularly as their ability to intervene is constrained and advocating in relation to these issues must be undertaken with care.

Fear. There is no employment security in the field of international education. Educators reported that mistakes can and possibly will be construed negatively against them, which lends to a fear of consequences. This was an aspect of life as an international educator, regardless of context according to Corey, Izzy, Morgan, Parker, Shane, Nat and Cassidy. Corey explained:

> You can want to do things, but it is difficult to know how far you can take it. And, when the backlash hits. … As international educators, we all know people who have suddenly been walked off campus, and given 2 weeks, 1 week, or less to clear out, Visas cancelled. That is real.

Nat commented, "When I taught in South Korea my university fired 80% of the faculty. Just like that. And that was a typical thing." Morgan stated "We are aware that regardless of any issue, if we can be blamed, we will be at least partially in order to save 'face.' You can be on the next plane out that day and everybody here knows it." Izzy stated, "Part of this is 'face.' If an international person can be at least partially blamed for whatever the issue is, then the Emirati, or whatever context we are speaking, is not to blame. That is our reality. You have to be careful what you do and say." Corey related a recent event:

> A member of faculty in passing made a remark about [a local] charity. Basically, this person said she had given enough money and if Dubai cared enough there were plenty of rich people here to contribute. She was reported and accused of criticizing Sheikh Mohamed. She had to go through this whole ordeal. Now, you have to question yourself, at what point it is a bit like the days of witch-hunting and the inquisition. Here, sometimes the truth must be masked. Universities are famous for expressing viewpoints. Here, you can't as openly.

Morgan believes that there existed a connection between being an international educator, educational administration, decision-making, and use of power. Morgan stated:

> We have to put up with very oppressive administrations, with very bad decisions made at times, we are totally on our own and personally held responsible for anything and everything. Thus, we have become excellent self-censorers.

Educators Kelsey, Bailey, Corey, and Cassidy reported experiencing trepidation in particularly with field trips, where students were chaperoned by educators and taken off campus for a learning experience. DWC encourages that all students have one field trip per semester, but this is filled with tensions not encountered in other contexts. There are many restrictions regarding where students are allowed to go for field trips and in relation to their actions in public, off-campus, enforcement of which falls on the educators chaperoning the field trip. For example, no student is allowed anywhere unescorted, even the washroom. Students cannot be seen eating in public. All students must be dressed in the national attire, *abbayahs* and *shaylahs*, properly secured when on field trips or for public campus events. Corey explained:

There are so many constraints on where you can and cannot go, which no longer reflects the reality of our students' lives. It is quite insulting; the assumption is if you let loose, these girls will behave in an undignified and disrespectful manner and that is absolutely incorrect. But, field trips are fraught with danger. When [the teachers] come back into the college gates, we look at each other and say "we survived" (laughter).

Kelsey was both excited and concerned about field trips. When you involve students in field trips, choosing the place, figuring out the educational value, and making the arrangements, and when you consider the social standing of many of the students, a field trip can be an amazing experience that could not be replicated elsewhere. Kelsey observed:

Again, in this context only … we took an airplane and we flew on a field trip to Sir Bani Yas Island. Taking off in a huge military carrier and flying there – unbelievable – only here could this happen. Normally, you are faced with this context. It isn't just taking students on a bus with everybody responsible for themselves. You have to cover your ass in every respect. It's another symptom of what we have to do here.

A profound tension for educators related to fear of mistakes or reprisals for mistakes attributed to them regardless of merit. These educators were well aware that they could expect no employment security in their international experiences and operate with that understanding. Due to social standing of students, field trips warrant both tension and excitement for new encounters.

Public Pressure and Media Backlash. Drew, Alex, Parker, Morgan and Cassidy acknowledged that DWC faces the potential for media backlash due to its commitment to innovation, achievement and students' engagement. They recognized that some curricular elements taught and educational opportunities that are part of the DWC approach have the potential to be "blown out" of perspective by the media and public at large. Alex identified "The press are not very accountable and they will print whatever they think will sell." Drew noted "The media here are quick to pick up on anything that could be seen to be insulting to the culture or something that is taken out of context." Cassidy related an example:

Many of our initiatives push boundaries in a way that tries to balance the public concern. Prior to the Bazaar event, there is an assembly where student behaviour appropriate for a public open event is discussed: appropriate dress, wearing *abbayahs* and *shaylahs*, not too much makeup. … In any other context, this would seem odd. Here, it is required because the media focus their criticisms on the public appearance of our students and passions become inflamed with the traditionalists who don't really want their daughters to come to college anyway.

Educators in HD1 encountered tensions in their work that directly pertained to their foreign status. These tensions were: social justice, equity, and human rights;

fear; and public pressure and media backlash. Recognition of their role as international educators has a profound impact on their decisions regarding the 21st century curriculum design and implementation for learners at DWC.

Controversial Issues. The working life of an international educator does not have any sense of employment security and mistakes are costly; thus, self-censorship is a matter of survival. Educators believed that self-censorship is a fact of life; a skill that international educators discover and incorporate quickly into their day-to-day and professional and personal communicative exchanges. This does not mean that educators cannot create and implement educational opportunities designed to extend cultural boundaries and explore real societal issues. In fact, later chapters explore the nature of controversial issues embedded in the 21st century curriculum they designed and implemented. There was a degree of professional freedom afforded to these educators, but all efforts in relation to curriculum and implementation were mediated by the awareness of employment insecurity and faculty abilities to self-censor because of fear of consequences. Alex commented "Here, you have to be able to know when to probe, when to offer alternative perspectives, and how to do it without imposing your view. It is fine-tuned and may sound hypocritical, but you have to be able to filter yourself." Morgan agrees and states "if you want to survive, you have to learn to self-censor." Parker commented "it is not that you have nothing to say, but really, is your view important? No, and it might shut down the dialogue because you might offend. Ultimately, we want students engaging in the dialogue. We want them to think and express with their voices."

According to these international educators, cultural boundaries can be and were explored in teaching and learning. The curriculum was also carefully controlled by the educators as they perceived that fault or complaint would be levied against them personally and professionally, and media backlash against the institution was an ever-present concern. For instance, both the Current Issues Forum and the Bazaar (discussed in Chapter 6) with the associated opening of the campus to a limited but public domain represented the two strongest curricular events that extended boundaries for students. But, these events also had the potential to invite discord. Faculty efforts to extend allow students to engage in controversial issues shared three characteristics:

1. Students' Control: Inclusion of controversial topics was research-oriented and student driven, and required students to locate alternative perspectives which must be evaluated, presented, and debated;
2. No Opinions: When controversial topics were presented by educators for discussion, these educators employed a heightened sense of self-censorship through asking questions but refraining from offering a personal opinion or conclusion;
3. Classroom Management: The conversation was managed to ensure that all students had the opportunity to express themselves.

These three elements allow the exploration of cultural boundaries to be *controlled by students*, rather than imposed on them by an authority figure. In addition, faculty were committed to censoring their own perspectives from the discussion. Neocolonialist approaches must be avoided at all costs if controversial issues are to be explored. These international educators in third space, who have no job security, understand that controversy need not be avoided altogether, but must be incorporated in a way that empowers students to construct knowledge, evaluate it, critique it, and use *their voices* to contribute to the dialogue about controversial issues.

These international educators recognize the need to develop advanced self-censorship skills, and a nuanced ability to understand what cultural boundaries they can extend. This is a matter of survival for international educators in third space due to lack of employment security, concerns regarding how their efforts will be perceived, and the recognition that ultimately students must debate these issues within their own culture and community.

Musings over Tensions. Interestingly, even given the above tensions educators experience, the tension that seemed the most troublesome for educators in third space revolved around conversations about their decisions to live in a Middle Eastern country. This tension occurred in 12 educators' discussions regardless of their nationality. Many of the experiences shared by these 12 educators indicated that upon their return home, they encountered both ignorance and/or distain for the Middle East, Arabs, Muslims, and the UAE. This appeared to indicate a significant level of intolerance and lack of knowledge. In particular, Arab women, their roles in society, and their choice to wear a veil or not were topics of debate upon the return home for these educators. These moments were filled with tension for these educators as they attempted to inform and educate. All educators acknowledged that various assumptions of life, learning, and living in the UAE, or in other international contexts do not necessarily conform to ideas held at home (Getty, 2011). Many societal changes in the UAE are evident but are not evident to those at home. For instance, this generation of women in the UAE are officially and educationally empowered to define their roles as suited to their beliefs and how they wish to determine their future. Educators revealed that people in their home-lands found this information both surprising and shocking, likely due to the lack of knowledge many people in various places have about women in the Middle East.

These educators indicated a lack of willingness on the part of those who have not lived an international life to hear that their perceptions may be misguided, or to learn that they are not as open-minded as they initially consider themselves to be, a finding Getty (2011) also observed. Several educators discussed the narrow vision of educators "back home" who are unwilling or unable to see the world through "others" eyes, even though he/she believed this is part of their obligation as educators. Twelve educators disclosed the animosity others feel when their assumptions about women in the Middle East were discredited. Two educators discussed being accused of "going Arab" when they attempted to enlighten certain values Muslims hold.

While these educators in third space discussed openly their sincerity in learning about their community of residence, it appeared that their hybrid mindset was not welcomed or understood upon their return to their homelands. In some cases, it appeared international educators' sincerity was treated with animosity during interactions with people in their homelands. In some cases, international educators in third space, upon their return home, have had their sincerity perceived negatively by some people, both at home and abroad, who have difficulty conceptualizing an international educator respecting Arab culture and religion.

CONCLUSION

The results of this study indicate that there is more to third space theory than hybridity or sense of symmetry in oppositional forces. There is also more to being an international educator than enjoying travel and being qualified as a teacher. These international educators actively seek the opportunity to become the other of themselves (Bhabha, 1990, 1994) and sincerely embrace their learning in new international contexts. Educators had a highly developed spirit of community and identify cultural curiosity as a prime motivating factor. This indicates that these international educators in third space have a nuanced sensibility toward others' knowledge, and as a group have a sense of support for each other. They embrace a willingness to let go of "their" way, embrace "other" ways, while they formulate "new" ways to create educational opportunities in curriculum and implementation for their learners to whom they are devoted.

Further, educators disclosed that one of their tensions regarding their hybridity involves their roles as defenders of their hybrid nature to those who cannot understand an international life. This is often perceived as uncomfortable or disagreeable to those "back home." As well, these international educators appear to feel little desire to return to their homelands. Some are unable to return, and some to varying degrees discussed their feelings that they were already in their homelands, the global landscape. Indeed, they had developed a sense of "home" in their "homelessness."

International educators are a unique group. These are not educators who are merely travelling through for a short time; they make being international part of who they are and what they value. International educators occupy third space (Bhabha, 1990, 1994) as they mediate between the amazing experiences and grueling tensions which can shake an international educator to the core. This is particularly true in relation to differing conceptions of human rights in international contexts.

NOTE

[i] Significant aspects of this chapter have been published in: Saudelli, M.G. (2012). Unveiling third space: A case study of international educators in Dubai, United Arab Emirates. *Canadian Journal of Education, 35*(3), 85–100.

CHAPTER 5

INTRODUCING 21ST CENTURY TEACHING &
LEARNING AND THE EMIRATI LEARNERS

INTRODUCTION

It is difficult to understand the nature of curriculum design and implementation practices without an understanding of the educators' approach to teaching and learning. It is also crucial to consider the nature of the Emirati learners in the design process. This chapter introduces the philosophical orientation the international educators bring to teaching and learning, which is described as a 21st century approach. This chapter also introduces the Emirati, female, higher education learners from the perspective of the international educators.

What is 21st Century Teaching & Learning?

What exactly do we mean when we refer to 21st century teaching and learning? Simply stated, 21st century teaching and learning refers to an orientation that recognizes the incredible change that has been ushered in by virtue of a dramatic technological evolution and advancements, globalization and cross-national migration of both people and information, and intense shifting of educational needs. It is often said we are living in the 'Information Age' which has a corresponding impact in the nature of knowledge. This educational shift described as 21st century epistemology, 21st century skills and knowledges, or 21st century ideologies. I prefer to use the term 21st century teaching and learning as a reciprocal process of knowledge creation, discovery and sharing in this interconnected and transforming spatial moment.

   Twenty-first century teaching and learning is complex, ambitious, provocative, and inspiring. Twenty-first century teaching and learning problematizes the notion of stasis in educational strategies, goals, standards, and approaches. Fossilized teaching strategies, pen and paper tasks, and read, write, answer a test approaches are relegated to the sidelines in favour of collaborative tasks, performance assessments, critical engagement activities, simulated learning, task and problem based approaches, incorporation of global issues and concerns, and inclusion of new technologies. Today's youth live in an increasingly diverse, globalized, media-saturated, and technologically savvy society. Education for the 21st century must meet that reality through teaching and learning that embraces these key aspects of contemporary society from both a local and a global frame of mind.

   With the advent of globalization, the global migration of human movement, and the interconnected nature of our global economy, political systems, and environmental concerns, students today need for more complex skills for successful futures. For example, the global financial crisis in 2008, and its aftermath, has resulted in highly competitive employment sectors in many parts of the world. Even a country like the United Arab Emirates, with vast oil and economic wealth, suffered devastating effects from the financial crisis. Companies collapsed, people became suddenly unemployed, and competition for employment became fierce.

Designing a 21st century approach to teaching and learning involves incorporating specific teaching and learning ideals (Saavedra & Opfer, 2012): a) Make it relevant; b) Teach through the disciplines; c) Develop thinking skills; d) Encourage learning transfer; e) Teach students how to learn; f) Address misunderstandings directly; g) Treat teamwork like an outcome; h) Exploit technology to support learning; and, i) Foster creativity.

Thinking through the characteristics of a 21st century society, Saavedra and Opfer (2012) assert: "Globalization, economic necessity, and low civic engagement compound the urgency for students to develop the skills and knowledge they need for success" (p. 8). Low levels of civic engagement as demonstrated by less participation in charity work, voting, and social activism highlights the need for education where students learn how to be involved, why they should be involved, how to participate in their community and why their voices are important (Levine, 2012). If we are to prepare our students for 21st century reality of rapid change, environmental degradation, advanced technologies, cross-cultural communicative demands and understandings, and for an uncertain and undefined future with new challenges, we need to arm them with 21st century skills. Wagner (2008) describes a set of 21st century skills that learners today need:

a. Critical thinking and problem solving;
b. Collaboration across networks and leadership;
c. Agility and adaptability;
d. Initiative and entrepreneurialism;
e. Effective oral and written communication;
f. Accessing and analyzing information; and
g. Curiosity and imagination.

Every educator at DWC highlighted the importance of all of the above skills as integral to their understandings of crucial components in curriculum, teaching and learning. However, they also added the following skills as crucial in a 21st century curriculum:

h. Collaboration and teamwork across cultural and geographical domains,
i. Interdisciplinary thinking, and
j. Abilities to think both globally and locally for short term and long term implications.

While these 21st century skills have international appeal and present long term beneficial skills sets for learners across the globe, it is interesting to note, every educator at DWC specifically highlighted the role of the last skill, the ability to think globally and locally for short and long term implications as specifically beneficial to these Emirati learners.

Curriculum designed to support these 21st century skills has the following characteristics: it is interdisciplinary in nature, experiential, and inquiry-driven. 21st century curriculum is balanced and interconnected: it brings into the classroom the community, the region, the national and the global. 21st century curriculum involves recognition that teaching and learning do not occur in a vacuum – they are intimately a part of every aspect of our interconnected lives. Thus, 21st century curriculum incorporates advanced technologies, multiliteracies, multiple skills, authentic resources, authentic assessments, collaboration, current real world issues, task and problem based activities, and higher order thinking skills.

Twenty-first Century Assessment

What do 21st century assessment practices look like? At one time, we spoke of assessment of learning as formative, diagnostic and summative, with the most prominent being summative assessment occurring at the end of a unit or semester. However, with 21st century assessment, we need to think of assessment with a different mindset. Ultimately, we want assessment that infuses measurement of 21st century skills with knowledge content (Drake, Reid, & Kolohon, 2014). Emphasis rests with substantiating assessment practices in authentic real world current issues (Drake, 2012). Twenty-first century assessment is performance based, with recognition to the multiple ways issues have potential resolutions to the problems, issues or tasks, while also allowing students to demonstrate their content knowledge learned.

Assessment literacy refers to the core understanding educators have in relation to the sound assessment practice. Inherent in this core understanding is usage of assessment terminology, design and utilization of appropriate assessment methodologies, and recognition of standards and quality in relation to assessment practice. It is important to note, 21st century assessment involves formalized assessment practices, information assessment approaches, and the central focus is embedding assessment practices as a mechanism to further students' learning (Drake, 2012).

In contemporary discussions we speak of assessment *for, of,* and *as* learning. Assessment for learning happens during the learning as learners progressively endeavour toward completion of the learning tasks. Assessment for learning occurs frequently as opposed to the end of a unit of study. Students are provided with explicit instructions, they are informed of what they are expected to learn, what is expected of them, with clear success criteria, and they are given detailed and operational feedback and advice on how to improve their work.

In Assessment *for* Learning, teachers use assessment as an investigative tool to find out as much as they can about what their students know and can do, and what confusions, preconceptions, or gaps they might have. The wide variety of information that teachers collect about students' learning processes provides the basis for determining what they need to do next to move student learning forward. It provides the basis for providing descriptive feedback for students and deciding on groupings, instructional strategies, and resources. (Rethinking Classroom Assessment, 2006, p. 29)

Assessment of learning is summative in nature and, arguably, is the most dominant form of assessment practice in higher education. The purpose is to indicate a quantifiable measure of learning and it usually occurs at the end of a unit of instruction or semester. In a 21st century assessment approach, assessment of learning is often performance-based, task or problem solving oriented, and contains both collaborative and individual components. Two primary concerns with assessment of learning involve designing an assessment that is: valid (do the assessment criteria measure what they purport to measure) and reliable (provides an accurate and consistent means to evaluate the learning achieved).

Assessment as learning refers to the sharing and constructing of understandings and the reflective process in relation to learning between both the educators and the learners. When an educator engages in assessment as learning, the mindset is to foster a shared understanding about learning intentions and success criteria of teaching and learning moments. This form of assessment is fostered through fair and open dialogue, self, and peer assessment. Assessment as learning involves reflection and responsibility. Reflection is in relation to honest and critical appraisal engaged by both educator and learner in relation to teaching and learning. Responsibility refers to the levelling of hierarchies in the educational moment – the recognition that both educators and learners assume responsibility for the potential for learning and both have a responsibility in the engagement of the learning moment.

A controversy exists in relation to 21st century assessment. The controversy relates to the balancing act of learning needs in 21st century assessment. Most of the debate focusses on the polarity between assessment that emphasizes accountability measures and assessment that emphasizes relevance or meaning-making (Baines & Stanley, 2006; Drake, 2012; Drake & Burns, 2004; Henderson & Gornik, 2007; Kauffman, Johnson, Kardos, Liu, & Peske, 2002). Which is more credible as a measure of learning? This debate is particularly highlighted in international education by virtue of the role of English as the language of instruction of many facilities in contexts wherein English is a foreign language for the dominating student body. Most higher education institutions worldwide require an institutional, regional or global standardized English assessment practice. DWC is no different. Because DWC is an English medium institution, and because all learners speak Arabic as their mother-tongue, English proficiency has an impact on the designed 21st century curriculum.

During the time period of this study, DWC requires that students successfully pass the Academic Version of International English Language Testing System (IELTS) in order to graduate (HCTAS, 2007), as the means of ensuring students' proficiency in English. IELTS Academic is an internationally recognized, standardized testing system that measures academic English language proficiency in five areas: speaking, reading, writing, listening, and grammar (British Council, 2005). The IELTS Academic test was created, and is provided, by these governing bodies: The British Council, IELTS Australia, and Cambridge University (British Council, 2005).

Ellis (2003) identifies that the IELTS and the North American counterpart the Test of English as a Foreign Language (TOEFL) tests are examples of common psychometric tests, which is a form of standardized, large-scale assessment commonly criticised (Altun & Büyükduman, 2007; Ellis, 2003, 2006; Zane, 2009). As Gipps (1994) eloquently summarizes, the critique focusses on:

> The emphasis on relative ranking rather than actual accomplishment; the privileging of easily quantifiable displays of skills and knowledge; the assumption that individual performances rather than collaborative forms of cognition, are the most powerful indicators of educational progress; the notion that evaluating educational progress is a matter of scientific measurement. (p. 14)

As students in the UAE (and other developing regions) are often accepted into English medium, higher education facilities with limited ability to use English (Mustafa, 2002), the result is that the DWC curriculum incorporates elements of English language instruction and IELTS Academic preparation into the curriculum to prepare students for this graduation accountability requirement.

Philosophically and practically, a tension exists regarding curriculum that endorses the students' achievement of standards, "accountability" (Drake & Burns, 2004; Drake, 2007, 2012) and curriculum that endorses a 21st century framework, often referred to as "relevant" or "meaningful" (Drake, 2007). The tension arises from the belief that teaching for success on standardized test performances, such as IELTS tests, results in learning specific only to the testing situation, as opposed to learning to understand concepts, content and subject matter (Baines & Stanley, 2006). Baines and Stanley (2006), Henderson and Gornik (2007), and Drake and Burns (2004) question: Can educators teach to both the test (accountability) and for relevance and meaning (through constructivist and transformative 21st century curricular approaches)? How does an educator ensure that 21st century curriculum design incorporates assessment of, for, and as learning? How does an educator assess for both accountability as required by the IELTS graduate requirement and relevance and meaning-making as required for a 21st century approach? What is the nature and educational background of the learners in this complex endeavour?

The Learners – The Nature of DWC Students

For the purposes of this body of work, I have delineated a distinction of Emirati nationals as a specific educational community because the implementation of DWC curriculum is exclusive to them. All educators specifically identified the importance of designing curriculum and implementation that acknowledges the fact that all students are Emiraties, female, have a specific culture, and are part of a particular community. For example, Bailey specifically identified this necessity even if you also have an Arab or Middle Eastern cultural background: "Everything is culture and religion here. Although I come from a similar Arab background, my background is still different. So, how we understand life and learning as Arab muslims will be different." All educators identified that education for Emiraties is unique due to the rapid economic and social changes that have affected the Emirati people. Drew explained:

> Thirty years ago [they were] Bedouins, our students. Our students 30 years ago they would not have been at school ever. That depth of understanding is necessary. Outside of this country, people don't realize how far it has advanced in 30 years.

Emirati female students are a unique educational community. Characteristics that the educators discussed to describe Emirati female learners included: Emirati graciousness, Emirati female restrictions, unprepared for higher education, and "When you teach, I learn."

Emirati Graciousness. All educators specifically discussed the welcoming nature of Emirati students to the foreign faculty. Alex states, "Emirati graciousness is second to none. Graciousness of foreigners characterizes this part of the world. They welcome you, want to know about you, and they want you to get to know them sincerely." In the words of Addison:

> The people of the Emirates are very, very welcoming people. They would take off the shirt on their back and give it to you. Very hospitable, they welcome you to their homes, weddings, or different occasions and share with you even their most intimate and personal occasions.

Educators discussed how students include foreign faculty into their lives through sharing information related to their culture particularly if they observe that the faculty are interested. Cassidy states, "They really want us to know about them, their families, their traditions, values, and ways of living and knowing." This sentiment was echoed by Corey who related a recent field trip experience:

> We went to an art exhibition of Emirati artists. This is something that is so sweet about teaching here: our students are inclusive, even as a foreigner they want you included in the experience and will share with you. Students were very interested in the names [of the artists]. Here, names are incredibly important. From names, students know if you are from slave origin, or Iranian origin, or from what they call the "Bedouin." They were explaining all of this to us as they went along – she is connected to this family and he is connected with that family.

Some educators noted students' acceptance of foreigners even during times of political strife: "In the UAE, if an international incident happens, you don't get resentment from students" (Taylor). Cassidy related this phenomenon to respect for the teaching profession: "Here, culturally and religiously, there is great respect for education. Here, teaching is an honourable profession." Jaden noted, "This is an advantage we are blessed to have – it doesn't exist in many other places."

Educators indicated the salience of faculty learning about Emirati social conventions, such as greetings, and particular expressions such as *bismillah*.[1] Awareness of Emirati social conventions may seem minor to foreigners but this knowledge represents significant moments of embracing students' culture and has an impact on the classroom dynamic. For example, Addison explained "Some teachers don't understand that in this culture we like greetings. We acknowledge a person's existence. That really, really, really matters here. It is shameful to me [when greetings are not exchanged] and I do take it personally." Cassidy related an example:

> Sometimes foreigners expect the culture here to adapt to them. Here, it doesn't work that way. You need to embrace Emirati cultural conventions. I used to feel annoyed when students arrived late to class with a greeting to all of 'Salam Alaikum' [Arabic greeting, peace be upon you]. Until I learned that it is seen as extremely disrespectful here not to express a greeting regardless of what it disrupts. Embrace their social graces – it means an awful lot to our students.

Teaching and learning in this context must recognize the graciousness of Emirati female students. Students were described as inclusive with faculty and willing to share experiences and personal information about their culture. Teaching is considered an honourable profession both within Islam and within Emirati culture. The salience in Emirati culture of greetings and social conventions cannot be understated in teaching and learning, and in all interactions in this context.

Nature of Emirati Female Restrictions. Although all HD1 students are Emirati females, there is diversity in terms of restrictions on their lives. Some students have very liberal families: they drive, go out by themselves, work, and make their own career and life decisions. Others are from conservative families: some do not leave the house, except to come to college, without their father or male guardian escorting them according to 11 educators. Corey stated "A lot of our students are quite sheltered. Many have not been out and about in Dubai, on their own or with other students. A lot of them have never been inside a workplace before. That can be a bit scary at first." Kelsey related the following:

> At one stage, I was trying to integrate business vocabulary and money concepts. One lesson dealt with banking. The ATM machine was in the cafeteria and I took the class down and I said, get out your ATM cards and your pin numbers and we will talk about the vocabulary and concepts. They looked at me blankly. "What is an ATM? My brother or father does this." They had no concepts for dealing with this experience. No concepts for dealing with getting money.

Drew explained:

> Coming to the college is a huge transformational process for students. They're able to explore what's happening in the real world. Many times this is the first time they are allowed to explore the Internet on their own without a brother or a father or an uncle being there watching every site they go to.

Eight educators noted that many DWC students have very limited contact with the large expatriate community of Dubai. Morgan explained

> How many places in the world do you have this kind of isolated population being educated in isolation by non-members of the population? You can't even look to other Middle Eastern contexts as the same, like Oman or Qatar. This is a very unique circumstance.

All educators noted that contact with the foreign faculty is often students' first international interaction with foreigners in a sustained way. Ellis explained, "What the Sheikh has in mind is he wants to create a safe international atmosphere where the students can gently experience. We are hired here as international educators to bring the world into the classroom."

The gender of faculty and students' social restrictions can have an impact on the implementation of curriculum. Nine educators articulated that few students are accustomed to interacting with men who are not in their immediate families. Kelsey described "If you are a male teacher here, you have a restriction as to the kind of interaction you can have with students. There is a wall." Bailey identified, "You need to be careful. When students have their laptops open and I want to show something … when I get close to them, I will say 'just take your hands off.' Proximity is very important here between men and women." This is challenging for students because most the HD1 faculty are men. Parker explained:

> In terms of their [prior] schooling, they only had women [teachers]. When they come to us, they are in shock when their first teacher is a man. It is a massive jump for them, but vital. It plays to [the reality of] going out to the workplace. Understanding that they are going to have to work with men, men are human beings, women and men can work together as equals.

According to educators (Parker, Ellis, & Bailey) many students become accustomed to male presence on campus. As observed by Ellis, "By the end of their year, they're usually quite comfortable to come have a bloody good argument at the desk of a man, which they weren't previously."

In addition to students' restrictions regarding contact with foreigners, and men, all 19 educators identified that few students have real-world work experience or exposure, an aspect that sets DWC's students apart from other educational contexts. For example, few HD1 students, if any, prior to college life, have ever had or performed summer employment, internships, household chores, volunteer work, any form of work-related task, or left the house unchaperoned by a father or brother.

It is important to note the role cultural restrictions on women as an aspect of understanding students. While some students are from liberal families, many are not. The restrictions relate to: lack of interaction with foreigners, lack of exposure to non-family related men, and students' lack of exposure to work experience.

Unprepared for Higher Education. All educators suggested that learners' prior educational experiences in elementary and secondary schooling leave them unprepared for higher education. This lack of preparedness affects implementation of DWC curriculum in four ways: lack of basic Math, English, and analytical skills; lack of study skills necessary for higher education; understanding of passive learning as an educational norm; and a fear of making mistakes in the classroom.

HD1 curriculum represents a significant transformation for students from all of their prior educational experiences. All educators agreed that most students arrive at DWC lacking basic English language skills, and in many cases lacking Arabic literacy skills (Morgan, Alex, Cassidy). Many students lack the Math and computer skills (Morgan, Taylor, Bailey, Shane, & Sam) necessary for higher education. Morgan commented:

> They can't work out 10% of 100 or figure out the order of operations to use in a given situation. That holds them back from understanding economics; they don't understand numbers. They don't see how zeros make a difference or that millions and billions are not the same.

Other comments regarding students being unprepared for higher education included:

- Alex: "This is part of our context. We know about the quality of many of the schools here. The 'English' teachers don't speak a word of English"
- Sam: "some of the teachers aren't even teachers – no qualifications, no experience"
- Parker: "Even their English classes aren't necessarily conducted in English"

As Taylor explained:

> Through no fault of their own, students do not possess analytical skills in mathematics. It is how they have been educated. I never underestimate their intelligence ability. It is applying critical thinking and logic with regard to mathematics analysis.

In addition to lacking basic English, Math, and analytical skills, all educators acknowledged that students arrive to college completely unprepared for the responsibilities of higher education. Alex responded "Our students, many of them have grown up in an incubator. Many of them have spent 12 years in a vacuum instead of in a school. They don't gain much from their [prior] school experience." Cassidy noted "Students can spend 12 years in school and some have never opened or maintained a notebook." All 19 educators acknowledged that student unpreparedness for higher education represents a significant implementation factor for HD1's task-oriented curriculum because students don't understand how to engage with this form of learning. According to Addison:

The college becomes a dumping ground, meaning they graduate from high school and they are thrown to the far end of the pool. They have to swim or sink. They don't really have an understanding of what it takes to be a college student. Students come thinking that they can carry on with the habits they had from high school.

In addition, students' prior educational experiences foster a passive form of engagement with learning with few interactive and collaborative learning opportunities (Drew, Parker, Addison, Sam, Kelsey, Jordan, Ellis, Jaden, Morgan, Alex, Izzy, Spencer, & Corey). Drew noted "In this context, the traditional 3 R approach, read, recite, regurgitate approach, and the sage-on-stage approach is very accepted in high schools and secondary education levels." The carry-over effect into HD1 is that students are well-versed with the Transmission Model of Education as the teaching and learning norm of instruction and expect this norm to be implemented HD1:

As passive learners [in] schools, they just listen to stories being read to them. The ability to see beyond what is said or beyond what is read is missing or eliminated. This is when you are engaged. It's active, you are brainstorming with ideas. It's the self-engagement that is important, but not happening yet in the UAE. (Addison)

Seven educators observed that students arrive to HD1 lacking meta-cognitive awareness (Cassidy, Morgan, Parker, Kelsey, Parker, Izzy, & Drew). Students arrive to HD1 without having thought about learning strategies, or given thoughtful consideration to how they as individuals learn best. Drew stated that "The biggest challenge is students' understanding how they learn and how they can improve their style of learning." Ellis noted "awareness-raising [about learning] … is a huge issue here" and was the underlying reason behind inclusion for many curricular elements. Parker stated "Our students, when they arrive here, don't know how to **be** students."

All educators observed that their students did not understand the concept of completing homework. In addition, if there is no grade attached to homework, they do not complete it. Alex, for example, observed that "Students haven't done homework. It is not part of their ethos." Sam indicates "they never have had homework before – homework? Why, school work should be done at school in front of a teacher is what they have experienced." Bailey confirms Alex's observation and also noted the lack of motivation to do homework: "With our students it is difficult. They don't give it a thought" and also states "If there is no grade on something, it is not done. That is the problem."

Further, in their prior schooling experiences, students arrive at the college with experiences that leave many students with a sense of trepidation of public exposure of mistakes, according to 4 educators (Morgan, Cassidy, Shane, & Ellis). Ellis observed that students feel "a great fear of making mistakes in this context. Ironically, by the time they leave HD1, they seem to have worked that out – at some point in semester 2 they think, 'I am not a bad student.'" Shane thought,

"From a cultural point of view, I don't know whether students feel comfortable [asking for help]. On a number of occasions, I learned that they did not understand and went to help them. They say 'we were too shy or we didn't want to ask you, or offend you." Cassidy explained, "The first hurdle is helping students understand there is no shame for giving the wrong answer. The classroom is where you can explore mistakes." Sam commented, "They are afraid when they have to make a decision. It goes back to that question/answer philosophy. Here is the question and the right answer is …?" Morgan noted:

> Students think if they give the wrong answer, they will be embarrassed by the teacher. That is a method of learning that is not gone yet from the public school system. Here, you do not admit that you can't do it, or don't know how.

Thus, in this educational community implementation of HD1 curriculum was affected by students' lack of basic skills in English, Math, and logic and analysis. Implementation was influenced by prior educational experiences that supported passive engagement with learning and by students' lack of awareness of their own learning styles and different learning needs. As Alex summarized, "They are underprepared [for higher education]."

"When You Teach, I Learn." Initially, most DWC students arrive unable to assume responsibility or assert independence over their own learning and are uncertain about what it means to be empowered as self-directed learners, according to 11 educators (Parker, Nat, Morgan, Corey, Jaden, Bailey, Addison, Alex, Drew, Kelsey, & Cassidy). Bailey stated "They are not independent learners." This aspect appears resistant to change: Corey observed "Our learners are not the greatest ones for taking notes or keeping records – stuff that at the college level you think you should not have to tell them to do." All curricular documents emphasize the importance of students assuming responsibility for their success in HD1 and the concept is continually reiterated throughout by all faculty and supervisors. However, initially as Morgan explained,

> Students come to us the first day of college with no pen, no paper. They don't keep handouts. They are not academically inclined in any way. They can't organize notes in a chronological order, and they don't use a highlighter. We begin by teaching things like: you have to bring a pen to class.

Addison attributed this to how students conceptualize education: "They think knowledge is like an aspirin pill" to be obtained in class as "students feel that learning is held in the teacher." Ideologically, according to 7 educators, many students feel that learning occurs directly from the teacher, so they do not feel compelled to learn independently. As well, many parents feel their daughters should be either at home or, if at school, in a classroom in front of a teacher as that is the locus of learning. Alex recited

The fights we still have when we try to keep students on campus. If students had a free period at 10, they wanted to go home. I probably spent at least 1/3 of my time talking to students and parents about the importance of using that time for reading, working on assignments, going to the library. [The belief is] "If she is not in a classroom in front of a teacher then she should be at home." The battle goes on.

Spencer confirmed "We are some distance from being able to get them to be independent learners and recognize the importance of keeping up with developments in their fields. We are not there yet."

This lack of self-directed learning affects implementation of HD1 curriculum, because there is a mental shift required on the part of students as they enter HD1. The design of the task-based curriculum is intended to scaffold students in developing self-directed learning skills, according to 9 educators (Nat, Taylor, Jaden, Morgan, Spencer, Jordan, Sam, Cassidy, & Drew). Nat explained:

There is far less hand-holding [in HD1]. Individual responsibility is an undercurrent of our curriculum. The biggest thing is that students need to grasp that they need to work on their own. That is a mental shift for them. They see the consequences [of not making the mental shift] in learning cycle 1.

The result was that students were initially confused about curriculum that is task-oriented and learner-centred according to 13 educators (Morgan, Drew, Parker, Ellis, Shane, Spencer, Bailey,Taylor, Izzy, Addison, Jaden, Alex, & Cassidy). From the first day of HD1, implementation of HD1 curriculum presented "a huge learning curve" (Drew). Jaden commented, "They struggle with the whole concept." Addison believed this was a flaw in the orientation process. Addison commented that students needed a "proper introduction about the link so they can move things from the head to the hand" a comment Taylor confirmed and explained in detail:

They have got to move into a more free thinking form of learning in HD1. The HD1 approach is "get out and find out how this stuff applies in the real world." That is a fairly big challenge for all faculty in Year 1 – to move them into that mode of thinking. They [the students] have the reins over their learning.

Interestingly, 5 educators (Morgan, Spencer, Jaden, Ellis, & Cassidy) reported that after the first semester, many students begin to make an ideological connection with self-directed learning and the curricular tasks they are required to perform. The tasks themselves supported students' engagement in the learning process especially as the tasks were public events. Morgan commented

They are achieving a lot in an anecdotal sense. They are able to articulate that now they understand why they have to do their own reading summaries, what they have learned. Meta-cognitively, they are making better connections between what it is the individual does [herself] and what the outcome is.

Jaden also made this point and believed that the curricular tasks supported students' development of self-directed learning: "If you can get this kind of student engagement in learning, which our curricular tasks offer, more learning takes place because it is much more memorable and meaningful for most of our students." In addressing the implementation of a task-oriented curriculum approach, Ellis and Spencer both identified that the most successful approaches to support and scaffold a self-directed approach were those that impose

> an external client [such as the Company Visit presentation] and external deadlines [Bazaar and Current Issues Forum which are open to the public]. It naturally builds a lot of the framework into it. The students know on that specific date they have to be prepared for the event. If they aren't, we are all going to look foolish and our reputation in the country will be ruined. Their external clients are going to be judging our students. Their public reputation is very important to them. (Spencer)

Five educators commented that a task-based learning activity with a public face lends itself to some of the strengths of the students (Spencer, Cassidy, Taylor, Morgan, & Ellis). Inevitably, regardless of the best plans, sometimes crisis situations happen: financing for a Bazaar business is delayed, a delivery truck is stopped in traffic, refrigeration breaks down, cash registers stop functioning, desert sandstorms, rain storms, or excessive heat happens, any number of fairly typical issues have the potential to arise and cause problems with any public situation. But, as Morgan noted, "It is like chaos theory. Students can adjust once pure chaos [hits]. They can respond – extremely well." Ellis stated "Our students have an incredible tolerance of chaos. They feel 'it is our responsibility. We have ownership of the event and people are looking to us so we will make it work.' This is their real strength. They don't give up easily" (Ellis).

Shane made an interesting comparison: situations where DWC students excel are the same situations where "In a Western culture, in this situation, there would be absolute bedlam from students." Cassidy relayed an experience:

> I was teaching in Canada and during an integrated task, a poster fair, the invitations that one student group were responsible to create and send out incorrectly identified the room. The whole class of students were agitated and had to be reprimanded in order for them to calm down. Absolute Meltdown! Here, for the Bazaar event, one group's booth decorations product was delayed in arriving on campus. Did the group meltdown? No – they called everyone they could to go and pick up any decorations available that they could think of. They just got on with it and found solutions to their own problems. It was awesome to see. One way or the other, their booth was going to be ready for the grand opening.

Morgan suggested "Here, students are able to pull together resources, usually at the last minute, to get the job done. They will enlist maids, drivers, brothers, whatever and whoever they can get. They pull it together to make a cohesive whole." While servants, brothers, drivers are expressly not allowed on campus, and are unable to help with the labour of tasks in the booths, they can pick up deliveries, collect paperwork for signatures, or other small tasks if a crisis occurs. Cassidy responded "If you have an activity with a public face, and it just has to happen, these students can respond to chaos and crisis and they can pull anything off like no one else. Come hell or high water, the public face will shine."

Educators indicate that students arrived in HD1 with a belief that learning rested in the hands of the teacher, and unless they were in a class, in front of a teacher, no learning occurred. This stemmed from both prior schooling experiences and ideologies prevalent in the community. For this reason, the task-oriented approach to curriculum was very challenging for students as they had to make an ideological shift, which appeared to occur during the HD1 academic year. As well, educators disclosed that students functioned and responded particularly well when a public "face" formed part of the nature of communication of learning.

CONCLUSION

The design and implementation of a 21st century curriculum has many elements that must be considered. First, it must embrace 21st century knowledge and skills development. These aspects must be woven throughout curriculum. Assessment in a 21st century curriculum incorporates assessment literacy practices of assessment for, of and as learning. Crucial is embedding performance assessment tasks throughout curriculum, however, a tension in relation to assessment involves the issue of accountability and relevance. A 21st century assessment must strike a balance in order to address policy and protocol needs while also maintaining the integrity of assessing the learning.

Any 21st century curriculum design must understand the nature of the audience – the learners. The learners at DWC were all Emirati female higher education students. Emirati students were described as incredibly gracious and welcoming of foreigners. There are some divergences in the nature of female restrictions: some families are quite liberal and others were not. Emirati students' prior education did not prepare them well for higher education and students believe knowledge rests in the hands of the teachers rather than themselves and their own initiative. Emirati students are very resourceful and "face" is an all important issue in learning. Twenty-first century education for Emirati students is a complex balancing act of all of these aspects in relation to the design and implementation of curriculum. This chapter provides the basis for understanding the integrated, transdisciplinary, 21st century curriculum designed and implemented in the 2008–2009 academic year.

NOTE

[i]   According to my private conversations with many Emirati and Arab individuals over the years, saying the word pays respect to Allah (God) prior to beginning any task or endeavour. A close translation is "By the Grace of Allah," or "Glory to Allah."

CHAPTER 6

MAKING LEARNING MEANINGFUL

Trans-Disciplinary 21ˢᵗ Century Curriculum

INTRODUCTION

This chapter outlines the integrated, trans-disciplinary curriculum designed by the faculty and curriculum leadership at DWC. Aspects such as the tasks, educators' thoughts regarding the tasks, assessments and tensions are discussed. It is important to note that all learners were provided copies of the curricular documents with complete outlines of all learning tasks, due dates, indications of group or individual work, assessments and rubrics.

Three Trans-Disciplinary Curricular Tasks

The Higher Diploma Year 1 (HD1) curriculum at DWC is constructed using the Higher Colleges of Technology (HCT) Graduate Outcomes as guiding principles and following constructivist learning theory framework. The graduate outcomes are standardized and guide teaching and learning throughout all 16 campuses of the HCT system in the UAE. The curriculum is constructed to conform to the HCT course outlines, which are also standardized throughout all 16 colleges of HCT in the UAE. Although the HCT Learning Model, Graduate Outcomes, and the HCT course outlines are common amongst the 16 colleges, the development of HD1's curricular documents, which uses a task-based learning approach and follows constructivist learning theory in orientation, are developed and implemented by HD1's faculty and are unique to DWC.

Task-based learning approaches feature prominently in discussions of constructivist curriculum (Henderson & Gornik, 2007). Task-based learning (TBL) is a strategy that focuses on the completion of a specific task or sequence of tasks through which learning emanates (Ellis, 2003). In TBL, the focus for the learners is not a simulation of a problem, but an actual task that is grounded in the reality of their learning discipline (Harden & Laidlaw, 1996) and transferrable to a real world (Drake, 2007) context. The emphasis in a 21ˢᵗ century curriculum is that these learning tasks should be collaborative, interdisciplinary and authentic tasks that foster the development of 21ˢᵗ century skills and foster transferable longevity to the real world context of civil society. This is the model for development of curriculum that HD1 at DWC follows.

The HD1 academic year is separated into two semesters each of which are 18 weeks in duration. Learning cycles 1 and 2 are completed in semester 1 from September through mid-January. Learning cycles 3 and 4 are completed in semester 2 from February through early June. Each learning cycle has a corresponding integrated learning document which provides details related to a primary learning task. These learning documents delineate the specific elements of learning for all four courses and identifies learning tasks that learners are expected to achieve during the learning cycle including all assessments (of, for, and as learning) and rubrics for evaluation if graded. These learning documents also delineate dates for assignments and events, and identify elements that are either collaborative or individual work. The primary task is specifically mandated as collaborative and learners are placed into random groups, usually by the Business teacher, or the Business teacher and English teacher. Copies of these learning documents are given to learners at the beginning of each learning cycle and an extensive, week-long orientation at the beginning of each semester familiarizes learners with understanding the nature of the document. Students performed and completed these primary tasks in groups. These tasks were public events and formed the core for students' achievement and learning for the academic year. All lesson plans and assessments emanated from these primary learning tasks for all four core courses: Math, English, Business and Information Technology (IT).

Semester 1, Learning Cycle 1

The task for learning cycle 1 consisted of a group visit to interview a manager or supervisor in a local company. The curriculum for this task is entitled "Research, Analyze, and Present." For this event, learners in their groups: chose a company in Dubai from a specific economic sector; made all arrangements to visit the company prior to October 12, 2008; and developed an interview protocol to learn about that company's place in the economic sector and uncover management strategies the supervisor embraces as part of his or her leadership style. This information was then collected from the interview and visit, collated and analyzed, and subsequently presented to the Math, English, and Business teacher in class using any form of digital communication the students' chose. The presentation forms part of assessment of learning, and continuous feedback throughout the learning cycle presented many opportunities for assessment for learning. For many learners, this was their first time off-campus into the "real world" without a teacher, parent, or guardian as chaperone. All presentations took place in class during the week of November 2, 2008. These presentations required the following: relevant research about the economy and economic sector; evidence that the group visited an appropriate company and understood details such as ownership, structure, company activities, key indicators, and competitors; a minimum of five different sources of information including the company website; statistical information about the economic sector, the economy of Dubai, and the UAE economy; and evidence of MLA referencing. The presentations were also graded for engaging and innovative use of technology to communicate their information.

Educators' Reflections Regarding This Task. All educators believed this first task provided the necessary induction for learners in relation to understanding the nature of learning through a task-based and collaborative approach. Specifically, educators stated that the Company Visit presentation caused "enormous conflict because the penny drops" (Nat). Nat stated, with this task came learners' realization that "if they don't work together, if somebody in the group doesn't pull her weight, then the whole group suffers." Cassidy, Morgan, and Perry believed that this task models for learners how professionals must work together to accomplish a task because it involved and was evaluated by 3 HD1 teachers, Math, English, and Business faculty modelling collaboration. Perry states "The three subject teachers sit in that presentation, each evaluating a different aspect. Sometimes, that is what it takes to inform the learners. That's where it is all brought together."

Morgan, Taylor, and Perry believed that this first task allowed learners to begin to make the "link between school and what is going on in Dubai's economy" (Taylor). However, 5 educators reported learners had difficulty making the extended connections in concepts or interpreting information beyond what was explicitly stated in the Company Visit presentation. For example, Perry noted in relation to assisting learners' in thinking through and planning the task,

> Students have trouble dissecting the topic. The most difficult aspect is getting them to identify the questions [for the interviewee] that elicit the answers to feed in to the information they need. When you ask them to make up questions to get particular answers related to theory, they have no idea where to begin. It is very important to foster students' understanding of these elements and help students think through the logic. I found that with each group, I had students engage in a group peer exchange of their interview protocols prior to visiting the company for peer feedback. This was very instrumental in students 'seeing how a question is asked has an impact on how it can be answered and what information it will elicit. [This was] very powerful learning for students.

The presentation itself is very challenging for students. In many cases, this represented students first time delivering an oral presentation and being asked questions related to their information. Part of the difficulty students had relates to nervousness and anxiety, and another difficulty rests with learners' synthesis of the information they have amassed from their research. Kelsey commented, "When learners are asked to interpret, extrapolate, or critically evaluate anything that is off the slides, many have great difficulty." Kelsey further explained:

> They had no difficulty speaking about Gross Domestic Product figures, but if you ask them to analyse or talk about them, students have very little idea as to what to say. With Maths, if you ask the learners to talk about a line in a graph [that they have used in their presentation], "what is the trend represented?" They can make the line appear but many can't or won't discuss what it means. This could be due to nerves, but more likely it is due to the difficulty understanding how to interpret implications of the knowledge they had presented, particularly as this facet of learning is new to most students.

Morgan identified that learners engaged in a traditional, transmission model of reciting learning in their presentation by speaking word-for-word information, without actually understanding the meaning behind the information during this first curricular task. Morgan explained:

This is what they know from their prior learning experiences in school. You memorize information, you repeat it; you don't question, deconstruct, conceptualize or synthesize what you have learned. It is natural that they would automatically present in this manner. It takes a lot of feedback and debriefing to help students appreciate these other skills and for the first task, perhaps it is more important that they just experience this kind of learning.

Interestingly, this value of the experience for students was a premise mirrored by 11 educators as they reflected on this first curricular task. These educators believed the real learning from this task rested with giving learners an opportunity to have an interaction with Dubai as a global marketplace, an engagement of presenting information and being asked questions on that information, and an experience of being responsible for the organization of the event by themselves. Kelsey commented "I feel that the real learning is in the experience – of going out and arranging, getting it wrong, getting it right, seeing the person, talking to the person." Izzy reflected on the learners' experience:

The company visit gets the girls out of their comfort zone and forces them to do things that a lot of them had never had to do: call up a company, visit a company unchaperoned to get information, ask questions, present publically. Those are the things that give them a real sense of satisfaction. It gives them useful skills: using presentation format, communicating, collaborating, encouraging language in a public setting. They can get a real sense of satisfaction out of that.

Nat, Morgan, Kelsey, Parker, Spencer, and Cassidy found that after the learners arrived back at the college after the company visit they were inspired. "Going out there, meeting people at the company. You could see it, they grew; it was a fantastic experience for them. The learning from this experience was responsibility and independence" (Nat).

Semester 1, Learning Cycle 2

Three different learning tasks were in operation during learning cycle 2 and their corresponding documents were entitled "DWC Bazaar," "DWC Bazaar Bank," "DWC Career Majlis." The Bazaar consists of HD1 learners, in groups, working with Higher Diploma Year 2 (HD2) learners' on-campus businesses during a 3-day, open to the public Bazaar event. The Bazaar event is intended to mirror the real world marketplace. Learners create a business concept, develop a business plan, obtain financing, create a website and marketing plan, and run the business during the 3 day Bazaar campus-wide event. The purpose of this event is to help learners make a connection between their learning and the real world of commerce in Dubai. For the Bazaar Project, HD1 learners must prepare a group report which chronicles: meeting their Year 2 business managers and listening to their ideas; brainstorming strategies, creating a summary of the Year 2 business plan; reading and understanding their employment contracts, job descriptions, and training, and learning about and critiquing the HD2 operation plan, finance, and accounting procedures; designing and recording their own sales and performance records and recording evidence and examples of Year 2's management for incorporation in Year 1's peer evaluation of the business; carrying out assigned duties during the 3-day Bazaar event while maintaining accurate records of developments; reviewing and understanding their performance review from their Year 2 employers; preparing a performance evaluation of their Year 2 employers particularly in relation to objectives; meeting their operations plans, marketing and evaluating financial skills and their business web pages; and evaluating Year 2's leadership style and delegation, conflict management skills, and decision-making skills.

For this event, a specific currency is created called DWC Dhows, which has cultural significance in Dubai as the dhows are the traditional Arab sailing vessels used for the pearling industry that once dominated the economic trade for the Gulf region. Year 2 businesses also created banks which handled the exchange of UAE dirhams (official currency) for DWC Dhows, the only currency allowed for the Bazaar event. Some HD1 learner groups were employed by the Year 2 banks. The learning document for this task is entitled "DWC Bazaar Bank." The purpose of the DWC Bank is to help learners make a connection between their learning and real-world situations in actual financial institutions with their Year 2 DWC Bank employers during the Bazaar. For the Bazaar Project, HD1 learners must prepare a group report which chronicles and evaluates: a description of the DWC Bank branch assigned including assigned duties; marketing strategy and promotion strategy for the branch; discussion of method of providing customers information about Dhows and method of ensuring that all businesses use Dhows; details of customer service, place strategy, and distribution channels; organization of staffing and plan of leadership; analysis of DWC Bank activity; numerical data for statistical analysis of the bank branch including discussion of cash auditing, transactions, Dhow exchange, and cash flow; and evaluation of individual and group Bank performance.

In the 2008–2009 academic year, learner numbers for HD1 were significantly larger than learner numbers in Year 2, so there were not enough HD2 businesses to employ Year 1 learners. The HD1 teachers, the Career Services Department at DWC, and the HD1 Chair made a curricular decision to implement a new learning task for two classes of HD1 learners during Bazaar. A new event called Career Majlis was created, and piloted during the 2008–2009 academic year, with a corresponding learning document. This task was specifically designed for the HD1 night class of employed learners (two classes), because they had practical, real-world knowledge of working life for Emirati women. The purpose of the Career Majlis was to help learners to make a connection between what they learn in their courses and a 'real world' situation of having a job in the UAE. The DWC Career Majlis is conceptualized as a non-profit service.

For the Career Majlis at Bazaar, learners created an outside, open, Arab-style discussion area (called a "Majlis") where they presented information in groups to visitors regarding topics they believed to be relevant to Emirati women working in Dubai. The topics were all learner generated and chosen during an in-class brainstorming session. For the Career Majlis, learners were required to prepare group reports chronicling: a career earnings projection and trajectory for the future; family monthly/yearly budget with statistical analysis and projection. They were also expected to include critical analysis of authentic experiences they had in relation to their chosen topic and how those experiences impact the nature of their working lives grounding their analysis with multiple perspectives and literature related to the issues. These reports were shared and presented to visitors to the Majlis. Each group was required to facilitate a discussion and questioning forum to encourage audience participation and engagement in the issue. Subsequently, each group created a summary of the participants' contributions. Each group developed the marketing message for their topic and marketed the Career Majlis to other learners and their families (visitors to the DWC's Bazaar) to ensure they had an audience during Bazaar. Each group managed the Majlis and observed, audited, analyzed, and evaluated the service during each shift and elicited visitor feedback on their information sessions.

The creation of learner-generated presentations in the manner of a Career Majlis has cultural significance, as a majlis is the forum for discussion prevalent in this region, still used to this day. A majlis refers to a place of sitting and it is a special area both in private homes for entertaining guests, and public offices for meetings, and special gatherings among common interest groups: families, administrations, and social, religious, or legislative groups. To this day, any person wishing to be heard at the Royal Majlis is welcome regardless of nationality.

The entire bazaar event operates according to specific guidelines and faculty fulfil many roles during the event. For example, faculty are on campus during the set-up of the event; they are expected to monitor the event and visit booths ensuring that learners are adequately and safely set up, ensuring that dress codes and behaviour conduct is appropriate, and assessing different booths for decor, customer service, originality, and cleanliness.

This particular campus-wide event is moderately open to the media and the public, but under strict access and security rules. DWC is a facility surrounded by walls with entry gates monitored by hired security staff to ensure that only learners, faculty, and staff are able to get in or out on a daily basis. Opening this facility to the public, even moderately, requires strict faculty supervision and monitoring during the event. The following 'open access' schedule was implemented:

- day 1 is the opening ceremony and the campus is open for industry guests, faculty and staff, and other female school and college educators in the region;
- day 2 is a ladies-only day only ladies and children (boys under the age of 13 years) allowed;
- day 3 is family day when fathers, husbands, and brothers are welcome to attend (Memorandum to faculty November 16, 2008 re: Security for Bazaar).

The protocols for security were:

1. Pre-registered male guest (husband or brother only) can come through the main gate only.
2. A currently enrolled learner must check in the male guest.
3. The security will check and register the identification of the learner and the identification (driver's license) of the guest.
4. All female guests and all children under 13 are welcome.
5. Male national guests *must* be family members (fathers, husbands, brothers).
6. Male Emirati guests must be signed in and accompanied by a DWC learner who is a family relation at all times.
7. If a male guest would like to enter the premises and a faced-covered learner is trying to sign him in, a female security person must check the identity of the face-covered learner.

Educators' Reflections Regarding Bazaar. All educators commented that the Bazaar task of learning cycle 2 in semester 1 was a curricular high point. All educators identified it as a highly collaborative, important educational event for learners for two specific reasons:

1. it was an authentic learning task where students demonstrated their learning in a manner that represented the real world marketplace, and,
2. it was representative and highly relatable to Emirati culture.

The curricular task of the Bazaar was to transform the entire campus into "a huge souk. It's a wonderful opportunity for the ladies. They come back to class after Bazaar changed. They became aware of the broader picture" (Ellis). Four educators appreciated the potential of Bazaar to allow for innovative business ideas from learners. Cassidy commented "I loved the costume portrait studio idea." Parker elaborated further:

> You get some really entrepreneurial girls. Some girls started a car washing service, which was fantastic. They did the cleaning and they buffed the cars and they made a lot of money. Girls had a business where you could hire gyroscopic controlled balance machines to stand on. You hire them and go around the bazaar. There have been some real interesting ideas.

Alex and Addison both identified the entrepreneurial spirit of the learners in relation to raising financing for the on-campus businesses.

> In this context, where it is easy to just go to a father or brother who probably owns a business or a bank, some of our students were far more innovative. One of the bank groups, created on online website where they were eliciting Emirati support and asking for financing partners from multiple sources. What a great idea, instead of going to a potential financier with a business proposal as required by the program, they posted their business proposal,

marketed it, and allowed the financing to come to them. Brilliant. These ladies will likely do very well in finance. (Alex)

Sam, Kelsey, Bailey and Nat spoke to how students realized the importance of precision in calculating currency exchange rates and cash flow. Sam stated:

The Bazaar Bank made numbers have hard core meaning for students. They were calculating profit and loss, figuring out why floats were either short or over, identifying how to represent these issues on balance sheets. After the bazaar, math class had a very different spirit. Students were making connections between their experiences working in the Bazaar with the concepts introduced. That is powerful learning especially in this context.

Educators' Reflections Regarding Career Majlis. Educators felt this curricular innovation represented their ability to adapt to changing circumstances. During the academic year of 2008-2009, just prior to the beginning semester, enrolment of a very specific group of Emirati women increased significantly. This specific group consisted of female Emiraties who were already employed at some level in the workforce but desired the continuation of their education. Many were married and had children as well. These women were working very hard on their education, but also had many demands on their time and their resources. This meant that the totality of HD1 learners outnumbered HD2, which meant that there were not enough HD2 businesses and banks to employ all HD1 learners. Thus, there were two full cohorts of evening students who would be unable to contribute to Bazaar in the same way as the full time day students. As it is a curriculum requirement to complete the Bazaar task, and given their working schedule and life experience, a new learning task was created by the HD1 team in collaboration with the Career Services Department that would capitalize on knowledge and skill while also providing a meaningful learning experience not only for them but for all visitors to the Career Majlis.

Thirteen educators stated the Career Majlis was the most significant learning task for all of HD1 during the academic year. Addison commented "this is learning that matters, relevant, real, and shared knowledge that is learner-driven and emphasizes the issues our women will encounter in their lives. These are the important issues – the controversial issues that mean something to our community." The Career Majlis consisted of a learner-designed and decorated discussion area where learners in groups created presentations and facilitated discussions with the regular day learners and visitors about issues of working life and family life they deemed as important to Emirati women. The topics themselves were entirely learner generated, chosen, and researched: Creating a Family Budget (all groups); Working for a Foreign Supervisor; Women's Roles; Emiratization; Time-Management; Marriage and Emirati Women; Change, Tradition and Modern Life; Conflict in the Workplace; and Work Challenges and Strategies. Cassidy summed it up nicely, "Everyone walked away inspired with these students and with new understandings of the realities they face on a day to day basis. They are inspirational in their devotion to their learning, their work ethic, their values, and their commitment."

Drew concurred with other educators regarding the learners' learning through this project:

> Career Majlis during Bazaar [was exceptional]. There was a strong collaborative effort between the Career Centre, the HD1 teachers and the HD1 learners. The night before, learners were setting up, walking around [promoting their majlis], running around in circles. They realized that they weren't organized with many things they needed to do. They managed to make it happen, mistakes or [problems] and all. It was a rich learning experience. I saw the groups of the morning learners sitting at the majlis talking about the work place, and people were really engaged in the discussion. People were listening, these students were empowered – their voices were heard and valued for their substantial contribution they made to participatory progress for Emirati women.

Ellis also acknowledged learners' learning from these curricular tasks "The sheer complexity of life, stimulates their curiosity." Parker noted too that "These curriculum tasks, especially this one, really do animate them."

Semester 2, Learning Cycles 3 and 4

HD1's curriculum demonstrates a change for semester 2 from the norm. Instead of having two learning cycles and two corresponding curricular tasks, semester 2 became learning cycles 3 and 4, with one curricular task, the Current Issues Forum (CIF). In late 2008, a devastating, world-wide, financial crisis occurred. This financial crisis had significant, long- lasting ramifications on Dubai's economy. All educators believe that a salient feature of a 21st century curriculum is that it needs to be responsive to current real-world issues and events, and adapt quickly and effectively to change in Dubai's society.

Significantly according to 12 educators, DWC's students appeared to have little awareness of anything pertaining to the financial crisis. Jordan explained: "[We are] at the height of the financial crisis and at the height of recognition that our students have no clue what is going on around them." Further, students who were aware of the crisis did not realize or believe that it had any impact on them regardless of its devastating impact on Dubai's economy. Shane elaborated on a recent class during a questioning period with students regarding the impact of the global crisis: "Everyone said, 'Well it doesn't affect me. We know it's going on but it doesn't have any bearing on us whatsoever.'" But, the crisis did have an acute effect on the economy of Dubai and, consequently, both residents and Emirati citizens as well. Morgan clarified

> Our students are quite sheltered from negative occurrences. When the financial crisis hit, it was very real. Some students' families lost a great deal of money, many of our working students lost their jobs. Dubai was not

insulated from what was happening, but our students very seldom think about what happens outside of Dubai, or even about issues that happen in Dubai. The financial crisis was major, but educators, in talking to students, discovered that students had no idea that a crisis existed. In November, students had total blank looks [on their faces]. We had to do something to address this.

In response to students' lack of recognition of the financial crisis, the theme of the Current Issues Forum was specifically geared to this crisis. The title of the learning task was "Global Economic Crisis: The Impact on My Career and Community." For this curricular task, students were required to conduct primary and secondary research, learned about a specific aspect of the financial crisis, and presented their findings in a 3-day, open campus, HD1 student conference. The current issues were randomly assigned to groups and the list is appended in Appendix A "Current Issues Forum: Issues and Booth Allocations." They thoroughly researched their topic, located alternate perspectives, critiqued the research, and created a presentation to be held in booths, which they decorated and marketed to the audience for the open event. During the 3-day public event, students were required cover all shifts, advertised their booth, publically presented their topic, and fielded questions related to their topic from faculty and visitors on campus including invited industry and government from within the UAE. Morgan believed:

> The success of the curriculum can be observed at this time by whether or not they are able to work independently, willing to work with other people, and almost the corollary, the amount of conflict that you see or don't see is a good measure of whether they have learned the group norms to accomplish the CIF project. Are those skills built? Has it worked? The observable behaviour is what the curriculum is designed for. A huge outcome is the students actually started to read the news, very surprising. The number of students who said on the last day, "what I learned this year is that I need to read the news so that I know what is going on in my town." That is a big achievement this semester.

Eight educators commented that the Current Issues Forum, with its associated topic themes relating to the financial crisis, was a highly successful curricular inclusion (Drew, Cassidy, Parker, Jordan, Jaden, Spencer, Ellis, & Shane). All educators believed that students learned a great deal from the event as it exposed them to the effect of the crisis on both Dubai and the world. Sam elaborated on the salience of the CIF: "The event helps them learn what is going on around them. They became aware."

Working through these tasks as elements of curriculum, and as they are moderately open to the public (during Semester 1) and fully open to the public in general (during Semester 2), requires that female learners, and their families, must accept cross-gender communication, interaction, and presence in proximity to members of the male gender who are neither relatives nor spouses nor teachers, and representing their public voices and fielding questions in relation to controversial and sometimes contentious topics. This is a new circumstance for many female learners and some find it to be culturally unacceptable (Burden-Leahy, 2005; Patai, 2002). But, this also represents the Business and IT workplace reality because in these fields, in Dubai, most of these workplaces are not gender-segregated. In this respect, it is the curriculum and the educators teaching this curriculum at DWC who stand at the forefront of these kinds of issues that are respresentative of working life in the UAE.

Educators' Reflections Regarding Current Issues Forum. Due to the controversial nature of the CIF, specifically during this academic year when there was great change as a result of the global financial crisis, all educators recognized that there were implications for both learners and instructors. Drew explained that "We are trying to get learners to think at a deeper learning [level], explore, push the boundaries. Some learners perceive us as imposing or pushing the boundaries too far. It takes quite a bit of sensitivity." Perry commented "teaching the learners open mindedness. It is an obligation for us to get involved." Parker explained the nature of the tensions involved in exploring controversial issues: "More and more, those issues are more acceptable here. Slowly. You have to have a highly attuned antennae, here." Morgan elaborated on the newness of having Emirati explore these issues:

> Learners do not see issues the way [others' do]. One group's topic was the "UAE Relying on Domestic Workers." Here, maids here are not covered by labour laws …. That group did an amazing job of presenting opposite perspectives. They included statistics that 50% of maids in the UAE are abused …. Some of the current issues we deal with now could never have been approached in the past: labourer rights, Thalessemia Disease and blood testing prior to marriage. Another new topic was genetic abnormalities and consanguineous marriage which is common here. These are issues that have impact on the health care sectors, which have also been impacted by the economic crisis. But, these are very controversial especially when you consider many of our students' families may be CEO's or have governmental positions that control some of these issues.

During the Current Issue Forum, students learned about highly controversial topics for this region. One group presented about the lack of labour rights in the construction industry in Dubai. It is important to consider that many of these students' families made their wealth from this industry. Some students' parents own some of these companies and families were invited to the event. Students debated the issue of consanguineous marriage in a country where first-cousin marriage dominates as the norm amongst Emirati people. Students researched and presented their findings regarding domestic labour abuse prevalent in the UAE. This is significant because almost all Emirati families have at least one and often more foreign maids, and domestic labour is not officially governed by the labour laws of the UAE. Students heard, read, questioned, considered, and wrote about these and other challenging new topics that may or may not have contravened their worldviews.

The international faculty created the opportunity for learners to drive the task. These educators did not present these controversial topics in class for debate, which likely would have resulted in negative connotations for the teacher. Instead, the international faculty created the situation for learners to explore the issues through research, readings, and presentations. Learners responded with well-developed presentations with multiple perspectives and their own opinions valued. This strategy has the potential for learners to expand their worldviews because they are required to consider alternate perspectives. This has the potential to contribute to learners' positive self-perceptions in a public forum because they are being seen and heard discussing difficult social and economic issues.

All educators specifically identified that the reason why curriculum follows a task-orientation is because of the need for experiential learning for these students in this context. They further identified that students generally arrive at Higher Diploma Year 1 without the skills they need for success in their learning. All educators acknowledged that students leave Higher Diploma Year 1 armed with work-related experiences, better test-taking strategies and skills, and exposure to real world issues and concerns. They leave with abilities to present and express themselves in public forums and abilities to question and evaluate the information they locate or receive. Students reflected on their identity and how they will define their roles in society while maintaining their integrity to their cultural and religious beliefs (explored in more detail in Module 3). This is a thought-provoking issue that all students must define for themselves.

The HD1 curriculum tasks attempted to support change, but in a manner that honoured Emirati society through "empowerment of Emirati women to be their own agents of change. Our curriculum tasks support them, their voices, their choices. Some of the topics in the CIF are controversial, but we give them the chance to speak on them, publically. That's important – this represents to students that their voices matter particularly in relation to these real world issues" (Cassidy).

STRENGTH: EXPERIENTIAL LEARNING, AUTHENTICITY & RELEVANCE

Twelve educators specifically identified that the strength of the HD1, 21st century curriculum rests with the fact that it required learners to engage in real-world tasks and respond to real world issues that are authentic to life in Dubai, transferable to a work context, and open to a public audience. Kelsey stated "We take learners outside their comfort zones and put them in situations where they will be [in the future], the employment context." According to Ellis, "We give them real-world experiences. They have to go out and talk to managers and they have to go out and see how companies operate." Morgan noted that "We give them work because we are trying to educate them to become functioning members in a working society. That is our mandate." Perry, Kelsey, Corey, and Taylor commented specifically about the value of Bazaar. Perry noted "It is entrepreneurial, public and real." Spencer also acknowledged that "It is beneficial. It energizes learners and it gets them to employ a broad spectrum of skills which is similar to the workplace."

Learner engagement was a factor that impacted learners' learning. Morgan, Corey, and Alex emphasized that the importance of the development of a task-based curriculum in this context rested with having learners do—the requirement of doing a task. Alex explained:

We made that shift to task based curriculum with emphasis on authentic tasks because we feel it results in deeper learning. Our learners in particular need to know how to do things, because they don't *do* many things in their daily life. When kids grow up in most parts of the world, they learn how to ride bicycles, they do chores, they are involved in charity work, and so forth. They do physical and mental things. They had part time jobs and household responsibilities. Most of our students have servants, they are often catered to, they don't generally have part-time jobs or responsibilities other than to their families. Students in other parts of the world have a connection with themselves and with the world they live in that is much more advanced than most of our students.

Ellis elaborated:

The most satisfying part of what we do is turning our learners into learners who don't panic. They can keep a grip of the situation and solve problems, make decisions, the work together and negotiate through conflicts because they are exposed to all of this messiness through our tasks.

Corey commented on a very important element representing the authentic nature of Bazaar: "Learners can be sacked. I have had learners sacked and they were speechless. These are the kind experiences that they really learn from. All the appropriate procedures of documenting performance issues, encouraging opportunities for performance to improve with clearly delineated success strategies. But if improvement doesn't happen, the student can be sacked by her Year 2 employers in consultation with the teachers." (Corey). Taylor explained the immediacy of the hands-on experience:

They are the employees. There is no getting out of it. You [learners] are going to have to walk around and try to sell to people. And, it is going to hurt. You have to promote, you have to market, you have to engage in customer service. You have to be alert and attentive. You have to be precise. They don't want to do that. In fact, they can't think of anything worse. One said to me "I have to clean the table but I don't know how. The maid has always done it."

These curricular experiences require engagement in the performance and completion of tasks that mirror authentic work experiences in the business world in Dubai in a manner that corresponds to the culture of the UAE, but also has the potential to extend the boundaries of cultural norms. For example, 12 educators specifically indicated that curricular experiences such as Bazaar, Company Visit, Virtual International Exchanges, Career Fair, Current Issue Forum as pivotal events because culturally they extended the repertoire of experiences for learners, which "generates curiosity and a need for learning" (Ellis). They offered public exposure for learners, were occasionally unchaperoned off-campus events, with cross-cultural interaction or cross-gender interaction, while at the same time being acceptable by most Emirati families. These events were acceptable as long as they were perceived as "safe and controllable" (Kelsey) by the Emirati community.

However, Taylor, Corey, and Shane would like to see these curricular tasks become "freer" culturally. Shane explained that "Learners are too hidden from what happens outside [the college]." Corey explored some of the problems with the authenticity of these learning experiences existed at this time:

> The purpose behind the Bazaar is to expose the learners to the realities of an open market. In actual fact, it is not – they are limited as to what they can sell. No chocolate, fizzy drinks. No music allowed. That is not a free market enterprise. For the bazaar, why are those restrictions applied? So we are saying to learners "go run a business, but don't do this and this and this." It is a little false.

Similarly, Taylor elaborated on the constraints:

> These events, career majlis, bazaar, the company visit are very good socio-culturally but could be freer. However, you have to answer to the parents. If there is a major incident, if affects the name of the college. Sometimes, I just feel it is a little bit too protective because Dubai is a very modern city and moving fast.

According to all educators, a task-based curriculum must reflect the realities, provide experiential opportunities and reflect the relevance of the community for which it is intended. Spencer noted "Authenticity is probably the most important thing for a successful result. When it has the feel of authenticity, they take it more seriously." Morgan explained "We have to give our learners authentic readings, authentic case studies and situations, authentic tasks. All of the readings are current and culled from various sources: media, government sites, journals" Kelsey added regarding the learning learners' experience: "It forces independence. They have to do things themselves, which inevitably go wrong. That is the learning." Seven educators commented on the challenges. Parker noted

> The challenges that come up are the ones we want to come up. It is those problems we want them to solve that come up in real business endeavours: communication, shift work, and Year 2 supervisor problems. Absolutely, that is what we want. We want it to be a chore that our learners accomplish. We don't want it all to be easy.

Ellis particularly stressed the value of representing reality in authentic curricular tasks and emphasized the value of learning from experiences that go wrong and the chaotic nature of the curricular tasks, particularly the Bazaar:

> I believe order comes out of chaos and these girls don't have enough messiness in their lives. I celebrate the messiness. When things go wrong on

the booths, they have to solve these challenges and this is really good for HD1 [learners]. Most of them, their rooms are tidy because "someone" tidies it for them. Everything, possibly even choosing a husband, are not messy experiences for learners. But, we could do more to help them prepare. "This is going to be messy but you've got to keep a clear head." (Ellis)

Morgan reflected on the resources used in the program:

We only use authentic materials. We use Zawya and UAE Interact online databases, we use the Chamber of Commerce's data. We use the Dubai Statistics Centre data. Learners will use these sites when they enter the workforce. This is data they need about their country. It's real. It's relevant. It's transferable.

In addition, all English language materials were generated from authentic, real-world media and governmental texts. Nat commented "Using authentic texts exposes learners to real English with all its multiple variations." Nat also stated an additional benefit being that "I always look for local texts. This covers a lot of the religious, cultural, and political concerns I may have about appropriateness of the content for this context and these learners."

The English team constructed lesson plans using source materials from: UAE governmental reports, the BBC, Dubai Eye (radio program), Al Jazeera English, English Breakfast (radio program), Khaleej Times, The National, Gulf News, UAE Interact, and various other sources. This includes the texts for all English exams. However Cassidy cautions "If the topic is controversial, I always include a response from a powerful Emirati such as the lesson 'The Dark Side of Dubai' (a BBC documentary chronicling negative implications of the development that was occurring in Dubai). Otherwise, you can run into 'face' problems. But, these learners need to think about these issues." Parker explained the value of culturally relevant lesson planning and resources:

I am committed to our approach particularly for these learners. They come from a totally different [educational] philosophy – rote learning. They don't actually know how the learning can be applied in their lives. That is always my starting point: authentic experience and texts that can be applied. When I am creating lesson plans, I think about what is valuable, needed by our learners. I think about how it is going to feed in their courses, their careers, their lives.

Three educators, Morgan, Taylor, and Parker further cautioned that the authenticity of curricular content and tasks must represent the reality of what is going on in the real world at the current time, which for Dubai is one of continual and rapid change. Morgan explained the critical need for current curricular content: "All of the examples I use are local. The topics that we cover are the ones that are from the newspapers during that particular semester. We don't include stuff that is 6 months old." Parker also stated "The authenticity of what we bring into the classroom has to reflect what is true out there now, not what was true 5 years ago."

All educators in this study believed that the strength of this curriculum rests with its experiential nature, relevance, and authenticity. The curriculum was experiential because learners were engaged in doing tasks to support their learning, particularly with events that had a public audience. The content materials were relevant to learners because they were drawn from current authentic media sources about the world of business in Dubai, which was the world these learners will be part of when they seek and obtain employment. The tasks guiding the curriculum authentically represent aspects of participation in global marketplace. Educators saw this as crucial for HD1 learners, but some educators wished the learning opportunities were less constrained.

TENSIONS: HD1 CURRICULUM

As much as educators were enthusiastic about the learning opportunities presented with their curriculum design and teaching and learning approaches, tensions emanated from implementation of HD1 curriculum. Specifically, the educators' discussed: Semester 1; teaching critical thinking; and teaching learners to conduct research.

Semester 1

Semester 1 appeared to be extremely challenging for learners and educators, particularly the first task, which was the Company Visit presentation. Seven educators reported that the dramatic curricular approach change from what learners have previously experienced in schooling, the full curricular requirements, the many assessments, and the time off and shortened days for the religious holidays of Ramadan, Eid Al Fetr, contributed to the "frenetic" (Taylor) semester.

Eight educators noted that the ideological shift required for learners as they enter Semester 1 placed them in a state of confusion and frustration, particularly the shift from learner dependence on the teacher to the requirement for learners to develop a sense of autonomy over their learning experiences: "One of my objectives was for learners to understand the projects [better]. Our learners come with the idea that they are going to be told everything. It's hard to move them into a more independent learning space in their brains" (Drew).

Interestingly, 7 educators observed that although Semester 1 was a significant challenge for learners, this was the moment when they "begin to get switched on. The company visit task is life changing for most of our learners. They come back after meeting a total stranger and interviewing them. They become motivated, changed" (Morgan). Therefore, as difficult as Semester 1 was due to the ideological change required, it appeared that this represented a significant experience for learners in their motivation for learning.

The Challenge of Teaching Critical Thinking

Teaching for critical thinking is a Graduate Outcome for HCT and a required element in the course outlines. All educators reported that they believed in critical thinking as an essential skill for learners. However, 6 educators commented that there exists a contradiction that impacts curriculum and teaching practice. Izzy noted that "We want to develop critical thinking in our learners, but we work in a culture that does not encourage critical thinking." Morgan observed as well that "There is a lot of exaggeration of numbers in various media sources as a simple example. Our learners need to be critical thinkers in their assessment of information to recognize what is true and what is not true."

Eight educators cautioned that navigating this element of curriculum was very challenging. Jaden noted that teaching for critical thinking is present but contended that

> It is sort of a cliché. How do you teach it? How do you get people to become more critical in their thinking? The approaches to problem solving and the tasks do aim to make learners think more about issues or give them strategies for ways of looking at an issue which may encourage them to be more critical.

All educators commented that the nature of task-based approaches to curriculum supported opportunities for critical thinking. Morgan observed

> We teach them to identify fact, opinion, perception, interpretation. When I ask them, "what is your perception of the company from your company visit," they have a real hard time responding. We ask, "how would you interpret that behaviour." They can give you the definition of interpretation, but they have great difficulty with the applying, the predicting, and the interpreting or inferring.

Seven educators supported the inclusion of the DeBono critical thinking concepts and models as a means to incorporate critical thinking into teaching practice. Nat, Corey, and Cassidy used the De Bono's CoRT Thinking Lessons (2009) through analysis of relevant issues according to: Plusses, Minusses, and Interesting (PMI), Consider All Factors (CAF), and Other People's Views (OPV). Corey explained this approach:

> We looked at a newspaper article on educational reform and the proposal to open the HCT system to non-Emiraties; now, there we have learner engagement because they are *so* against that idea. We used De Bono's PMI and CAF about the issue, which require a critical approach from the girls. Then, we got to consideration of "Other People's Views." In groups, they were assigned to represent: The Ministry of Education, the Ministry of Higher Education, teachers, parents, and learners. Each group had to look at the issue and proposal and formulate a response from the viewpoint of whom they represent. Suddenly, responses went from "oh, we have no opinion" to

quite informed opinions. They were able to identify with the group they were assigned.

Eight educators also endorsed the use of 6 Hats Thinking Models as a critical thinking approach for lesson planning and HD1 curriculum. De Bono's 6 Hats Thinking assigns a coloured hat for a thinking pattern. When engaged in a problem-solving activity or a thinking activity, the learner was to think about each coloured hat and analyze the situation accordingly to the characteristic attributed to each hat: information gathering, analyzing emotions, negative thinking, positive thinking, creative thinking, and operational control thinking. Eight educators acknowledged that 6 Hats is a formulaic process of teaching learners to think about their thinking initially implemented in Business and then "reinforced in English" (Perry). Perry elaborated

> They look at what influences thinking generally: bias, perception. We give them case studies to pick out particular biases and perceptions. They look at elements of what good critical thinking is. It needs to be reinforced though. They do use the model. I have witnessed learners using 6 Hats for a problem.

The De Bono models were popular with learners and teachers. Taylor commented "I endorse the 6 Hats. I use them, learners like it. I have seen them use it." Jaden also noted "They enjoyed and engaged with it. It transferred to other learning. Learners in year 2 and 3 refer to the technique." Morgan believes that these models are good for this context, but also had concerns. Morgan thought the problem was not the model, but that more scaffolding was necessary in this context:

> With 6 Hats one of the steps is to look at alternatives. Learners will only look at one alternative. They will not evaluate a number of alternatives and come to a conclusion that one alternative is better or worse than another with [supporting] reasons. Those later steps they don't seem to be able to handle at this stage. I wonder if it is because they can't or don't or won't predict in some ways.

Three educators observed a lack of learners' will to question or predict as an impediment to critical thinking. Corey and Kelsey believed that comprehension of the language was the impediment to learners' ability to predict. "For a prediction about what is going to happen, you have to understand exactly what has happened. I wonder how much of the text they understand. It is a second language" (Corey). Similarly, Kelsey pointed out that "This is the first time [they have been asked to think critically] so I know it is new learning for them – applying criteria to choices and decisions." Cassidy also believed "The insh allah [God's will] way of life here has an impact. If everything is God's Will, and believe me, everything here is insh allah – then what is the point of predicting or questioning anything?" Morgan further explained "They are told that to do as a daughter and as a learner. They don't tend to question what they are told."

A further complexity identified in the teaching of critical thinking related specifically to the way negative comments could be perceived according to 11 educators. Teaching critical thinking was difficult in this context because negative comments about the UAE by foreigners are seen as offensive. Corey stated "Nobody criticizes the government here. Not even a whisper." Izzy, Kelsey, Morgan, and Cassidy noted similar observations. Kelsey observed "Even talking about the Sheikhs or the way things are run here – we can't." Cassidy explained

> We are hindered by what can be accomplished because of our context. There are so many issues we can't talk about or that can only be approached superficially. For example, how can you approach social and political consciousness, if you are seen as a guest to the Emirates and should never criticise anything about your host.

Drew, Cassidy, Morgan, and Izzy also explained the difficulty in teaching the difference between fact and opinion and the care required. Drew observed "Some learners get upset and I have to do some careful counselling with teachers and learners, to make sure we don't have a blow up of misunderstandings." While this is an aspect of education that can occur in education, globally, Drew further elaborated "it is more of an issue here where learners are very sensitive."

Teaching learners the difference between fact and opinion, and teaching learners critical thinking, appears to involve tensions that relate culture "face" and linguistics (discussed in more detail in Module 3). Five educators believed the concept of "face" became involved in the discussion. Cassidy articulated "Face is a concern here because learners will not engage if they are concerned about their public image." In-class discussions were challenging because "Many learners are unwilling or unable to discuss because others in the class will disapprove of their point of view" (Izzy). Cassidy further explained:

> Often opinions are stated as facts, so the issue is deciphering the meaning behind the words. Also, here, we may be teaching a concept of opinion, but a learner will say "But, the Qur'an speaks of this." Then you have the dilemma of religious belief, and opinion becoming intertwined with conceptions of fact. Here, if it is referred to in Islam, then it represents truth and fact for our learners.

Morgan, Izzy, and Corey identified further limitations regarding teaching critical thinking. "Our mandate as educators is to educate citizens to think critically. But, you can think critically about only certain topics. (laughter). You can't think critically about how your country is developing for example" (Morgan). Corey and Izzy specifically identified that the HCT system wanted to generate andragogical strategies to teach critical thinking, but does not want critical thinking from faculty or learners, in relation to system-related activities, rules, or objectives. Corey clarified:

> Here, there is little scope for people to do anything other than agree with the hierarchy. Critical thinking questions those in authority, the social hierarchy. This is a constant tension. The college wants you to facilitate critical thinking. But you can only critically think about, what we tell you to

critically think about, which in itself doesn't make sense. That is where the HCT system is falling behind Emirati society; it is not set up to encourage questioning about its systems and ways of doing things. Emirati society has moved on. If you start applying critical thinking, you should be willing as an institution to open your system to critical thinking.

Although educators acknowledged that critical thinking as a challenging aspect of curriculum, all educators agreed that it is an important aspect of learners' learning. Drew explained "It's that whole thing about, what are we doing in HD1? We are getting learners to think more, deeper learning, explore. Some learners perceive us as imposing on their boundaries too far. They don't quite understand why we are doing that."

Reflection was a prevalent component throughout the HD1 curriculum. Seven educators stated that learners at first have difficulty with reflection. "We do ask them to reflect quite a bit. Reflection is very difficult. They have trouble differentiating between reflection and description" (Morgan). Perry commented "Don't forget the level of HD1 learners. They struggle with English so the concept is difficult." However, Morgan, Cassidy, Perry, Jaden, and Nat indicated that by the end of the academic year and with "constant reinforcement, providing models for the 'how' of critical thinking, individual learner conferencing and operational feedback, by the end of the year learners are much better at thinking about their thinking" (Cassidy).

Corey raised an interesting point: "if what we want is students to engage in thinking about their thinking, then it is important to recognize that their expression of thinking about thinking may be very different from what is conventionally accepted as critically reflective thinking. The whole construct is problematic in international contexts where students are approaching knowledge from very diverse perspectives." This was also a premise supported by eleven educators who identified that Emirati students can and will engage in critically reflective thinking, but that their outputs from this activity cannot be separated from their beliefs and values systems (discussed further in Chapters 7–9). Cassidy stated:

It is a discussion all educators in HD1 have. What are we really looking for in critical reflection? Some kind of easily recognized formula of what critical reflection is or looks like or something more germane to these students and their lives? Frankly, if my students can engage in a deep exploration about what their values mean to them, and can explore alternative values consider the how's and why's of differences among others, then I feel that a great deal is accomplished. Fact is, I find students are quite willing and able to speak to value systems in a very engaged and reflective manner.

Drew further identified that this is an important consideration that must be explored among the global educational community. Drew indicated "So far, the education systems have very narrow visions of what critical reflection is. Perhaps we need to explore this on a deeper level as to what exactly we want from students in various places, with various different ways of being and knowing in relation to reflection."

Thus, teaching critical thinking in this context was very challenging. Some of the challenges related to the potential for cultural misunderstandings, linguistics, and the fact that critical thinking is only allowed in relation to some issues, but not for issues related to the social system, Dubai as an Emirate, or the HCT system. Educators reported the De Bono 6 Hats, CoRT thinking, and reflective thinking as successful. It is important to note, eleven educators question what critically reflective thinking is or should be in this and other international contexts.

The Challenge of Teaching Learners to Conduct Research

One of the main thrusts throughout HD1's task-based curriculum was to teach learners information literacy and to conduct and evaluate research. The entire HD1 curriculum throughout the year required learners to seek information, think about it, explore alternative viewpoints, and develop skills to communicate that information. However, learners arrive to HD1 lacking research abilities according to all educators. As well, culturally and historically, an oral tradition is the norm according to 7 educators. Morgan commented "They don't read and it is not a culture that encourages reading." Corey claimed "Learners do not like to read. Anything. Ever." Addison was concerned about learners' resistance to read and articulated:

> Reading is important. Knowledge passes through different elements of touching, feeling, being and all of that [is supported by reading]. Involving all and extending beyond. Here, it's completely different. Reading is bypassed; it is not felt to the same degree in this part of the world.

In addition, three educators noted a lack of curiosity in learners. Alex and Addison extended the discussion further stating a desire for learners to become curious as a product of their learning from HD1 curriculum. Alex explained:

> The learning process has to stimulate their curiosity. Ironically, we have to start out far from the independent mode. Here, we have to force them to learn how to do things. We have to force them to learn to be curious. We have to force them to take an interest in their own education. That strikes new faculty as being hypocritical. But, here, we are not interested in having new faculty perpetuate their own self-reference criteria. We are interested in getting results, having learners see their value and importance in society, in changing the behaviour of our learners so that they can go out and make a difference.

Similarly, Addison indicated "I think what's lacking is desire for knowledge. Learners start the year just wanting to do what will get them through or enable them to pass exams. It's not an exam that illustrates how well informed a person is. Learners think knowledge is like an aspirin pill." For all of these reasons, teaching learners to conduct and evaluate research was a necessary component of curriculum.

In this process of teaching the HD1 curricular tasks, particularly the first task of learning cycle 1, the Company Visit Presentation, were specific, integrated learning activities driving the learning about how to engage in research-driven tasks. Izzy explained:

> For most learners, it is their first experience with research, going to the library and locating information. It is starting with the bare bones of things like actually how to use a library. How to find valid information? How to assess if information is true, and then how to select information that meets the criteria? Other people might not understand this, but we have to begin here so students have the opportunity to learn how to access information and what criteria guide information.

Taylor described learners' research skills during semester 1 as "chronic." But, according to 12 educators their research abilities changed by the end of the academic year. Nat summarized:

> Semester 1 was successful in that the learners went from zero to being able to research and present something. It could be seen as unsuccessful because they really struggled with questions [from assessors] in the presentation. The teachers asked probing questions to see how deeply they understood. Learners showed they had a very narrow and limited understanding. But they have gone from zero to some understanding.

After Semester 1, learners still had a narrow vision of how to approach research-driven tasks, and of information literacy constructs such as: discerning and disseminating relevant information, evaluating information, presenting and fielding questions regarding research according to 10 educators. With the realization that learners needed far more instructional assistance with information literacy and conducting research, the HD1 team collaborated with the Library team to develop a new learning activity that was implemented throughout every HD1 class. Development began on altering the Semester 2 curriculum documents to incorporate a lesson called 'The Big Six.' This was implemented by the Librarians, in class, to all HD1 learners, with the HD1 English faculty assisting and all educators (Business, IT, and Maths) reinforcing the learning in their classes as well. The Big Six represented a step-by step approach to seeking information and evaluating information, including a discussion of the emotional elements involved in the process.

For this task, at the beginning of Semester 2, a librarian and the English teacher facilitated two lessons that specifically taught The Big Six model for conducting and evaluating research. Initially conceptualized by Mike Eisenberg and Bob Berkowitz, is a common information literacy model. The Big Six model consists of: task definition, information seeking strategies, location and access of information, use of information, synthesis of information and evaluation of information (The Big Six, 2008). The goal of HD1 was for learners to develop skills to become information literate individuals. According to the Information Literacy Competency Standards for Higher Education (Association of College and

Research Libraries, 2014) this entails: determining the information needed; accessing the needed information effectively; evaluating information and sources critically; incorporating the selected information into one's personally held knowledge base; using information to accomplish a specific purpose; and considering and understanding the economic, legal, ethical and social issues related to the use of information (Association of College and Research Libraries, December, 2014).

Seven educators believed the inclusion of the Big Six, and collaboration of the HD1 English teachers with the librarians, provided an effective mechanism to support learners through completion of Semester 2's research elements, and in their ability to disseminate and evaluate information required for the Current Issues Forum. Morgan commented

> The AHA moment was they said they had learned about research [from Big 6]. They identified that Google wasn't the only resource. Here, this is huge. One learner identified that magazines are in the library. One learner said "Before, I didn't realize that reading the newspaper could give me information." Quite a few learners were pleased that they improved their research skills, found good information, cited somewhat correctly. We actually accomplished a good thing.

Taylor added:

> With The Big Six the learners could relate to the library. With the Librarian coming into the classes, they could see a person that they knew and had met and knew they could go up to help. That was an important part – drawing a relationship between the library and learners.

Morgan further reported at the end of the academic year in the final interview that:

> It is the first time that most learners were able to suss out the connection between this class task and the curricular task. It worked, but it took the entire semester and constant reinforcement with the English, Maths, Business and IT teachers and the librarian.

Thus, the entire academic year required an emphasis on research, but learners struggled during Semester 1. Their struggle was attributed to their lack of previous exposure to this form of task, this new kind of learning, and their conceptions of learning that negate reading and research skills. The HD1 Business and English team, and the librarians, collaborated at the end of Semester 1 and created and implemented a new curricular item implemented the first week during Semester 2 to address this. The curricular inclusion was called The Big Six Information Literacy Model. Educators reported this inclusion as successful, but required a lot of time, reinforcement, and collaboration on the part of the English and Business faculty and the library.

CONCLUSION

The 21st century curriculum designed by the HD1 team of educators was highly focussed on active learning participation through the use of a task-based, integrated trans-disciplinary teaching and learning approaches. Students had 3 primary learning tasks that were collaborative. Public exposure was carefully scaffolded from the beginning of Semester 1 to the end of the academic year. Educators commented on students' engagement with the tasks, and the kind of learning students achieved. Discussions of the strength of this curricular approach focused on the authentic nature of the experiential learning focus and the relevance to students' current reality and visions for the future. Some elements involved tensions such as students' initial confusion and trepidation with this new form of learning engagement, difficulties with teaching critical thinking in this context, and also assisting students' development of research skills. Various models to address these issues were presented and discussed. It is important to note that educators question the nature of critical thinking and critical reflection in this context in relation to what it is or should be. Some educators discuss students' expression of these skills as being potentially different given the unique context. The next chapters explore the nature of students' engagement with curriculum and Islam (Chapter 7), Emirati culture (Chapter 8), and Dubai as a globalized society (Chapter 9).

MODULE 3

DELVING INTO THE LEARNING CONTEXT, RELIGION, CULTURE, SOCIETY AND LANGUAGE

CHAPTER 7

ENCOUNTERING ISLAM IN THE CLASSROOM

Faith and 21ˢᵗ Century Curriculum

INTRODUCTION

Arguably, no other area is as controversial as the role of faith and education. Some parts of the world have a long standing tradition supporting a separation of "church and state." Other areas have faith-based educational systems. But, if we accept that our world is increasingly becoming interconnected and given the salience of faith to individuals, what does this mean for 21ˢᵗ century education?

These international educators are aware either intuitively, or based on extensive global experience, of the primacy of faith, in this context Islam, to understanding learners, their experiences, their values, and their understandings of self in relation to learning. This level of understanding their learners has a profound impact on 21ˢᵗ century curriculum, meaning making and exploring learning experiences. This chapter begins with defining religion, spirituality, faith, and values in relation to teaching and learning and discusses how Islamic faith impacted decisions regarding the design and implementation of HD1 curriculum. Shared are educators' perceptions regarding how students conceptualize knowledge, and specific curricular inclusions and exclusions based on religious sensitivity. This is followed by a discussion related to the tensions involved with censorship and self-censorship.

Defining Faith, Beliefs and Values

Religion is one of the most powerful forces driving individuals, communities and societies. It shapes how people relate to each other, how people understand knowledge, how people think and why they behave as they do. Faith guides how an individual, and/or a community, understand reality, truth, knowledge, teaching, learning, and life. Drawing from the work of Patrick Slattery *Curriculum Development in the Post Modern Era: Teaching and Learning in an Age of Accountability* (3ʳᵈ edition, 2013), religion, identity and culture are interconnected. Slattery eloquently describes:

> There are many people whose religious identity is a cultural imperative and not necessarily an act of faith or spirituality .... Some people are eclectic and ecumenical – they embrace the best practices of many world religions ... others prefer to seek wisdom, insight, enlightenment, or spiritual experience outside the context of formal religion .... For many people, religion and spirituality require a personal commitment to a deity, many deities, or

possibly a cosmic force such as harmony or justice. Religion may involve adherence to certain scriptures, rituals, values, clothing, initiation rites, and community worship. For many others, however, religion means only participation in cultural holidays, family rituals, public ceremonies marking the beginning or ending of life, or preparing and eating specific ethnic foods. (pp. 75–76)

However one engages or understands religion or spirituality, and given its salience to human beings, it will have a profound effect on 21st century teaching and learning. Slattery refers to discussions of religion, curriculum, teaching and learning as a "very complex and complicated conversation" (p. 78). This conversation is equally complex and complicated in an educational context such as DWC where international educators come from across the globe, embody various faiths, and all students are Muslim. Prior to discussing the role of faith in the classroom at DWC, it is important to have a way of defining the key terms in this chapter, religion, spirituality, faith, and values.

For the purpose of this book, religion is defined as "a set of beliefs, symbols, and practices which is based on the idea of the sacred, and which unites believers into a socio-religious community" (Scott & Marshall, 2009, p. 643). Any reference to religion, unless specifically stated otherwise, refers to the religion of Islam, which is the religion of the UAE. Spirituality is

> that which gives meaning to one's life and draws one to transcend oneself. Spirituality is a broader concept than religion, although that is one expression of spirituality. Other expressions include prayer, meditation, interactions with others or nature, and relationship with God or a higher power. (Burkhardt, 1989, p. 70)

As the nature of faith-based systems of the international educators who contributed to this book is quite diverse, I have chosen to use the word "faith" to encompass the personally held, individual connection to a religion, spiritual connection, or belief system. It may be formally recognized or not, and it may be based on wisdom, deities, connections to the divine, connected to cultural identity or could involve only an individual belief in the nature of the world. Faith is personally held and may be collectively valued. But, it is intimately experienced and is central to a person's being, ways of knowing, meaning-making, conceptions of world views, experiences and realities. Thus, faith is central to the human being; it is central to the adult learner and adult educator.

Faith-based values are intimately held understandings that are aligned with an individually held belief system. These may include moral or ethical understandings, ideological or doctrinal understandings, altruistic or virtuous understandings, social/cultural/political understandings, and/or aesthetic under-standings. These values may align with community held values, for example the Islamic value of modesty may be collectively held, but differ among individuals in terms of what mode of attire constitutes modesty.

Perspectives on Faith in Education

Arguably, no topic is more controversial or sensitive than the role of faith in social interactions. While various school systems may identify as faith-based schools (such as Islamic schools, Catholic schools, and so forth), in higher education the question of how to approach faith in the classroom makes many educators feel uncomfortable. This discomfort is particularly troubling for educators in relation to curricula that often assert a 'value-free' label. Regardless of whether or not a value-free curriculum is possible, and I do not believe that it is, in many contexts faith is generally avoided in the classroom and specifically in North American contexts where postmodern movements generally call for the recognition of different religious belief systems, while also advocating for separation of church and state (Slattery, 2013; Simon 1998). Even higher education classes designed to empirically and objectively explore faith such as World Religious Studies, or Philosophy and Faith can involve challenges and sensitivities because learners and educators come to the learning situation with a wealth of experiences and orientations that may be in contradiction with the content being studied.

However, gaining in prominence in recent decades, are other educational movements in relation embed the concept of faith and education. Embodied knowing (Merleau-Ponty, 1962, 2002) rejects the notion of mind/body dualism (also known as Cartesian Dualism) and embraces the role of the spiritual, or faith, as central to the embodiment of knowledge and learning. Gendlin (1981) drawing from Merleau-Ponty, spoke of the intricacies of "bodily sensed knowledge" (p. 25). Lakoff and Johnson (1999) have discussed embodied knowing as a challenge to Western thought in relation to learning. Contemporary discussions of embodied knowing explore the integration of "as an existential whole, the experiential history of individuals with their current experience. It implies an education that trusts individuals to learn from their ability to attend and to listen to the information they are receiving from the interaction of self with the environment" (Sellers-Young 1998, p. 176). Thus, embodied knowing is experiential knowledge. It involves the whole being in the experience including the senses, perception, and mind/body action and reaction (Matthews, 1998) and the spirit (Irigaray, 2005; Kelan, 2011).

As faith is an integral part of the nature of experience, and therefore a central component of understanding adult learning, learner's actions, and epistemologies, 21st century teaching and learning that involve aspects such as reflection, questioning, critical thinking, and open consideration of knowledge can be quite sensitive in relation to a faith-based perspective. How do these international educators teach for transformation through curriculum design and practice in an effort to make learning meaningful address the role of faith when it surfaces in a 21st century international classroom?

What Does it Mean to Teach in This Islamic Context

Dubai is a global marketplace, and diverse in terms of the people who reside in this Emirate. Dubai is also an Islamic Emirate, as is the entire the country of the United Arab Emirates. This means that all national holidays and recognized Holy Days (such as Ramadan, Eid al Fetr, or Eid al Adha) and all regulations and ways of living are governed through the tenants of Islam. This includes higher education.

All educators were expressive and adamant that understanding curriculum design for these learners means recognizing the primacy of learners' faith in their lives. Thus, these educators' decisions regarding the design and implementation of curriculum were first explored from the lens of Islam. Cassidy explained "Here, Islam is not part of life – it *is* life." Corey commented "The impact is huge and cannot ever be ignored or forgotten" and further noted that in class Islam "is going to come up." Morgan believed "It forms a strong anchor for what they believe in, what they are willing to listen to, and how and why we do things the way we do." All educators emphasized that students understand the nature of all knowledge and experience through Islam. In 21st century education, this is the premise for which to begin: what is the faith of your learners and how may this impact curriculum design and teaching practice?

Designing the Learning. All educators specifically stated that they began their design of the learning with close examination of the approximate dates of the Islamic Holy Days. The exact Islamic Holy Days dates are fluid in terms of the exact beginning and ending because the Islamic calendar is lunar; months begin when the first crescent of a new moon is sighted. The number of days in a lunar calendar year is not uniform with the typical 365 day (leap year 366 day) calendar year of the Gregorian calendar. Ramadan occurs during the 9th month of the Islamic calendar. According to '*Understanding Islam*' (2010), fasting during Ramadan is one of the Five Pillars of Islam. Thus, during Ramadan, Muslims fast (no food or water) from dawn to sunset. Usually, Muslims also read the Qu'ran during Ramadan and increase both prayer, charity, and self-discipline as well (Ibn Habaj Abdul-Hussain, Hadith, 2013).

During the Ramadan time frame, no off campus tasks were incorporated into the schedule or design of the curriculum. In fact, the international educators focussed this time frame of teaching and learning concepts that connected with Ramadan (such as social responsibility, giving to charity). Many educators' efforts were focussed on inclusion of prominent guest speakers. Some of the guest speakers addressed: the role of education and change, women and Islam, Islam in the workforce, and globalization and female empowerment. All of these topics were presented by either Imams in the area, prominent Emirati business leaders, or prominent Islamic scholars. Izzy stated:

> Having these guest speakers arrive on the campus during Ramadan was essential. They spoke to important issues that came up again and again during the year. The timing was crucial as students are thinking about their beliefs during Ramadan anyway so this created opportunities for students to reflect.

Reflect on themselves, their country, their roles as Emirati women, and how they will represent themselves as modern, Muslim women. The speakers were perfectly chosen as they did not stray from the hard questions – but challenged students to think about the hard questions and determine their answers from their own mind and their own beliefs.

All educators identified that designing instruction during Ramadan requires great care. Although the rest of the curriculum did not shy away from controversial issues, great care was given to waiting until after Ramadan to incorporate difficult or controversial topics or tasks.

In most Islamic countries, the work/school day is shortened and this is true of DWC. As the educators designing the curriculum were aware, Ramadan fell during the middle of September to the middle of October. All classes for this time frame were designed to recognize a 30 minute in-person class, with students who are tired and often hungry. All educators used blended learning techniques (Blackboard was the learning management system) to create learning engagement in virtual space wherein students could access the content during the evening after Iftar (the meal that breaks the fast). In many cases, this is when the discussion boards were the most active. Parker states: "You know, there is no point in going into any heavy material during the day. Just doesn't work. Entertain them, create really enjoyable in-class activities, and then post serious work online for students to read, address, or complete." There were chat rooms with large group discussion questions and group tasks, portfolio activities, small group discussion, questions and answers and online tests occupying most of the typical course content during Ramadan.

It is important to note, many faculty members, whether Muslim or not, also engaged in the specific practice of fasting during Ramadan (7 non-Muslim faculty members specifically indicated they fast during the day for Ramadan). Morgan stated: "it is humbling and that is an important message. I love this message." Cassidy felt it was important to recognize the laws of the context:

Ramadan is an important time of life here. Part of our students' lives. What is the message you send to students when you come to this wonderful country but flout their laws. It is actually illegal here to be seen eating in public. I think it is important to recognize their country, their laws, their national belief systems. Proud to honour them.

Nat fasted to engage and connect with students: "If my students are fasting, so am I. Besides, I love the meaning behind Ramadan."

Islam and the Classroom at DWC

According to all educators, students' conception of knowledge directly relates to Islam and the Holy Qur'an in this context. Izzy commented "It's an Islamic environment and their views are based on Islam. [Students] perceive everything to link to Islam." Cassidy elaborated:

Islam governs their beliefs about their ways being and knowing. It is not unusual in class for students to take a concept being taught and express a connection to either an Islamic principle or to the Hadith. When this occurs it tells me that they understand in a way that is important to them. Some teachers in some contexts are fearful with this, which is unfortunate. As long as you do not critique the connection to Islam, students seem to appreciate you for respecting this and honouring how they understand knowledge and learning.

Corey explained "In the Qur'an, one of the purposes of humanity is to investigate and think. Use your brain for a higher purpose. When students say they don't feel like doing something, don't want to think, or just want the answer, I remind them of this." Corey commented that sometimes, students "try to get out of [doing] something or knock you off by bringing up religion – 'Whallah' [in God's name] kind of thing. You have to recognize this when you teach here." Corey elaborated on how Islam assisted in teaching a language issue:

The word "perfect" is overused here. Students want to write so that "Everything is perfect" or "in a good and perfect way." I say, in Islam, only Allah or God is perfect. The minute you remind them of that, they understand. Nothing man-made can be perfect. That gets the point across.

Morgan and Cassidy discussed relating ethics and social responsibility course content to Islamic ethics in order to make the concepts meaningful to students. Morgan explained "When you talk about behaviours you have to talk about the value system that those behaviours are part of. Family values and religious values tend to be the top 2 whenever we do values exercises." All educators confirmed that you cannot separate Islam from learning or from students understanding of experiences: "It can be an excellent teaching strategy because it builds on something students know intimately and genuinely want to talk about" (Bailey).

Therefore, the religious faith of Islam is central to students' lives. Educators in this context recognized this. Some educators used their knowledge of aspects of Islam to help make content meaningful for students. All educators recognized and allowed students to incorporate faith-based connections to content, particularly pertaining to class work regarding ethics or values.

Faith-Based Sensitivities and Controversial Issues

One consideration of religious complexity in this context, according to all educators involved the interpretation of Islamic beliefs that is debated within Islamic societies themselves and controversy can be upsetting depending on the topic. In fact, all educators recognized the plurality of understandings represented among Emirati students and among faculty. Because several Islamic aspects are debated within Islamic societies, and among Islamic clerics and scholars, so sensitivity is integral. Izzy articulated "[What is important] is how Islam is interpreted and applied in different parts of the world, by different people within Islam."

During the second semester, educators were required to have all classes engage in a Virtual International Exchanges with students in a different country. One educator at DWC connected with a colleague at a Canadian college. They decided to create a learning moment that would focus on understanding different personalities and collaboration. Two classes of DWC students and 2 classes of the Canadian students engaged in a Personality Dimensions workshop at their respective campuses. Afterward, all students were placed into groups and were tasked with creating posters that was designed to indicate a pictographic representation of aspects important to them as an individual, a group member, and a community member. These posters would eventually be shared between the Canadian students and the Emirati students which would then be discussed among all via video conference.

Morgan discussed observations about the event:

We held a class debriefing to discuss this. Look at the size of the Qur'an in the poster. The Qur'an is bigger than the globe, which is an indicator of importance. The other group, independently, came up with a big, central figure of an Emirati woman reading the Qur'an. One group had the word 'Allah.' There was great discussion in Arabic and English. Students are approaching this issue from very different perspectives. All indicate the importance of Islam in their lives, but their practices in relation to Islam and what they believe they can and should do in this pictographic representation, is very different.

Some of the discussion that emanated between the Canadian group and the Emirati students focused on the differences in the posters between the two groups. During the digital exchange, the Canadians observed that the Emirati posters contained themes of the word 'Allah' and 'Islam,' a picture of an Emirati woman reading the Qur'an, or a picture of the Qur'an itself. Every single Emirati poster contained a connection to Islam in some respect. The Canadians also asked about hijab and female modesty; some Emirati students were fully veiled with a niqab (face covering) and gloves, while some Emirati had their *shayylas* (head scarf) sitting only partially on their head, partially covering their hair. This led to an informative discussion of whether veiling or covering hair is an Islamic or a cultural requirement. The Emirati students observed that the Canadian class was gender mixed with females and males sitting together. This led to discussion of the roles of females and males in Canadian society, and issues related to feminism. The Canadian posters had a pictures related to multiculturalism (clasped hands with different skin colours representing diversity), hockey sticks, a crucifix, a spiritual wheel (Indigenous symbol of Aboriginal peoples in Canada), music and celebrity, technological devices, maple leaf (symbol from flag). Emirati students questioned the items and learned that Canadians valued diversity and patriotic ideals. The Emirati students were very curious about the spiritual wheel and learned about Indigenous beliefs in Canada.

Dialoging with the educators' afterword, they indicated no surprise that both gender and faith was represented between both the Canadian posters and the Emiraties posters. Morgan indicated:

I am astounded when anyone tries to tell me Westerners have no transcendental beliefs and no real culture. This activity was all about what do you value as a Canadian/Emirati. They represented their values. It was a real bonding moment between students across the globe to discover that there are many values that are congruent with each other. Students totally got the meaning behind the Spiritual Wheel. No question.

Sam commented that the healthy dialogue of Emirati women and modesty and gender contact among the Canadians promoted understanding of different ways of being. Sam states

I grew up here, and I have seen change in how women engage their understandings of modesty. It is healthy for students to see that modest relationships between and among genders can 'look' different in different parts of the world. Men and women of all beliefs have to work together and be together. It helps if the dialogue about modesty can encompass many perspectives. Canadians and Emiraties can learn about gender, roles of women, modesty and beliefs from each other.

Another controversial moment happened during the Career Majlis event in Semester 1. Addison stated, "We have to remember, there is diversity in understandings within Islam including Shi'a and Sunni muslims. And, we have a very diverse teaching faculty." Sam states, "Some controversies in Islam are debated among Islamic scholars themselves." During the Career Majlis event, Emirati students, who are also full time employed working women, had a different learning task for the Bazaar event. They were to create a discussion-focused area on campus and they created presentations focused on relevant issues crucial to Emirati working women. One of those issues was entitled '*Marriage and Emirati Working Women.*' Learners created a questionnaire for married Emirati women that they had their friends, family members and colleagues complete. The questionnaire was only targeting married Emirati women. This information was then synthesized and presented to attendees at the Career Majlis. The goal was to have visitors at to the majlis area (regular day learners and their families) be prompted to explore the issues, question, share experiences, and engage in an authentic dialogue about the challenges of being a married woman, pursuing a career, raising a family, and caring for children.

During the discussion part of the presentation, an attendee asked if the questionnaire was also given to divorced Emirati women to answer. The learners identified that it had. The attendee then asked if women in Mut'a marriages were given the questionnaire. A Muta' marriage (a fixed term of marriage that is controversial in terms of whether it is allowed (Shi'a) or haram (forbidden) (The Four Pillars of Mut'a, 2014). Izzy stated "I had heard of Mut'a marriage, but I did not know it was still practiced – at least not until that moment. I still think it is uncommon, but the question does indicate not only ramifications for the discussion, but also this was a research-driven event. Should women in a Mut'a marriage have been given an opportunity to complete the questionnaire?" While the educators were listening carefully to see if this was going to be a tense moment, Kelsey commented "These students just gone on with it and answered that they had not asked if any of their participants were in a Mut'a marriage." This did lead to a very involved discussion among all attendees and the learners about the validity of Mut'a marriage, whether or not it was forbidden, connections to the Hadith (a very important book of readings about the life of Prophet, peace be upon him). Although this was one of the most controversial moments of the learning event, Jaden observed:

> There are religious sensitivities which sometimes come up in class, like the religious difference between Shi'a and Sunni. While most students are Sunni, there are Shi'a and Sunni faculty. The onus is on teachers to be extremely careful. Discussions highly emotive and controversial may be misinterpreted. Faculty have to be very aware of the tensions and be ready to mediate if necessary. BUT these engagements should be welcomed in the classroom. This is part of why we are all here – to open the dialogue. It's CRUCIAL.

All educators expressed that students naturally connect concepts taught through curriculum to their religious beliefs. Their faith is the most important thing in their lives and a critical component to understanding these learners and teaching to these students rested with faculty's ability to go deep in their own learning about learners' faith-based beliefs. It was quite normal for Islam to come up in class, which could be an excellent teaching strategy. It is also important to recognize that students are quite diverse in their understandings of Islamic beliefs. There is great plurality and what is important is allowing students to express their beliefs and connect their learning to their faith. This may involve controversial aspects within Islam itself and although this may be challenging for faculty, it was described as a crucial aspect in this time of life for these learners.

Editing Knowledge

Significantly, international educators expressed concerns related to editing knowledge. Awareness of the salience of Islam to students, and the recognition that many texts and digital resources are either not appropriate for these Emirati learners or contain content that would be deemed offensive made the question of curricular resources quite complex. Educators were diverse in their approaches related to how they managed this aspect of teaching and learning in this context. Bailey noted the governmental and collegial censoring programs that restrict access to Internet content deemed religiously or culturally offensive or illegal: "[Access] to everything is censored here. That can be a benefit in terms of ensuring you do not use something that can get you into trouble, but it can also limit the use of different information that may be quite beneficial" (Bailey). Cassidy related the following examples of visiting scholars and dignitaries:

The prof said she was aware of the censorship issues but she did not really take it to heart. She included a YouTube video in the lesson. YouTube is banned here so the "offensive to religious principles" message came up which shocked this prof. Also, there was the recent visit from [named dignitary] who included a picture of Michelangelo's Adam's Creation. Great controversy and trouble emanated from the complaints from students and families. This was important as it was religiously offensive here mainly because students objected to the representation of Adam in a pictographic format.

Resources had to be carefully edited and scrutinized for content that is offensive to Islamic principles. This included concepts that other contexts do not find objectionable. According to 12 educators the content to avoid or edit include "any criticism or potential reference to any negative aspect of Islam, any graphics with exposure of skin such as shoulders or legs or representation of an important person in Islam" (Cassidy), any discussion of "anything to do with sex. Including discussions of other religions must be undertaken with care so it is not seen as proselytizing" (Kelsey). Izzy commented "Most teachers are functioning in an environment of fear in terms of making a mistake. We are afraid of the consequences [so we edit everything]." Parker explained that censorship was required: "Not because most students are genuinely culturally or religiously affronted by what you have introduced. But some will object just because they are being belligerent. They will play the religious card. You have got to read the class" (Parker). Morgan explained "If it is open in the press, it should be ok for the classroom, because the press is censored as well. So that is one of our strategies."

With textbooks, according to 6 educators (Cassidy, Parker, Spencer, Corey, Kelsey, & Morgan) often good materials could not be used because they were designed for a different student body and contained themes or pictures that depicted: pre-marital dating, sexual orientation, particular aspects of the human body such as genitalia, different religious celebrations in other faiths. Or, they raised issues that are "*haram*" (Cassidy), which means forbidden to Islam. Corey explained:

> It is not that the students don't want to discuss these subjects. But, students leave the class and tell their friends and families. That has, in the past, found its way into the local press, particularly Arabic language press. You suddenly find out it is being discussed and always, you are found to be at fault. The college does not support you [the teacher]. It is always the case where "That teacher should learn to be more religiously and culturally aware" – the big stick that gets thrashed around.

Parker elaborated "When you are choosing a text, think, is this going to be all right? You have to go through it carefully. The Health and Wellbeing course that we are writing, the course book, is excellent. But it has content on sexually transmitted disease, which doesn't happen here (small mutual laughter)." Perry commented "We are trying to expand these girls' horizons, but with respect to their religious beliefs. It can be an editing tightrope" Spencer recalled an incident: "There was the time a graded English reader contained a paragraph that said 'the Muslim conqueror' and a student was offended: 'Muslims never conquered. Islam is spread by persuasion. Muslims never conquered anywhere.' Now, I censor everything."

This editing of knowledge to respect Islam is not just felt by faculty; it is also felt by students. Students, according to Morgan "Are very concerned about people knowing and speaking about Islam, correctly." During the annual speech competition, many of Cassidy's students spoke about Islamic topics but first "they went to their religious leaders for guidance, the Sheikh or Imam." They become quite anxious when "either they or someone else misrepresents Islam" (Cassidy). Morgan relayed a recent class event:

> My class had a virtual international exchange with Canadian students who suddenly asked about Islam. A few students told me how threatened they felt because they were afraid they would be wrong [in their representation of Islam]. They are afraid to give a wrong answer or a wrong interpretation. They want to represent the religion correctly.

Therefore, the selection of resources and content materials was affected by pervasive governmental and collegial censoring programs that restricted and censored access to information. As well, all curricular materials were carefully scrutinized for content that could be deemed offensive. Visiting dignitaries or professors may be aware of requirements for censorship, but this sensitivity was also not fully realized in terms of how it affects teaching and learning. Occasionally, occurrences of sensitivity that was not fully understood by visiting dignitaries caused difficulties. At least part of the concern with regard to editing knowledge related to respect for Islamic principles, and also a concern about potential misrepresentation of Islam or Islamic principles felt by both faculty and students.

Censorship and Faculty Self-Censorship

Data reveal that implementation of HD1 curriculum and the salience of Islam in this context can produce tense classroom moments and faculty approaches during these moments are crucial.

Strategies discussed by educators to deal with tension when it occurred was avoidance (Izzy, Spencer, Jaden, Morgan, Nat, Kelsey, Parker, Ellis) and control (Corey, Cassidy, Drew, Alex, Addison, Sam, Shane, Ellis). Educators avoided specific topics such as anything related to sexual orientation, sexually transmitted disease, alcohol or narcotics, and negative comments about Islam or Sheikhs. In addition, they "avoid expressing personally held opinions or drawing conclusions" (Parker). In terms of control, Corey commented "I deal with it as it comes up. If I feel it is getting too heavy, or that one more religious student is trying to impose on another then I diffuse the situation but not get too involved." Cassidy noted

Students enjoy these discussions, they are relevant: for example, the "hijab debate." It is fascinating to listen as students' debate the wearing of hijab as a religious or a cultural requirement. I control the conversation in terms of allowing all students to speak, but I don't ever offer my thoughts even if asked. I always ask students to summarize the discussion at the end so they can acknowledge the differing students' beliefs.

It appears that success as an international educator is related to abilities to self-censor. Thirteen educators reported that self-censorship is a normal aspect of life as an international educator and that HD1 faculty are particularly skilled in self-censorship. Kelsey explained "It is an aspect that you learn very quickly if you are going to be here. Censorship." Corey commented "We self-censor. We don't draw conclusions. We don't state opinions about certain things. You pick up fairly quickly when it behooves you to listen and not comment." Cassidy elaborated: "Students are curious about us, but comments could be interpreted as proselytizing—punishable by firing and immediate deportation. Most students are aware of teachers' vulnerability, so we are careful and students respect that." Corey raised an interesting point. Corey identified that learners were never asked what was offensive to them and related an example:

At our workstations we are not supposed to display anything related to Christmas or mention Christmas because this is an Islamic society. But, there is no basis in Islam for not discussing the birth of Jesus—which is in the Qur'an. I think about these interpretations of what will offend [students] and what won't are made without anyone ever sitting down and asking [students] "Do you find this offensive?" Dubai malls are filled with the biggest Christmas trees in the world. So, who is censoring whom. Who is censoring what and why?

Parker reported:

It is rare the students that are bothered [Merry Christmas cards on desks]. It is the authorities from above who are concerned. I have had Christmas cards from students. But, we have to be careful. Something we consider small might hit the headlines. We know what happens. That Christmas card at your desk, the headline [in the news] will be "DWC holds a Christmas party." That is how it would be reported.

Not only were teachers prohibited to have any religious iconography visible to students but they had to be very careful when asked questions regarding their religious faiths to defray negative consequences for the teacher and the learners. Both Ellis and Cassidy contended that this was unacceptable to them. Ellis elaborated

We should be able to express, we celebrate like Easter as long as it's done in a diplomatic way. [But if the topic comes up] the hairs stand on the back of one's neck as one heads into it. When the students prompt me, and I say "why don't you do a bit of research and find out."

A further tension was that sometimes, according to Nat, Cassidy, Ellis, and Alex, learners wanted to discuss aspects or problems they experience in their own lives with teachers with whom they share a bond. This has the potential to be problematic for faculty as Alex noted "There is nothing in my training manual for some of these issues." These educators' reported that learners sought some of their teachers specifically to discuss sensitive topics, such as family pressure to marry, consanguineous marriages, or family problems, because the teachers were from different backgrounds. Jaden explained "Students may talk to you about issues because of who you are. They just feel more comfortable. In some cases, they just want to talk. They want to voice their concerns and they want you to respond to them in some sort of sympathetic way." Nat noted "[In reference to] boyfriends. I don't want to know. I don't want that burden of information and having to deal with it because [then] it is my responsibility."

Cassidy believed that it was normal for a teacher and learner to bond. "Our students are human. They have relationships with people, sometimes with men. They have problems they want to discuss. We spend so much time together it is natural for a connection to form." Nat explained that when the learner bonds with the teacher, often "There is a level of trust. If they have had you as their teacher for a while, they know what you are like. They know they can tell you things in confidence." This sentiment was mirrored by Cassidy who related a recent occurrence:

> A student wanted to talk about *boyott* [girls with boyish attributes or behaviour] after the Bazaar assembly [appropriate student appearance and behaviour]. This student was very upset. She had been called a *boyott* by another student and she felt disrespected. But, she felt she could not do anything about it. She didn't want to talk to Students Services or anyone in her community because *boyott* is *haram* [forbidden in Islam] and she felt it would have brought shame on her and her family to reveal she was called this name. She wanted to talk to me about it. All I was able to do was listen as obviously this moment was loaded with implications for both of us.

Therefore, educators specifically identified the need to develop strong self-censorship skills, particularly in relation to students' questions about their cultural or religious values and beliefs. Occasionally, students approached faculty with family problems or concerns about their lives, but these kinds of discussions had to be undertaken with great care, if at all. Given the necessity for faculty self-censorship, on the occasions when students wanted to talk about religiously sensitive or culturally sensitive topics, educators stated that they cannot and either listened to the learner only or followed DWC protocols for their own security and to ensure that problems were avoided.

CONCLUSION

The religious faith of Islam is central to students' lives. Given the diverse backgrounds of the international educators, faith was very important to them as well and this had an impact on what and how they approached curriculum, teaching and learning. Educators supported learners' connection of their learning to their belief systems and their identities. These educators recognized that although all learners are Muslim, they have very different personally held values that form their individual understandings of how to be a Muslim person. Some participants used their knowledge of aspects of Islam to help make content meaningful for learners. Some teachers allowed learners to incorporate religious elements, particularly pertaining to class work regarding ethics or values. All educators avoided topics considered *haram*. Development of abilities to self-censor and manage tense moments characterizes a skill an international educator must learn in this context.

CHAPTER 8

BALANCING ISSUES AND EXPLORING BOUNDARIES

Emirati Culture and 21ˢᵗ Century Curriculum

INTRODUCTION

Culturally relevant teaching (CRT) is a pedagogy often characterized as "good teaching" (Schmeichel, 2012, p. 212). CRT refers to pedagogy that displays high levels of cultural competence. Teachers skilled in CRT display teaching capabilities in making course material relatable to specific aspects of culture and context. Coined by Dr. Gloria Ladson-Billings (1995), many scholars believe CRT "empowers students to maintain cultural integrity, while succeeding academically" (p. 465). The most common discussion of the role of CRT is in relation to higher education in a North American contexts, and often in relation to people of colour (i.e. Brown-Jeffy & Cooper, 2011; Gay, 2010; Lipman, 1995; Schmeichel, 2012). In an Arab context with Emirati students, what does CRT look like? What are the issues related to CRT and 21ˢᵗ century curriculum design and practice?

This chapter describes how educators understood the issues that surfaced in their efforts to embrace CRT and 21ˢᵗ century curriculum design and practice. Specifically, in the UAE, where there exists a significant population imbalance of expatriate foreigners (85%) to Emirati citizens (15%), it is important to embrace and balance internationalization and nationalization in an effort to engage in 21ˢᵗ teaching and learning. The factors related to Emirati culture that educators identified as impacting 21ˢᵗ curriculum design and teaching practice were: capitalizing on students' experiences; sensitivity with culturally controversial issues; collaboration and tribal affiliation; and teaching for students empowerment vs. rules, rules, rules. This chapter will explore these factors and situate them in the context of curriculum design, teaching and learning at DWC.

What Does it Mean to Teach for Cultural Relevance?

Culturally relevant pedagogy (CRP) has been described as possessing the following characteristics (Culturally Responsive Pedagogy, 2013, pp. 4–7):

1. Social Cultural Consciousness: Culturally responsive teachers recognize the privilege their positon offers in relation to their role in the classroom, which has the potential to affect the teaching and learning experiences of learners. It is recommended that CRP educators engage in self-reflection regarding personally held biases and the impact of distribution of power and privilege relative to social identity and the teaching and learning process.

117

2. High Expectations: Ladson-Billings (1994, 2001, 2011) asserts that the perceptions and expectations educators have in relation to learners' success have a profound impact on their achievement and well-being. Brown-Jeffy and Cooper (2011) specifically indicate that CRP integrates excellence and equity through a curriculum that is nurturing, inclusive and respectful of the cultural experiences learners have while adhering to high expectations of learners' success.

3. Desire to Make a Difference: Educators devoted to CRP embrace equitable and inclusive education as inherent in engaging learners for educational success. "Culturally responsive educators are committed to being agents of social change" (Culturally Responsive Pedagogy, 2013, p. 5). CRP educators incorporate learning activities that are both challenging and culturally relevant.

4. Constructivist Approach: Embrace of a constructivist approach means recognition of the lived experiences of learners as foundational to their learning. Bringing this recognition into the learning event will bring "the curriculum to life" (Culturally Responsive Pedagogy, 2013, p. 5). These lived experiences are resources for educators as they design a culturally relevant curriculum.

5. Deep Knowledge of Learners: Without in depth knowledge of learners' lives (i.e., families, relationships, culture, faith, social concerns, tensions, etc.) as individuals who are integral to the learning event, little can be accomplished in designing a culturally relevant curriculum. This knowledge and interest in the learners promotes mutual respect and a collaborative approach to the learning moment. It levels the hierarchies between the teacher and the learners. This theme within the context of culturally responsive curriculum embraces the belief that learning moments infused with respectful and reciprocal dialogue and shared understandings as critical to successful, culturally responsive pedagogy. It is about the "caring, relationships, interaction, and classroom atmosphere" (Brown-Jeffy & Cooper, 2011, p. 77) that teachers must generate as educators who are have vested interests in learners as individuals and as members of the learning event.

Educators of culturally responsive pedagogy acknowledge the "cultural uniqueness" of each learner. In fact, these educators nurture this uniqueness and understand that this is integral to design effective and inspiring conditions for learning (Brown-Jeffy & Cooper, 2011).

It is important to recognize that all of the above characteristics are defined from a North American or European perspective and embracing of an inclusive classroom supportive of diversity and multiculturalism. In the context of the UAE, where all the students in the HCT system at that time were exclusively Emirati, and faculty were foreign, how are these characteristics nuanced for CRP at DWC?

Balancing the 'Here' in Culturally Relevant Pedagogy in the UAE?

It is significant that all educators acknowledged the unique nature of teaching and learning in the UAE. This acknowledgment is exemplified by the educators' use of the word "here" during their discussions of teaching, learning and curriculum. In fact, the word "here" prefaced or followed almost every comment from the educators in this study. This suggests that in-depth consideration of context – of "here" is integral to discussions of education, constructivism, transformation, curriculum, and culturally relevant pedagogy. These educators approach their work giving thoughtful consideration to: issues affecting education of Emirati students as a specific educational community, the learning needs specific and meaningful to them, the cultural change issues that impact the nature of their lives, the manner in which to design meaningful curriculum for the learners, the tensions involved with the creation of learning opportunities for students, and how all of these factors coalesce in education in this context. This knowledge, according to the educators is crucial, but must be presented in a manner that embraces the local needs and voices – the "here," while also representing change and globalization. In essence, balancing the local with the global.

To illustrate, curriculum at DWC is impacted by a complex interplay of various specific contextual factors such as the nature of students' experiences, culturally sensitive issues, tribal affiliation especially in relation to group work, and the tensions involved with teaching Emirati female empowerment while also adhering to cultural rules. The curriculum also incorporated content and learning moments designed to bring the 21st century skills, such as questioning and critical thinking, into the classroom. This proves to be a complex balancing act as curricular content that elicits questioning in relation to societal differences, hierarchies, or social roles must be undertaken with great care due to cultural mores inherent in this context. It is essential to understand that the cultural background of the Emirates is one of "nomadic desert tribes" (Al Fahim, 1995, p. 152) that impart strict terms of loyalties and traditionally emphasized cultural roles in society: "allegiance must lie with the two beings who would care for and protect them – God above and the chief of their tribe here on earth" (p. 152). As well, the UAE is a political monarchy, not a democracy, with defined allegiances that are not only politically asserted, but they are also connected culturally. For example, it would never be allowed to publically critique or call for any questioning of the Sheikh in any fashion in the classroom. Thus teaching for cultural relevance means embracing and employing strategies to balance the nuances of competing values – the "here" and the 21st century in the teaching and learning process. In this regard, educators must go deep in their learning about Emirati culture in this educational context.

Embracing Students' Experiences in Teaching and Learning

Kelsey stated "People often come here thinking that students are so restricted in their lives, they have no real experiences to ground their learning. That is just not true – but, their experiences are different from that of other contexts." Kelsey's comment was mirrored by each and every educator who was involved in this study. They all agreed that students do have experiences and relational connections can be made between the concepts of the curriculum design, but it rests with the educator to uncover those experiences and figure out how to incorporate them into their teaching. Morgan noted a challenge for foreign faculty:

> We don't know exactly what Emirati culture is because: it is not out there for us to easily grasp. There is very little written about it. Even those who want to learn about Emirati culture sometimes have difficulty finding out. And here, understanding this context is vital.

In an effort to meet this challenge, eleven educators specifically stated that learners' themselves are a wealth of information about their culture and the best resource as they are very willing to share. Cassidy relayed an example:

> I had trouble teaching professional writing until students began sharing their stories about social etiquette with wedding invitations and parties. Students do not necessarily understand formality in professional writing, like an introductory email for the company visit. Professional written etiquette is not easily relatable for them, but they absolutely understand social etiquette. So I created a lesson on Email Etiquette as a form of social etiquette. That makes a bridge in their learning. But, you have to be willing to go real deep in your own learning here. You have to talk to students, go to the Cultural Foundation, talk to people, ask questions, let your students know you want to know them and embrace every opportunity to learn about their culture.

Five educators reported that learners also responded to and made connections with narratives, details, or discussions from teachers about their lives, families, and their homelands, especially if humour was incorporated. Taylor stated "They have got brilliant senses of humour." "I find that the more I use analogies, stories, the better. They relate it to a real world experience. They are fascinated by the similarities of my culture to their own cultural background. The reaction is amazing" (Shane). Corey also stated that students loved stories of the educator's experiences and believed this was important particularly in this context. Corey commented:

> Here, stories work very well. There is a long tradition of storytelling here that is an excellent teaching practice. Creating lesson plans that connect stories to the content, students' stories and your own, makes everything relatable. Here, with many students who are coming from a restricted environment, they love to ask you questions about your world, your home, what you have learned. They are amazed that you know things. I think that is a big part of what we bring. We are not really very typical of other teachers. We are ambassadors of our nations, but in actual fact I don't think our nations recognize us (laughter) as being of our homelands. They also want you to ask them for their stories. They want to be ambassadors of their own culture for you. In fact, this is how I teach reflection by the way … I have them narrate their story of a something that relates to the course content, then ask them to share

it with a partner, then the discussion turns to alternative perspectives, uncovering values present in the narrative, tensions involved with the narratives, exploring how to question and inquire about motives … It works.

Regardless of differences in restrictions in learners' lives, all learners have had opportunities to engage in specific cultural experiences in the home and community. Fourteen educators commented that these experiences can inform instructors as they consider implementation that related curricular content to students' lives. According to 14 educators, all students had participated in events such as: planning and organizing weddings, caring for children, organizing servants, welcoming and entertaining guests, organizing for religious events such as Ramadan, Eid al Fetr and Eid al Adha, and in-home entertainment. In addition, some learners at DWC have travelled with their families to places such as England, Syria, France, Jordan, Egypt, and Iran and have been involved in organizing for these excursions. Morgan discussed:

> Weddings and the planning of them are a BIG deal here. Every single female student can relate strategic planning instructional content to the strategic planning required for weddings. Students always get it when it directly relates to something important in their personal lives. Contingency plans, etiquette, communication skills, decision making, and problem solving – you can relate them very easily to their personal lives and the issues they encounter in their group work (Laughter).

Seventeen educators identified that capitalizing on these experiences was important because students understood those activities. Students had this background knowledge that would make the learning meaningful and "relating our content to what they already know intimately as part of their lives, makes the information understandable, relevant, and important to students" (Cassidy). In addition, recognition of experiences students have as part of their lives "leaves them with a positive feeling" (Ellis). These kinds of connections with learners' experiences were important because they needed these connections in order to comprehend new and seemingly strange learning concepts particularly as the concepts are taught in English – a language challenging for most learners. Addison explained the importance of scaffolding learning on learners' prior experiences:

> Students need to be taught things that they can relate to in their own lives. If I am teaching them about teamwork, an example that they can associate with is a wedding. An Emirati wedding requires team work. Throughout the wedding plans, all members of the family are involved. Somebody has to take care of the cards, flowers, cake, dresses, and somebody must supervise. During the wedding, they make sure that their customers are satisfied, their visitors and guests at the wedding. Protocols must be followed and working together is crucial. The following day after the wedding is a feedback session, who came, who didn't come, who was wearing what, what was nice, what went wrong, how they can improve for the next wedding. They understand teamwork from this exercise. Otherwise, what is team work? They have

never played sports. They have never had a part-time job. They have no concept of team work. If you want to teach them something you have to start with concepts that are close to their heart, close to their environment. Here, this is what makes a difference in their learning.

Thus, the scaffolding of learners' experiences that were typical and representative of their lives made a bridge between the new content and their ability to learn. Foreign educators in this context learned as much as possible about learners' lives and culture in order to create optimal learning opportunities, which was not without challenges. However, learners themselves were identified as valuable resources. In addition, some educators believed this sharing was reciprocal. Learners desired to learn about their instructors as well.

Sensitivity with Learners' Personal Issues

According to all educators, discussion of personal student issues (especially related to family circumstances) must be avoided or managed very carefully due to cultural and religious differences and the international faculty. DWC has an official policy governing this issue because, "When it comes to things like this, it's just a minefield" (Izzy). DWC has a Student Affairs department staffed mainly by Emirati females, many of whom have graduated from DWC. When learners approach faculty with cultural, family, or personal problems, the official protocol for faculty is to either inform an Emirati staff member in Student Affairs about the concern, or send learners directly to the Student Affairs department. This protocol was followed if faculty suspect any issues that might affect learners' well-being, including: concerns about mental or physical health, suspected learning exceptionalities, issues possibly related to abuse, or concerns about interactions between or among learners and educators.

This protocol protected the integrity of the interaction between foreign faculty and Emirati learners. Alex explained "Even after all these years in the UAE, I realize there are things I don't have the competence to deal with. Our Emirati Student Affairs people can give me guidance and insight." However, Nat and Cassidy identified that, although they follow this protocol, they did wish they could engage with learners and offer help when needed. Nat elaborated

They don't want to talk to the counsellor and they *do* want to talk to you. And it is really difficult because in my heart I do want to talk to them and I want to be there for them. But, I don't want that responsibility for knowing what is going on. Sometimes, students have boyfriend issues, or family issues. One student came to me wanting to talk about her mother who was a third wife in the family and not Emirati. She felt her mother was not treated well by the other wives. What can I say? I am a Muslim myself, but I come from a country that does not allow multiple wives. What can I say to this student? Here, all I can do is listen.

Cassidy also commented "They come to us genuinely wanting to discuss an issue, and I say 'I can't talk to you about that.' It feels disingenuous and hypocritical." Ellis noted:

I believe that we should show them that our views on life are different. Otherwise, the whole point of bringing us from around the world is lost. We're not just education models, we're culture models that they're going to find out in their work place.

Culturally relevant pedagogy can involve tensions particularly in relation to learners' personal, cultural issues or problems that may come to the educators' attention, but may be beyond their capabilities to address in a culturally appropriate manner. Due to the nature of understanding challenging, cultural issues and the status of the international faculty and Emirati learners, DWC employs a strict protocol that all learners with highly personal, cultural, or religious concerns must meet with an Emirati staff member in Student Affairs. Faculty were not allowed to get involved, which troubled some educators who believed their voices or even their ability to bring a different perspective may be helpful for learners. In some cases, all the educators could do was listen. International Culturally Responsible Pedagogy (ICRP) must recognize that embracing culture in teaching and learning may result educators learning about personal issues for learners. These moments can be very difficult for educators because they may involve issues for which they may not be empowered to intervene.

Group Work & Tribal Affiliation

An aspect of culturally relevant pedagogy not discussed in the literature relates to the sense of awareness and an ability to respond to group work conflict and issues particular to this Arab context. DWC's educators designed curriculum to incorporate group work throughout the academic year. In addition, all educators identified the value of group work in their day to day teaching practice. As the HD1 curriculum required extensive group work for the completion of the curricular tasks, it is salient that culturally relevant pedagogy recognizes that group work in an international context may involve issues and considerations different from group work in Western contexts. Corey commented "At first, students do not work well in groups. There are a huge number of variables as to why – personality, tribe, social status, behavioural issues. Some girls just resist working with other girls. We need a deeper understanding of why groups don't work well here." Tensions related to group work that were specific to this context were described by all educators as "tribal," "clan," "family affiliation," "wife status" and "father's name." Drew noted:

Here, there is tribal caste system based on the background of the Emirati people. Some [backgrounds] are: Yemen, Iran, Iraq, and African Middle Eastern countries. It impacts on the nature of our students. Emiraties are a minority here, in some ways a privileged minority because of economic wealth. But, there is a caste system here that is alive and well. It even affects intimate relations such as those between half-sisters. It is not unusual for us to have sisters with the same father but different mothers. They can be in the same grade, or even the same class.

Emirati culture traces its roots to tribal affiliations have not always been cooperative according to all educators. Morgan described:

It's a tribal society, historically and today. Tribal animosities carry over generations and manifest in the classroom. I have seen students verbally abuse each other, storm out of the classroom, refuse to work with other students, not speak with other students, not acknowledge the presence of the other students – no existence.

Corey acknowledged "Bullying, ganging up, students arranging to meet outside college time is happening right now with a group. In this part of the world, conservative families don't allow daughters out. So, the rest meet, make decisions. She is excluded from the discussion but blamed later for missed meetings." Cassidy explained:

You have to be aware of this. The teacher could easily and mistakenly come down hard on the student who missed meetings or is being bullied because she could be seen as uncooperative. Some of our students are from perceived less important family names, perhaps from a 4th mother who is foreign, or they are from very conservative families and this can manifest in negative group behaviour. Here, you have to always have tribe, family name and social hierarchy in mind with how it impacts on group dynamics.

Invariably, some learners were placed in a group consisting of members with whom they did not wish to work. When group conflict difficulties arose, underlying issues of tribe may not be easily discernable to expatriate teachers, according to 13 educators. Izzy commented "One of the problems that we face is we come from different cultural backgrounds from the students and we are unaware of, oblivious to, or unable to deal with the undercurrents in the relationships between students." Some of these conflict issues related to tribe, socioeconomic status of the family, mothers' status, and ethnic background according to 10 educators. Jaden commented "Emirati society is small in numbers, but diverse. Sometimes you don't realize that, you see them as fairly homogenous but there is diversity: socioeconomically, culturally, ethnically, linguistically, tribal." Jaden claimed the issue is further complicated by the fact that often students will not inform the faculty of in-group problems. Jaden clarified:

Here, you have this issue with expatriate teachers and local students. There are tribal problems, ethnic problems because of different heritages and [first, second, third, or fourth] wives. There are things going on that are not apparent to an expat teacher. Students don't communicate these issues to teachers or they may be couched in different terms. Teachers have to be good observers in order to pick up on subtleties, or to know if and when intervention is needed.

According to Morgan, Izzy, and Cassidy the issue was compounded by the fact that there was little ability for teachers to specifically address these issues directly with learners in depth due to the nature of the issue. As indicated, while faculty must be sensitive to learners' personal issues, many of these issues can only be explored or engaged through the Student Affairs office with Emirati staff and faculty must be very careful when they observe group dynamics that have broken down.

Izzy noted a further complication: "This is a taboo topic, which is hard for others to grasp. We cannot talk about this in depth, and there is little to no information available if you try to research this phenomenon so that you can become aware of these issues. You have no means or ability to analyze them. It is complicated. There are so many factors: inter marriage, Indian or Egyptian mothers … It is unimaginable to us how important it is [to them] – but, no one is allowed to really explore the issues." Cassidy explained the protocols: "We are supposed to send students to Student Affairs when we suspect these issues. Often, students won't go, because of 'face.' They have to speak about their ethnic background or mother's heritage or 2nd, 3rd, or 4th wife status."

Tensions in relation to group work is also discernable in the form of group difficulties in collaboration and leadership. According to 6 educators, collaboration in this context this can be challenging because "Students want to defer to one person so it is not collaborative. Power issues are always huge – who is in control, balance of power" (Nat). Morgan commented "They have a very tribal sense of leadership. Somebody at the top makes all the decisions, usually a male, authority figure. Because he is the leader, they will be good decisions and in their best interest." Morgan further explained "There is also a female pecking order that is based on tribe, position, and family. These interrelationships are important." Parker elaborated:

> It is illustrative of how the students operate and gets to the heart of what makes our job difficult. It is a tribal society based on a **very** strict cultural code. There is only 1 opinion, the tribe's. You can't have a rebel in the tribe. Individual opinions get constantly suppressed. That is one of our big tasks – getting them to think as individuals in a way that won't offend. Not always being or conforming to the group. Not always imposing a decision or an idea. Embracing the collaborative. We try to spark a debate, but getting debate here is difficult. A group of Spanish, Italian, or British students will run with it. But our students, they just don't.

According to educators this is also an aspect of cultural change as tradition and modernity meet and this generation of Emirati learners are currently experiencing. Morgan says "They are actually in a massive transition period now. Their leaders are promoting individuality and entrepreneurship, and that is a cultural clash happening within this generation."

125

All of the main curricular tasks, the Company Visit, the Bazaar, and CIF require group work and "It is enforced" (Nat). Student groups are formed through a random assignment, or the Business and English teachers meet and assign students to groups. According to 7 educators the premise for random group allocation is to mirror work place circumstances. Kelsey noted "This is something they have to overcome." Morgan considered "[At work] they don't have the option of saying 'I won't work with that person. She is from a different tribe.' One of our roles is to prepare our students to work in a multinational, multilingual, multi-religious working environment," a comment mirrored by 5 other educators. These educators felt conflict with group work provided an opportunity for real world learning for learners. Izzy reported "Eventually, they will be working in situations with other nationalities. This forces them to step outside their comfort zone. It's a learning curve that ultimately can be and generally is successful." However, Kelsey and Izzy noted a concern regarding this premise:

> We form these groups and expect them to function the way they would in an academic [or work] environment where you separate your sociocultural identity and your work identity. For these students, that is not something that they are used to doing and many are not capable of doing it yet. (Izzy)

Interestingly, aside from undercurrents in the group relationships, 9 educators reported learners enjoy work. They reported that learners were "natural, cooperative workers. They love it." Parker commented "In his environment, these students can work well together because they are very family and group oriented." Spencer reported that learners "Love it. They eat things like this up."

Five educators who had taught or supervised Year 2 and 3 noted a marked maturity in relation to this issue as learners continued through their college life toward graduation. Izzy explained "By year three, they tend to mature and deal with group work [better]." Perry commented "That is one of the first comments made from industry as these students go out [to the workforce]. Students are so used to working in groups [from college], they reasonably well settle in [on the job]." Addison believed "It [the curriculum] is empowering them. They feel valued and invested in. It brings them together, they congregate, they congratulate, they chat, and they get to work. It elevates their self-worth to one another."

While educators discussed these issues with group work, two educators, Corey and Cassidy identified a concern pertaining to discussions of tribe, clan, or family affiliation. The foreign faculty and supervisors attempt to understand issues pertaining to tribe from their experiences with learners and knowledge of context, as foreigners. Only 1 educator in this study is an Emirati national. This meant that how faculty conceptualize and respond to issues of tribe was critical. For these issues, the Student Affairs department was appropriate for intervention, if needed. Corey stated "Remember we are not from here. Most of us are not Emirati and we are not anthropologists. When conclusions are drawn and labeling happens, it is an issue." Cassidy also commented "The majority of staff in Student Affairs is Emirati, thank goodness. I am not an expert on Emirati culture so for these issues I always send students there for counsel or I ask Student Affairs for advice." Nat summarized "We as teachers are aware. For group work, students might need counselling or observing and that has to come from within the Emirati culture."

Educators in this study acknowledged that the curricular emphasis on group work, while mirroring a workplace environment, was not without tensions. These tensions have not been addressed in discussions of CRP but are present in this educational context and likely present in other educational contexts internationally. Some of the tensions related to clan, tribe, or family name and some were attributed to the nature of learners desiring to defer or assume leadership rather than collaboration. In some cases, this resulted in bullying of some learners. Educators believed teachers need to be very aware of group dynamics and be concerned about issues not easily apparent to foreigners. Potential intervention for these issues may be referring the student group to the Student Affairs department for advice or counselling from an Emirati staff member, particularly if the tension pertained to any of these culturally-based issues. It is crucial for international educators to recognize the boundaries of their ability to intervene due to the sensitive nature of some of the tensions. Recognizing the needs of the learners, recognizing the role of culture in education, and creating opportunities for 21st century curriculum design teaching and learning, and understanding the boundaries a foreigner has is a complex balancing act.

Teaching for Emirati Female Empowerment vs. Rules, Rules, Rules

A paradox existed in relation to the curricular emphasis supporting female Emirati empowerment, embracing CRP, and educators' beliefs and learners' assertions regarding elements of perceived disempowerment through strict enforcement of rules mandated by DWC, HCT, and necessary due to cultural factors of this unique context. To illustrate, 7 educators reported they questioned the strict enforcement of the rules governing learners' behaviours pertaining to field trips, mobile telephone use, attire, chaperoning, security at public events, and attendance. Taylor commented "God, they have got enough rules on them here. Why so many?" Kelsey noted "The contradictions are rife and it affects the integrity of what we do here." Nat summed up the issue: "We are saying 'you need to be professional and mature,' but yet we are treating them like children. "The campus is secured. You can't [leave campus] because 'You might meet a man.' 'You can't use your phone.' Huge restrictions. Here, it is a real dichotomy. A contradiction." Eight educators identified that learners themselves questioned the issue: "Students ask us why we teach them to be entrepreneurial, empowered as Emirati females, to take leadership roles in their society. Why when they will have their mobiles taken away from them if they use them on campus. That they have to be chaperoned when they use the ladies rest room on field trips. What can we say?" (Cassidy). Alex confirmed that a contradiction exists, and acknowledged that is difficult for new faculty to understand:

> We talk about learner independence on the one hand and then the faculty will get an email message saying "We have got a Nobel Laureate coming to give

us a talk and we want you to get every student there, accompany all students and take attendance." If you are a new teacher you say "what a bunch of hypocrites (laughter). Students should be independent learners. They are 18 years old. They can make their own decisions." That doesn't work here. (Alex)

Some curricular tasks were open to the public, but remained restricted in terms of campus entry, codes of conduct, and attire. "Absolutely, it is a protected environment" (Alex). Taylor noted how the restrictions imposed on learners in relation to public events stifled the attempts to encourage innovation and progressive thinking. Taylor explained:

Our college has a super strict interpretation of how students should dress based on the necessities encountered here. The emphasis given at the assembly [before the Bazaar, focusing on proper Emirati dress and behaviour for the public]! People were so vehement. That takes away the credibility of the event and the role of self-determination. The event is about Emirati women as business leaders owning and operating a business entity – but the emphasis on their makeup, hair and dress? Really? It is important to retain their culture and modesty but [shrug shoulders] ... shoes can only be 2.759 cm high or [height of] hair cannot breach the 3 cm rule – it makes it challenging to teach about Emirati women empowerment and then enforce these strict codes. You can't ask students to be innovative and progressive in college work and then subject them to this.

The dichotomy appeared to relate to the issue of educating learners for empowerment, but denying learners' voice, ability to self-govern attire and behaviour, and accept personal responsibility regarding the following: attendance, properly fastened *abbayahs* and *shaylahs*, height of hair and shoes, cosmetics, mobile phone use, unchaperoned departures from campus, boyish behaviour (referred to as "Boyott"), and social restrictions all of which must be enforced by HD1 teachers, staff, and supervisors. Ellis commented about the pre-Bazaar assembly where learners were lectured regarding appropriate behaviour and dress in public:

The assembly began with a discussion of bazaar & clothes, but it was heading in very interesting territory. The question of: Who are these women in essence and how are they going to define their identity when these walls come down? That is what is great about task-based curriculum. It is a great method for bringing these issues out to deal with, an aspect of the not so hidden curriculum. The students' faith in Islam, their Emirati culture, and their understanding of what is 'right' and what is 'not quite as right.' It seems like a side issue, but really, it is the main issue. The hidden curriculum is the curriculum and these students are at the heart of these decisions. Who are they, what do they believe, how are they empowered or disempowered, why, and what do they envision for themselves in their future and according to their belief systems in their country.

Four educators recognized that, at this moment in time, if the rules did not exist, and if the campus were not as securely protected, gated, walled, and restricted, then few female learners would have been allowed to go to college:

> If those restrictions, security, and constraints weren't here, then our college wouldn't be here. We have to conform. With the wall around the college, the gates, then the parents know "my daughter is there." If it were open like the men's college, then we wouldn't be here because we would not have students. (Taylor)

Educators in this study noted a contradiction between the curricular focus on empowerment and the fact that learners must comply with many strictly enforced rules governing their behaviour and attire. Several educators noted that learners themselves were questioning this issue. This particularly arose during the assembly before Bazaar, which was the first open campus event. Some educators acknowledged that regardless of the contradiction, if the rules did not exist then the college would not exist. What is required on their part is locating the balance between educating learners for empowerment and the Emirati cultural needs of context. All educators noted that regardless of the tension between these issues, they believe the value rests with learners themselves noting the contradiction, and balancing the issue in relation to their own personally held Emirati identities.

All educators noted that many HD1 curricular topic inclusions, especially in Business and English, specifically spoke to the issue of Emirati identity and female empowerment, particularly in preparation for the CIF task (Drew, Morgan, Shane, Alex, Sam, Parker, Bailey, Corey, Cassidy, Addison). The issue of Emirati identity is in fact an Emirati cultural concern that was, and still is, being discussed both within education and throughout the UAE in business, governmental and political realms. Because this represented a concern within the nation, it became a specifically designed inclusion in HD1 curriculum. Shane explained "It is all part of the fabric of what we do." Alex identified "You don't need confidence to sit at home and drink coffee. You do need confidence to interact in your world in a way where you do make a difference, contribute in some meaningful way. That is part of the reality of this part of the world." Addison further explained:

> [Our curriculum] empowers them with the fact that they need to work. Emirati women don't want to position themselves as burdens. They want to be agents of change. The idea, here, is to empower them by exposing them to their abilities and to sense, steer and guide their own career and their ambitions in life. To be effective members of their society.

According to educators, part of the reason for the emphasis on Emirati Identity emanated from the concern about loss of culture amongst Emiraties due to the changing nature of Dubai and the strong foreign presence. Corey illustrated "There has been a lot of discussion about what makes you Emirati. We look at issues like language. The replacement of Arabic for English in schooling. Many of them feel their language is under attack." Morgan, Shane, Corey, Addison, Alex, and Cassidy discussed learners' concerns in relation to themes of Emirati Identity including concerns about their loss of culture, particularly in relation to expatriate actions, beliefs, or ideas that many Emiraties find offensive. "Students worry about assimilation and loss of their culture and this is a legitimate concern" (Cassidy). Corey specifically related the issue of Emirati identity with the fact that the UAE is a developing country. "That is why the college is important. It gives these students the environment in which they can discuss their identity, Emirati – and the fact that so much of this country is run by non-Emiraties. It has been interesting unpacking this issue." Morgan described the political debate affecting students:

> We are starting to hear discussions – traditionalists and modernists; students are starting to talk about it. Emiraties are watching foreigners move in, bring in less than moral values in their viewpoints, and undesirable elements like alcohol, loud music, skimpy clothing. The strength of the community, these tight tribal family structures is being changed through exposure to the foreigners and many families do not like this change. Many Emiraties believe they are giving the country away.

In response to potential threats to loss of Emirati identity, the Higher Colleges of Technology declared 2008 as The Year of National Identity in the UAE and created a conference event at Sharjah Women's College called "Mosaic 2009 – Know Your World: Proudly Emirati." The aim was to generate dialogue and engagement with learners regarding who they are as Emirati young women. Through this process, the expectation of this curricular inclusion was for learners to begin the dialogue regarding their changing society, to envision Emirati place in the modern world, with values that embrace "tolerance, self-confidence, and national pride" (Proudly Emirati, 2009, p. 14). Morgan elaborated on the relation between the conference task and HCT expectations:

> The year of Emirati Identity was just made a political priority in 2008. Our curriculum is about raising awareness: who they are, their country, and their place. The country has changed significantly; but our students grow up behind a wall. That is what we are trying to help them with, and that is why context is so important. They need to come to a personal understanding of what their context is because it is not the same as their mothers, and it is not the same as their grandmothers, or older sisters.

The HD1curriculum responded to this UAE regional and educational dialogue regarding national identity through creation of many opportunities for learners to engage with this issue. Ten educators discussed the inclusion of these themes as "absolutely crucial in this time of change" (Morgan). Ellis stated "We are preparing them for the situation they will be in, not for the one they are in." Drew noted that "the Sheikhs [identified] that as part of the strategic goal."

Inclusion of curricular content related to Emirati identity during the 2008–2009 academic year was varied but prominent. Two research topics for the Current Issue Forum were: Emirati Identity, Change and the Financial Crisis; and, UAE Women – Identity, Entrepreneurship and Innovation. In learning cycle 1, students were encouraged to choose an Emirati female supervisor to interview for the company visit task. In English, themes of considering Emirati identity could be found integrated into lesson plans, listening activities, and articles students are required to read. The reading exam at the end of semester 2 contained two readings that were chosen by the reading team specifically because they focussed on Emirati identity: "Who Are You," and "Whatever Their Judgements We Define Who We Are." All educators reported that these themes are strong curricular inclusions and developed in a manner that opens the discussion, but are also culturally acceptable to Emiraties. In fact, these inclusions are welcomed. Cassidy predicted the impact of these curricular interventions:

> Our ladies will leave us and move society forward. Hopefully in a way that honours their culture and tradition in the contemporary world. They are the ones to define what Emirati culture is, to themselves, their husbands, their children and the next generation. And, this should be done on their terms, not as defined and imposed by others. We have to create the opportunity and they have to engage in the discussion.

Addison articulated the reasoning behind the curriculum presentation of these ideas as

> [Students] need to learn how to work with a vision – a vision of themselves. They need to imagine themselves somewhere and they need to inspire themselves and motivate themselves. They need to assume a leadership position. Events such as the Bazaar and the Majlis, everything we do empowers them. They feel valued and invested in.

Morgan concurred and reflected that "Dubai is constantly changing and students don't have their traditional anchors to guide them. [This inclusion is] so they can come to a personal understanding, an anchor. That is why [understanding] context is crucial."

A specific curricular theme of Emirati identity and female Emirati leadership was included specifically due to the nature of social and economic change that is occurring in Dubai. Emirati identity is a relevant governmental concern due to the demographic imbalance of foreigners in Dubai and the perceived need to define what it means to be Emirati. Female empowerment was included because of the specific need for women in this context to envision themselves as participating leaders in their world, and defined on their terms, particularly as their future is very different from their mothers and their older sisters. According to educators, it was crucial for these students to think about these issues now, while they are at the college.

CONCLUSION

It is important to note, while all educators and supervisors (save 1 Emirati supervisor) are foreigners to the UAE, all have gone very deep in their learning about Emirati culture and designed and implemented a curriculum that balanced the needs of being culturally responsive while providing a forum for transformation. This is not without tensions and concerns particularly as CRP in this international context must mediate different cultural issues. International educators must understand the limits of cultural sensitivities and controversies within the culture itself, possibly bringing in assistance from within the culture, such as that provided by the Student Affairs department. These educators recognized learners' experiences as valuable mechanisms for making learning meaningful, while balancing the tensions that surface in the design and implementation of a 21st century curriculum that seeks to have learners explore boundaries in their construction of knowledge, and a culturally relevant approach to teaching and learning. In all, exploring cultural boundaries through 21st century curriculum design and practice is a complex balancing act.

CHAPTER 9

GLOBALIZATION ON STEROIDS

21st Century Curriculum and Societal Change in Dubai

INTRODUCTION

Dubai as a changing Emirate has been described as a society experiencing "globalization on steroids" (Moorehouse, 2008, p. 1). Moorehouse explains that in a few short years, "it has undergone the kind of transformation that a city might experience once in a lifetime" (p. 1). This small Emirate in the UAE has witnessed unparalleled change, which has a corresponding and profound impact in higher education for female Emirati students. This chapter will explore civic minded education, an integral component of 21st century curriculum design, from the perspective of a context experiencing this "globalization on steroids" phenomenon. Aspects of teaching for societal relevant pedagogy in this international context will be discussed.

Why is Societal Relevance Important in Higher Education in the UAE?

Today's multinational environment means that it is typical, and must be expected, that people regardless of nationality or homeland will encounter and must be able to collaborate across nations, geographies, communities, and populations. This requires a level of exposure and engagement with multiculturalism and multinationalism. The United Arab Emirates, and particularly Dubai, is one of the most diverse countries in the world; people from across the globe have migrated to this fascinating and welcoming region. In this text, any reference to "society" refers to this multinational conglomeration of diverse people living, working, and interacting within the cosmopolitan city/Emirate of Dubai, UAE.

The Higher Colleges of Technology was, at one point in time, exclusive to Emirati learners only (this changed in 2010 and expatriate learners were welcomed to the HCT system so long as they had the minimum grades for acceptance and finances available to pay tuition). However, the number of expatriates in the Higher Colleges of Technology system, and at DWC in particular remain very small in comparison to Emirati learners who have free tuition. According to all educators, most HD1 learners had little interaction with the demographically diverse nature of Dubai except through the international faculty, primarily due to prevailing cultural restrictions on women. Parker elaborated:

It is different for the Men's College because they are allowed access to the social sphere much more so than our students. Our students are very much

133

confined to a domestic sphere. The idea of women in education, in the workplace, in the social sphere, is still relatively new in this part of the world.

Society in Dubai is multinational and part of the nature of the curriculum is to prepare learners for the diversity represented in the society of Dubai. Jordan commented "We are trying to prepare students for this workplace, which is multicultural." Addison, an Emirati supervisor, explained:

> This is a diverse, metropolitan city. There are 200 nationalities living in Dubai that will interact with our students. They impact the society at large and in so many different ways and we really need to understand "the other." Respect is something students need to look at. Diversity and tolerance for people, their religion, and their different sociocultural backgrounds. This is an attitude towards self and toward others and this is an aspect that has dramatically changed in Dubai over the last decade or two. Many of our students are sheltered from this aspect of change and this is why what we do in this regard is important. We prepare students for a different lifestyle than the one I grew up in Dubai, the one their parents grew up in, the one their sisters grew up in and the one their children will ultimately grow up in.

According to all educators the highly multicultural element of the society of Dubai, together with learners' limited exposure or interaction with the international representation in society, impacts curricular inclusions and related teaching and learning strategies in this context. Drew noted about the HD1:

> [We are] trying to get them [the students] to understand the multicultural/international perspective. This is the work place out there and you [the students] might work with people from other cultures and faiths. They will likely have a supervisor who is not Emirati – certainly they will have colleagues who are not Emirati, Arab, Muslim, et cetera. They need to understand the impact of international influences on the UAE and in the business and IT world. We need to integrate the [diverse] social and cultural context into the content of their subjects. We need to bring the international to the classroom.

Therefore, implementation of the HD1 curriculum was affected by the limited knowledge or exposure students had to the diverse and multinational population of Dubai. It was deemed important that learners were exposed to multicultural/ international perspectives as when they graduate and enter the workforce they will encounter, interact and collaborate with people from around the world.

It is stated within the Vision for the Future and specifically within the Mission and Shared Values of DWC to ensure learners had the knowledge, skills, ethics, and behaviours that would ensure their employability in either the private or public sectors in the UAE. As such, educators believed that embracing a 21st century international approach inclusive of elements of multiculturalism, multinationalism, and civil-minded education within and among different peoples was a necessary inclusion so learners were be exposed to this in their learning and be prepared for a highly globalized society when they graduate. How did these educators create opportunities for Emirati learners to engage with civic mindedness, Emiratization and the multinational diversity represented in the UAE through the design and implementation of 21st century curriculum?

Civic-Minded Education in the 21st Century

Contemporary discussions of 21st teaching, learning and curriculum speak to the roles of civic engagement and globalization in teaching and learning. Any discussion of civic-mindedness involves a complex set of issues such as: national identity, global migration, intercultural understandings, societal change, and multiculturalism to name a few. Judith Torney-Purta and Britt S. Wilkenfeld (2009) in their report on 21st century competencies advise that "Civic education, especially when it is interactive and involves discussion of current issues, is an important way to develop the skills that young Americans need to succeed in the 21st Century workforce" (p. 7). A 21st century approach to teaching civic mindedness is complex in international contexts, particularly a country such as the UAE due to the fact that the national peoples, Emiraties, represent a very small portion of the population. Further complicating the notion of civic education are issues of Emiratization and social and cultural segregation especially in relation to female Emiraties. Female Emiraties in the UAE are not only segregated in relation to cross-gender social interaction but also in relation to the kinds of engagements they have with other nationalities in their daily lives.

Adding to the complexity is the generational change represented in the UAE in a very short timeframe. Foreigners who have lived in Dubai from 2004 to the current day attest to the phenomenal change that Dubai has undergone. All of the educators in this study (most resided in the Emirates during this timeframe) speak of HRH Mohammed bin Rashid Al Maktoum's vision for change with great respect and admiration. Sam said with great pride:

> Although not born here, I grew up in this country. When I came here as a boy with my family, we had nothing. We fled a homeland that had experienced devastating loss, violence was normal, our cultural and national identity had been stripped. Here, we were welcomed foreigners – but we were a minority in this country at that time. Now, I am part of the foreign majority. My children know this as their home, but they are NOT Emirati nationals and can never be citizens. HRH Rashid [bin Saeed Al Maktoum], HRH Maktoum bin Rashid [Al Maktoum], and our current leader HRH Mohammed [bin Rashid Al Maktoum] welcomed us to their country, provided opportunities for health care, education, a life. Now, look at what has been created. I am filled with pride for this land. I want to give my students that sense of pride – I want them to work with change and support the vision of HRH. HRH wants his people out in society, participating, visible, with voice – all of his people, not just men.

CHAPTER 9

Because of the fact that rapid societal and developmental change is a fact of life in the UAE, particularly Dubai, 21st century curriculum must reflect this ability to work with change and foster support for changing roles in society as an embedded component within teaching and learning. Eight educators believed "Our curriculum reflects that change here is normal and happens fast" (Sam). Kelsey commented "Here, you can change things and things change around you. I feel like you can come up with any idea here and it will fly." Corey elaborated:

> Dubai is expanding exponentially. It is no longer trying to *'catch up'* with the West. They are taking the best of the West and the best of the East and the best of the Arab world and the best of anything else that they fancy and are creating their *own* way.

Morgan explained: "In 1971 we had a mostly illiterate, itinerant population. Now 30 years later, we have 25,000 college graduates. Changes happen fast here, overnight" (Morgan). If change, conceptions of civic mindedness and globalization form part of 21st century curriculum, teaching and learning, how would educators and educational leaders conceptualize students' success in relation to this changing society?

Conceptions of Learners' Success

Conventional discussions of learner demonstrations of successful learning are often attributed to elements such as convocation, grade point average, or possibly learning concepts or interests that have developed in relation to a discipline. DWC educators described learners' success quite differently. These international educators attributed learners' success to engagement, identity, empowerment, and a vision of their role as Emirati women to participate in the civic minded, globalized society of the UAE – a 21st century learning ideal.

According to Alex, the primary goal for DWC is "Everybody working as a team for students' success: faculty, supervisors, Student Affairs, The Career Centre. That is our goal." Educators discussed learners' success in two interrelated ways: ability to obtain employment and confidence in the public domain. Five educators (Alex, Drew, Jordan, Taylor, & Morgan) connected learners' success to graduating and obtaining employment in society. Taylor stated:

> My ultimate goal is to get these students to graduate because it will improve their life circumstances. If they miss out on learning a skill but graduated, I would prefer that than learning a lot of skills and failing … failing, here, potentially affects the whole quality of life [for students] for the rest of their lives. (Taylor)

Fourteen educators attribute learners' success to engagement and confidence in a public, globalized and communicative sphere. Both descriptions of success involve Emirati female learners' ability and confidence to engage meaningfully with their changing and competitive world. Alex stated:

We are about preparing Emiraties to be useful citizens by working and taking their place in this society: the technical competence, the ethical behaviour, and the confidence. You need confidence to interact and contribute in your world. This developing country is 95% expatriates in Dubai and the leaders want Emiraties to participate. It is important that our curriculum consider the practicality of values, skills, knowledge, and attitudes of students so they can go out there and compete with those expatriates.

Importantly, all educators noted that the hidden curriculum elements of teamwork, consequences, responsibilities, and confidence with skills and abilities for public task performance and communication that emanated from the 21st century curriculum is crucial to learners' success. Ellis noted "What students have learned [in HD1] is the invisible curriculum" and is not present on any form of assessment or accountability measure, such as:

Our students can walk in a room, look you in the eye, and smile. They work well with other people. They have skills and can function in a business environment with professionalism. These are classic task-based learning results. Ironically, things employers like about our students are not reflected [in assessments]: It is our students' ability to communicate and express ideas, not a 1,000-word tested vocabulary that is important here. (Ellis)

Educators' conceptions of learners' success is based on their ability to engage with confidence and professionalism in the real world environment of Dubai. However, how do these educators characterize unsuccessful learner achievement and why?

Deferring Success. Learners' lack of successful achievement in this educational context is characterized as 'Deferred Success.' This may sound like a semantic ploy to avoid using a word like "failure" or "underachievement" but it also represents an institutional approach to promote the notion of every learner being "able to achieve – it is within their control" (Alex). Spencer notes "Failure is not an option. Failure is not even a hypothetical possibility." Cassidy states "Our students *do not* fail." "They defer success" (Kelsey), which is "the politically correct term here" (Parker). Deferring success means that learners' progress throughout the academic year has not met the expectations for moving to the next academic year. They 'defer success,' the implications of which mean that the learner must repeat the entire year's curricular content.

However, rather than emphasizing learners' control over success, according to all educators, implementation of HD1 curriculum is impacted by institutional and learners' expectations for successful achievement in this context. Drew commented, "Students have high expectations that they will succeed but do not really grasp, at least during the first semester, how to reflect on their performance and appraise their capabilities for success." Morgan identified

Semester 1 is always difficult. This is when you really have to spend time with students, helping them see that just because they are in class does not mean they automatically get an A. They have to accomplish their tasks, perform their roles in the curricular events, work hard. This is a big hurdle for most students and some don't get it. Every year, we have students who just do not show up for their shift in Bazaar. Sometimes, a student will be 'fired.' Or, she will decide not to go with her group for the Company Visit. In this case, the student will quite rightly defer success and have to return the following year to do the semester again.

To illustrate, Izzy, Morgan, Drew, Spencer, Sam, Bailey and Cassidy observe that "Our students don't understand how to evaluate the quality of their work, because they have never had to do it. They have great difficulty relating quality of work to their grade, process to output to outcome" (Cassidy). Cassidy and Kelsey relate this issue to learners' lack of understanding of consequences. "When students run across an unwelcome consequence, like a poor grade, culturally, they have gone to someone higher up to deal with it. They don't necessarily look to themselves. They use their culture, tradition, family name because this is what they know for fixing their problems. It is part of their culture." In addition, Izzy indicated that:

> If one of your students defers success, you as an educator better be able to prove you provided early intervention, engaged in frequent discussions and provided every opportunity to assist that student. The institution expects that you as the educator have a strong guiding role and you must embrace this. You have to frequently and effectively engage in interactions and interventions to ensure as much as possible that students' success will be achieved.

Educators Corey, Addison, Sam, Spencer, Parker, Ellis, Kelsey, Bailey, Morgan and Cassidy state that they believe that continual monitoring learners' work and holding frequent debriefing sessions are implementation strategies imperative to learners' success in this context. Corey notes, in relation to portfolios "As a teacher, if you don't take a participatory role, [throughout the semester], it will be done the night before it is due, and likely not be done well. But, if you show you are guiding the students through successful completion, you will have a very different result. Because, the students really do want to do well." Cassidy states "Debriefing sessions are essential here. Students need that one-on-one attention so they can understand self-evaluation of their work as an ongoing and thoughtful process." According to Morgan debriefing post evaluation has the benefit of promoting learners' ability to develop discriminatory skills in relation to their own work after completion. Morgan states

> Never in their school career have they had a grading rubric. They have never had to individually assess their own work. HD1 is the first time they are given the grading rubrics. 'If you do this you get an A. If you do this you get a B, C, or an F.' It takes a lot of reiteration and reinforcement. Conferencing helps our students develop a sense of grading. It is not easy to explain the grading unless you sit in a teacher/student conference and go over the work in detail, explaining the difference between an A, B, C, or an F. You need to do

this throughout the semester, but sometimes it does not really have meaning for students until you do the same activity post evaluation.

The DWC conceptualizations of success and deferring success in this context represent an institution awareness that Semester 1 presents a significant change in teaching and learning for learners as they adjust to a 21st century curricular approach. It is important to note that these international educators are devoted to learners' ultimate successful completion of their learning, and engagement in the authentic tasks that form the curricular approach as this represents learning with the real world authenticity as a core value. This understanding of learners' success and learners' recognition of their role in their own success represents an opportunity to support authentic learning about success in society. This is crucial not just for students' learning, but also in relation to the national ideal of Emiratization, a political mandate to increase Emirati presence and ultimately leadership in the workforce in the UAE.

Emiratization

Politically, a mandate exists within this region for Emiratization which means an increased presence in the workforce of Emirati nationals. Emiratization is an affirmative action, governmental decree that mandates an employment quota, and preference in hiring in favour of Emirati citizens on all private businesses and governmental organizations in the UAE (Godwin, 2006). Strict financial penalties are imposed for noncompliance. However regardless of the financial penalties, the private sector has been slow to implement Emiratization and instead accepts the levy as a form of taxation (Godwin, 2006). Godwin (2006) contends that the private sector is lax in implementing Emiratization mandates due to: lack of skilled Emiraties, substandard work ethic, preferential labour laws that make dismissal of Emiraties difficult, and unrealistic expectations of Emiraties in terms of salaries and benefits. The result of this situation is that DWC publically and educationally advocates the need for a strong presence of skilled, capable, employable, Emirati women with a positive work ethic in the workforce. As DWC is a governmental higher education vocational institute, and the chancellor at the time of this study was HRH Sheikh Nahayan Mubarak Al Nahayan, design and implementation of curriculum that endorses Emiratization and these work-oriented ideals is expected.

Data from all nineteen educators revealed that a key feature to the HD1 curriculum is the political mandate for Emiratization: the curriculum emphasizes both employable skills and an appropriate work ethic in a multicultural society. Parker commented "Emiratization is the driving force [of curriculum]. From day 1 it's about work readiness, familiarity with the world of work, work ethic. These concepts are vital here." Addison explained the vision:

The focus has to be on the big picture, their country, their home, their people, their land. The need to buy into the idea [of working], invest in themselves, and take it seriously. We need to empower them to run the show.

To this end, behavioural training for the workplace was an important teaching and learning aspect of curriculum. Jaden discussed "We do a lot of behaviour training, things like punctuality, attendance, disciplinary things like [mobile] telephone use." Alex believed that this was crucial because "If you want to change behaviour and improve performance, you have to get them doing it, regardless." Cassidy commented "A key idea is 'Understand how to do the work yourself' because our students always seem to think 'Can't I just hire someone to do that for me?'"

Interestingly, Parker related some experiences of asking Dubai's employers about HD1 students: "If you ask an employer here what their main criteria are for employing an Emirati, they would say, 'I know if they are from DWC they leave qualified, hardworking, and their English [language skills] allows them to be trainable. What we do provides authentic workplace experience – Emiratization." Nat explained "We are supposed to be preparing students for the workplace. We are trying to produce professionals – so professionalism is expected and graded." Alex detailed the rationale:

> HCT is about Emiratization. The focus is on globalization and Emiratization at the same time. Dubai's leaders are ambitious for Emiraties to participate. You can do that with quotas, or you can do that by turning out graduates that can compete with all these other very able expatriates, many of whom are Arab, intelligent, driven and with fine qualifications. So the emphasis has to be on *doing*, and doing well.

Emiratization is more than a societal issue, it is an ideological shift for learners to embrace according to 15 educators. Often, Emiratization themes in the curricular content were focussed on changing perceptions regarding women's participation in careers, potential career options, and building enthusiasm for a career. Cassidy also commented on some of the learners' reactions: "Many students openly discuss their desire for a career and to contribute to society, but it is usually tempered with comments about what their future husbands and families want for them." Bailey further noted "We talk a lot about careers for women in IT. Students do not think about IT as a career because it involved the type of work which is 'men's work.' This is what students think." Alex explained the rationale:

> You have to have a vision based on the context, so, when this society really develops with meaningful work experiences, our graduates are out there doing things and not just occupying positions with no real responsibility, like some of their relatives. There are many UAE nationals with big sounding titles. They probably don't speak either English or Arabic very well. They probably don't read, and there is an army of people doing the work. Work is not perceived as something you do, it is perceived as a place you go. To this day, that is one of the things that we here at DWC have to overcome. This idea that work is something you do and you can get excited about the challenges of work. You get even more excited when you have done something well and YOU know it.

Several required curricular components were designed to generate opportunities for learners to engage with the working world of Dubai and to build enthusiasm about learners' opportunities through Emiratization such as Careers 2009. Careers 2009 is an annual event sponsored by the Dubai government. It is a massive career fair held in the Dubai Convention Centre and filled with prominent corporations in Dubai such as: Dubai World, Tanmia, Emirates Airlines, Dubai Media Corporation, Nakheel, HSBC Bank, and many others from all sectors. Significantly, Parker commented that the UAE Career Fair event began as a Dubai Women's Campus curricular event: "It was held in the cafeteria (smiles) and look at it now. Our graduates took it to the next level and made it one of the biggest exhibitions for Emiraties." Now, Career Fair is an annual, national event officially named "Careers 2009."

It was a curricular requirement that all HD1 learners attended Careers 2009, discuss employment issues with companies and collected information regarding hiring practices. In anticipation of the event, the Career Services department of DWC created a workshop which was delivered to each HD1 class about: What they should bring to Careers 2009, important points to remember, what to say and do, and provided a role playing activity for learners to practice approaching strangers at company booths. In addition, HD1 learners were required to formulate questions for company representatives regarding the effect of the financial crisis on hiring quotas and Emiratization compliance.

HD1's curricular importance of Careers 2009 was evidenced through assessment in English. For example, during semester 2, the mid-semester English writing assessment asked the following question of learners: "From your experience attending Careers 2009 discuss two or more company perspectives you learned that relate to: The effect of the Financial Crisis on Emiratization and hiring practices in the U.A.E. Support your answer with specific examples."

Eight educators believed events such as Careers 2009 were valuable because they provided the opportunity for learners to network with potential employers and consider possible careers in the UAE. All educators believed these events exposed learners to the competitive workplace environment in a manner that was culturally acceptable. Jordan explained "We need to get them thinking about work, potential careers, and career requirements." Taylor commented:

> They can establish some networks, which is part of the way this country and this culture works. It can lead to potential employment. It is a positive thing if they take the right approach to it. Go around and talk to people. Ask questions. Find out about their jobs. I tell students 'impress them because you may be back. Perhaps, you can walk into a job.

Careers 2009 also offered HD1 learners the opportunity to experience working at the registration desk according to Parker and Ellis. Parker discussed:

> It feeds into the mandate of Emiraties' opportunities, and employment. Employers from every sector are represented. It is only for Emirati nationals. They submit CVs, ask questions, and find out companies' Emiratization

quotas and policies. It is an eye opener for our students: (a) that there are opportunities and (b) that those opportunities require something of them. They are not going to walk into a job. They have to have something to offer. Every year the registration desks are run by our students. This year, we had almost 40 students involved over 3 days in various shifts, registering thousands of visitors every day.

Another important curricular event related to Emiratization is Current Issues Forum (CIF). Ellis referred to the Current Issues Forum as "a flagship event" that "forces students to address issues related to Emiratization" (Cassidy). The Current Issues Forum contained research topics related to Emiratization: Emirati women in IT, female leadership, Emirati employment laws, Islamic banking. Morgan explained the CIF inclusion of themes pertaining to Emiratization:

It provides a framework for the discussion of students seeing themselves as entering the workforce and having a role in the workforce – and more challenging – during this challenging time of dealing with the global financial crisis. It underpins the fact that they are going to have to go to work, perform at work, contribute to society, and the country's future. That is part of their responsibility for their country.

Jaden concurred and further explained:

The CIF tries to address these concerns through the topics, but within a context that has a broader view and allows students to look into issues affecting society: Emiratization Quota Mandates, Labour Law Issues, Allowing Foreigners to Purchase Real Estate, Labourer Rights, Law Differences Regarding Hiring and Firing of Emiraties, etc. This allows them to explore some of the issues in the workplace. They way workers are treated, where they are coming from, expatriate labour, women and men working together. It offers a really good focus. Even topics that may appear relatively safe, for instance "the real estate sector," can be controversial once students explore the issue. What are the implications of all this building on the environment? Or, people [expatriates] owning property? It gets them to think about issues from many perspectives – not just their own. It definitely broadens their perspective.

It is important to note, according to 9 educators that every year more controversial topics become included in the CIF. Morgan explained three new topics for the academic year 2008–2009:

Many topics taboo in the past are now included. Things are changing. Some of the current issues we deal with now are issues that could never have been approached in the past, i.e.: labourer rights, dismissal of Emirati employees, human rights in the UAE, foreign ownership of business and realty, female entrepreneurship, thalessemia and its connection to the cultural practice of Emirati consanguineous marriage, genetic abnormalities and consanguinity. I was afraid to mention the topics, so I got the director's formal permission for that last topic.

Cassidy believed that part of the hidden curriculum of the CIF related to changing learners' perceptions of the workforce. "Part of our hidden curriculum with the CIF is to reinforce that being a supervisor is not a figure head position ascribed due to Emirati nationality. Many learners think it is shameful to see an Emirati working for a foreign manager. It is a very controversial topic that gets a lot of attention and many opposing discourses especially in relation to Emirati women working for a foreign supervisor." Parker also discussed this aspect and elaborated:

> They need to understand that Emiratization isn't about men getting jobs. It has to do with all Emiraties – working. Our female students need to see that they have a role in Emiratization. With women in this part of the world, traditionally and now, these big questions, involvement, and decision making, have always happened in the Majlis, which is an area of the house mainly for men. That is where big decisions are made, and women don't contribute. Part of our job is to show them how this is no longer the case and it doesn't have to be in conflict with tradition, culture, or religion.

According to educators, promoting Emiratization through curricular content, events, tasks, and examinations, and job-readiness skills was of crucial importance. This curricular inclusion involved more than content, it was about changing ideologies that have been dominant, and remain dominant, regarding women's roles in society. However, it must be recognized that Careers 2009 was a forum exclusive to Emirati citizens as was the CIF (other than the teachers who attended). How then, can curricular context expose and integrate international communicative opportunities for Emirati learners? Other than the international faculty, learners' opportunities for international interactions are limited but important for learners' successful engagement in a multinational, highly globalized society such as represented in Dubai. How can educators create this form of learning opportunity in a manner that will be acceptable?

Virtual International Exchanges. As part of the endeavour to ensure learners have an interactive technologically relevant international experience, a virtual international exchange experience was designed using a variety of digital tools for telecollaboration across geographies. According to Guth and Helm (2011) "Telecollaboration in language learning contexts is internet-based intercultural exchange between groups of learners of different cultural/national backgrounds set up in an institutional blended-learning context" (p. 42). Due to the limited interaction Emirati learners generally have with the multinational population of the UAE, and with recognition of digital technologies as a communicative tool for meaning making, it was deemed crucial by DWC educators to create an educational opportunity for learners to digitally interact and engage in a virtual international exchange involving collaboration related to current issues affecting our global environment.

Guth and Helm assert that "The goal for language learners is to become intercultural speakers or mediators who possess the linguistic skills and intercultural awareness necessary to allow them to interact effectively in a foreign language with people from cultures that are different from their own" (p. 42). While traditionally, these exchanges were conducted with bilingual speakers, in more current telecollaborations the emphasis is the role of English as the language of interaction that focuses on "different cultural perspectives on local and global issues" (p. 42). These digital interactions offer value in terms of digital expression, online communication either synchronous or asynchronous, and cross cultural interaction, particularly for this Arab context and given the nature of lack of multinational interactions that Emirati students encounter (Lovering, 2012).

Hampel (2006), Hampel and Pleines (2013) assert that it is important to design these learning tasks with an understanding that the digital interaction will be different from an in-person, in-classroom encounter. Drawing from the work of Lankshear and Knobel (2006, 2011) three dimensions of VIEs will be explored through design and practice at DWC as a means to explore the learning and the constrains and the affordances offered by these interactions: the operational dimension (the multiliteracies skills); the cross cultural dimension (understanding issues such as etiquette, differing perceptions regarding current events, misunderstanding, cross-cultural accommodation and learning through digital interaction); and the critical dimension (reflective, consideration of power relations, awareness of those who are silenced or marginalized). It is important to note, learners' engagement in VIEs varied in terms of form and learning potential. Some were designed better than others, some implemented better pre and post learning experiences, some were more in depth than others. As VIEs were a new learning task, the success or lack thereof with the endeavour must be recognized as varied and highly dependent on the planning leading up to the event, engagement within the event, and the reflection after the event. If there was a lack of preparation in advance that would allow learners to research a topic, or create a digital artifact for discussion, the engagement and learning may be compromised.

VIEs formed a required curricular element for every class and every learner and was to be arranged by faculty and piloted during Semester 2. Although this was an ungraded aspect of learners' performance tasks, it was promoted by the leadership at DWC as a required part of learners' learning. Faculty were given full creative authority to locate an educational facility outside of the UAE, use any form of digital communication they wished, design any kind of collaborative discussion they felt was important to students' learning, and provide any guidance they felt learners would require in preparation of their VIE. This was the first time DWC engaged in any form of virtual exchange with an educational facility either outside the UAE or within the country.

VIEs in Practice. These exchanges were either in the form of Second Life, video conference, BlackBoard Vista or Web CT, a blog, or Facebook. The countries that participated in the exchanges were: South Korea, Bahrain, Japan, China, the United States, Canada, and the United Kingdom. All educators reported they felt there was value and "learning potential" (Kelsey) in these international interactions. Drew explained "It is one of the key goals. Every student will have an international experience." All educators acknowledged that the international faculty provided learners with some international exposure but not enough compared to the international marketplace of Dubai. Parker noted "We are from all over the world. There is no question that is one of our strengths; the diversity amongst the faculty who bring their knowledge here for the students' benefit." However, the international faculty was only one manner of controlled international exposure for learners and all educators felt it was not enough and it was too "controlled" (Addison). "Their global awareness is too limited even with the VIEs" (Kelsey). Drew explained the purpose of virtual international exchanges:

> [It] is for students to have global awareness because they live in a little pocket in their own lives. If they can link up with a student on the other side of the world, talk about the economic world or the effect of the economic crisis, it makes them think more globally. It's part of the (Sheiks') wanting students to have "glocal" (global and local) experiences.

Cassidy, Ellis, Bailey, Morgan, and Sam noted that the international exchange was beneficial, not only for DWC learners, but also the other learners in the exchange. It was clear that learners in the other contexts had very little knowledge of the UAE in terms of culture, ethnicity or in some cases, even where the UAE existed geographically. Bailey reported "I heard the questions the Canadians were asking. They were unreal [laughter]." Sam related:

> They got a 180 degree turn in their vision of the Middle East. The kind of questions our students were asked 'Do you drive cars?' and our students said "I drive a Porsche. I drive a BMW." I felt our girls were running the show actually, the others were just recipients. Our students initiated each country singing their national anthems as a formal closing and goodbye.

This fact alone was significant because, culturally "Emirati women don't sing in public" (Morgan). Morgan elaborated "This was profound for students. Every single class afterward, it was brought up. For me, it was a metaphor of moving out from behind the veil – an international video conference with strangers for the first time in their lives." Jordan commented "They were fired up. There is a richness and spontaneity in seeing the people and talking." However, the idea of video interaction had to be explored with care. Some learners were "reluctant with that idea because of the cultural issues of being video recorded or photographed. It is important to allow options in this regard" (Corey), an observation Morgan shared. Morgan further observed:

> The cultural mix, the cultural connections that were made between the Emirati students and the other students were absolutely astounding. Emirati students engaged not just with Canadian students, male and female, discussing issues pertaining to identity, but also there were several students in the Canadian group who can be described as 'goth.' There was also a student

who was male but had very long, pretty hair. The student later asked if he was transgender. One student said on her very last class where we have a reflection "I never in my life thought that I would be able to see and talk to a student from Canada – I really enjoyed it – I learned that they have very free identity." I think both groups of students needed to do a bit more homework looking at the other side. What they discovered about each other was the similarities and differences. That was very interesting to hear the students talk about that. What was quite different were the questions [they asked of each other]. It was a huge learning curve for both sides and it was hard to shut them off.

Morgan discussed the VIE video conference with a Canadian facility where learners on both sides of the world created posters of aspects important to their lives and discussed the various elements. Interestingly, the two posters created by HD1 learners contained two elements in the artwork that was quite unconventional of Islamic art: a pictographical representation of an Emirati woman reading the Holy Qur'an; and the lack of typical Islamic artistic elements of calligraphy. Morgan asked learners if the posters created would be the same if they were created for Emiraties and learners "wouldn't or couldn't give me an answer [at first]." Morgan explained "Later, students said they wanted to give [the Canadians] artwork that they knew would be understood [by them]. They put a Western face on it to suit the audience. The poster was about face." Learners were attempting to accommodate for a Western audience, but Morgan also commented that it was "unlikely" the recipients were cognizant of this accommodation to them.

Seven educators (Kelsey, Jordan, Parker, Ellis, Morgan, Cassidy, & Izzy) appreciated the VIEs' "learning potential" (Kelsey) but remained reserved in their opinions due to the "restrictions in engagement" (Kelsey). Cassidy believed:

> In hindsight, I wish I had collaborated with the instructor in Hong Kong better. I would have preferred to have students collaborate to create a digital presentation related to the Financial Crisis or researched something meaningful. It was superficial – hellos, interests, study goals, but there was not a lot of meat to the interaction. The potential exists, but I would like to see it freer.

Izzy notes that the learning potential was also hindered by the "lack of opportunity to revisit and reflect on the experience." Corey, Bailey, and Jordan believed that preparation of all learners in the exchange was key to the learning value elicited from the experience and to ensure "things go smoothly" (Bailey). Jaden commented:

> We had successes and some experiences that weren't. For the IBM Jam on the Environment, we didn't know what to prepare students for with the discussions [so their contribution was limited]. Students need preparation so they can contribute in a meaningful way.

The potential for value in the international exchange existed, but was not guaranteed. Parker, in discussing a Second Life VIE explained:

> Dubai Women's College has an island [in Second Life]. Again, it is the idea creating a safe environment, so people visit us on our island. My jury, at the moment, is out on VIEs. Part of students' education should involve having them have an international experience aside from just the teachers. VIEs do allow students to interact in a virtual space with people from different parts of the world. It was successful in terms of the girls doing it, being animated by it, and getting something out of it. There is value in it (shrugged shoulders) – if only just communicating.

However, Parker also believed the Second Life experience was "liberating" for learners because they created their avatars free of cultural restrictions. Parker elaborated:

> They create their virtual self which is a liberating experience for the girls. In their real space, tradition dictates that they have to wear *abbayahs* and *shaylahs*. In virtual space, none of them have to and none do. There are *abbayah* shops so they could if they wanted. Most will wear shaylas covering their hair. Then, they approach people and they talk using texts while they are seeing the virtual person.

Perhaps the most interesting element of the cross-national communication for the Second Life VIE related to the way the learners in South Korea and the learners in the Emirates perceived each other's communication mannerisms. In relation to the Second Life VIE, the two educators debriefed post virtual interaction regarding their learners' perceptions. The teacher in South Korea stated that her learners felt Emiraties were "rude" (Nat) in their communicative mannerisms, while the same comment resonated by the Emiraties in relation to the South Korean learners. Upon further discussion, it appeared that linguistic patterns that feature in each group were the issues that caused discord. To illustrate, an Emirati upon being asked a question answered "of course" very directly and with assertion, which caused the South Korean learner to apologize. The Emirati learners were confused as to why the South Korean learner apologized, and the South Korean learners felt that the comment from the Emirati was too direct and casual and the apology was not graciously received. In contrast, the fact that the South Korean learners preferred to engage in a dialogue using a messaging feature, which required writing the text, and Emirati learners preferred to use the oral feature to the messaging feature, because the messaging feature made it challenging to get reciprocal interaction in a sustained manner. In fact, all learners perceived "rudeness" in relation to each other (Nat, Spencer, Parker). This fact alone represents a compelling opportunity for future research in relation to VIEs.

According to educators, VIEs provided students with an opportunity to interact and ask questions of students in a foreign land. This had the potential to provide valuable learning experiences, but advance preparation, requiring students to engage in multiliteracies related tasks, and critical reflection before, during and

147

afterward are key meaning-making components. VIEs as a component of learning offers thought provoking area of future research in relation to cross-cultural communication, digital discourse, and digital etiquette.

CONCLUSION

Globalization on steroids is a compelling description of Dubai as an Emirate undergoing profound social and economic change. Dubai is growing, changing, developing, transforming and re-envisioning itself rapidly in a profoundly short time span. As the national peoples of the UAE represent a small population demographic, and as the leadership of the UAE desires an approach to education that supports nationalization and participation in the thriving workforce of the UAE for Emirati nationals, including women, a curricular emphasis for societal relevance was incorporated into the 21st century curriculum designed by these international educators. This incorporation involves these educators conceptualizing learners' success in a manner that embodies learners' growing confidence and professionalism in a public domain. This also involves bringing Emiratization into the curriculum so learners can begin to think about careers, leadership, and assuming their roles in society as they choose to define. As involvement in the UAE means interactive and collaboration with the multinational population, a curricular task of creating and designing Virtual International Exchanges with other higher education learners across the globe was piloted in Semester 2 to varying degrees of success. These VIEs as educational opportunities for teaching and learning offer an opportunity for future research.

CHAPTER 10

ENGLISH – A GLOBAL LANGUAGE

INTRODUCTION

The 21st century reality of internationalization of educational systems has embedded issues pertaining to language and communication. A growing area of scholarly study relates to the role of English as a global language, language varieties, and English as the medium of communication and instruction in schools, higher education facilities, and professional development opportunities across the globe. Linguists attribute the proliferation of educational systems using English internationally to the prominence of English as the language of technology, commercialization, globalization, and the Internet. In higher education institutions, this dominance of English has resulted in an increase in demand for English language programs, English testing preparations, and a corresponding demand for English language teachers across the globe. This chapter will explore the role of English as a language of instruction at DWC in the UAE. Presented will be a discussion problematizing English as a global language, followed by an exploration of English proficiency tests and teaching to the test or teaching for relevance – a balancing act of competing needs of context and internationalization.

English as a Global Language

As there are currently more non-mother tongue English speakers than mother tongue English speakers (Kirkpatrick, 2007; Lovering, 2012), English can be considered a global language with multiple varieties, dialects, mannerisms, purposes, and characteristics. English as a lingua franca has corresponding complexities for international education and higher education. As Jindapitak (2013) asserts "English is considered as the world's lingua franca which is most utilized to serve both intra- and international communication" (p. 118).

The resultant varieties of world Englishes have led to debates among scholars regarding adopting or accommodating multiple variations of English versus a privileged or dominating form of English (usually UK versions of English or American versions of English), embracing new manners of English meaning-making and communication, and standardization of English proficiency. It remains to be seen how the global academic community will respond to questions of recognition and embrace of English diversity, but what does appear to be an important factor is how the field of English language learning will respond to the issues of native, non-native and new varieties of English in international contexts where English may or may not be a nationally accepted language, but may still hold privilege in the education and employment sectors. The UAE is such a context

– most higher educational facilities use English as the medium of instruction and most professions, organizations and workplaces demand English language skills to some degree of internationally recognized proficiency. Options for employment are limited if English language proficiency to some internationally recognized standard cannot be evidenced.

As a form of intra-communication, in local usage, multiple hybridized variations of English in the UAE are common communicative tools to facilitate meaningful interaction among the diverse population living and working in the UAE including: Arabic-English combinations, Hindi-English combinations; Urdu-English combinations; and Philippian-English combinations. These hybrid forms of intra-communication have their own linguistic features. Ultimately, in many communicative interactions, direct translation of one language or another by two or more non-native English speakers frequently involves words, phrases and communicative devices that incorporate both languages – thereby creating a hybrid form of language (linguists call this a creole or a pidgin language). Indeed, and particularly relevant for Emirati students, it must be recognized that direct translation of Arabic to English and vice versa is problematic as the linguistic features and vocabulary often do not easily transfer in meaning. Thus, there is a metamorphosis of globalized English communication emerging – new varieties of both international and regional Englishes (Jindapitak, 2013) converging in the global communication discourse in the UAE.

As the UAE has the historical legacy of being a British protectorate (Al Fahim, 1995; Davidson, 2008) the United Kingdom variety of English has prominence in the region. But in the commercial sectors such as banking, finance, IT and commerce, North American English has a strong presence. Arabic is the national language and the mother tongue of learners. Many DWC learners also speak at least some Urdu, Farsi or Hindi as expatriates from Iran, Pakistan and India are significant in the UAE. The dominance of privileged forms of English is shifting from the diversity and varieties of languages and versions of non-native Englishes common in the region generating new communicative patterns that students incorporate in their communication both in school and in their daily lives. In fact, it is common for educators at DWC to hear Emirati learners communicating in a rather complex mix of Arabic, United Kingdom English and/or North American English, with elements of Urdu, Hindi or other languages incorporated into the mix.

How much of these new communicative strategies, and new language varieties, could or should, be welcomed in the classroom or in the real world of communication in the public sphere? Does this impede learners' ability to work with the "standard" of English they will need for their futures? Can standardized English proficiency tests actually evaluate the communicative abilities of learners' use of the English language? What is relevant about language: Communication for meaning with a diverse public in a specific context or ability to successfully work with the English required for the international English proficiency examinations? These are compelling questions for 21st century educators as corresponding issues are embedded: English proficiency standards vs. relevance of meaning making and communication; English proficiency standards and privileged status; what kinds of communication patterns are valued in international educational facilities and who decides and based on what criteria; and can educators make learning relevant if a standardized version of English language proficiency is mandated?

Problematizing English Proficiency: Standards vs. Relevance

There are two dominating, internationally recognized English language proficiency tests: The North American Test of English as a Foreign Language (TOEFL) and the United Kingdom International English Language Test System (IELTS) Academic. Both evaluate English based on five components, grammar, listening, speaking, reading and writing. Both have a paper based versions (less common in practice) and Internet based versions (very common in practice). English medium higher educational facilities decide upon a benchmark level of proficiency in relation to the five components that indicates a learner's ability to engage in higher education with English as the language of instruction. Hence, the English proficiency test becomes an entry requirement for acceptance in higher education in many higher educational facilities across the globe. However, for the Higher Colleges of Technology in the UAE, the IELTS proficiency scale is not an entry requirement, but an exit requirement. All learners must successfully pass the Academic Version of IELTS (HCTAS, 2007) with a minimum score of Band 6 in each composite area in order to graduate with their Higher Diploma certificate. As learners are often accepted into higher education facilities with extremely limited ability to use English (Mustafa, 2002; Lovering, 2012), DWC has extensive English language foundation programs for learners prior to their beginning of their diploma studies. It is not uncommon for students to spend 1-3 years in English foundations programs prior to their entre into their diploma or degree program. As well, the Higher Diploma Year 1 (HD1) program incorporates elements of IELTS Academic test preparation into the 21st curriculum task based curriculum to prepare learners for this graduation requirement.

This leads to a tension in teaching, learning and curriculum for English educators at DWC. According to Ellis (2003) psychometric testing, such as IELTS and TOEFL is characterized by delineations of discrete components (grammar, listening, reading, etc.), closed-form questions with specific answers, objective scoring computation, and statistical analysis of results in an effort for ensuring reliability and validity. But, this form of language assessment is commonly criticized (Altun & Büyükduman, 2007; Ellis, 2003; Zane, 2009). Critique focusses on:

> The emphasis on relative ranking rather than actual accomplishment; the privileging of easily quantifiable displays of skills and knowledge; the assumption that individual performances rather than collaborative forms of cognition, are the most powerful indicators of educational progress; the notion that evaluating educational progress is a matter of scientific measurement. (Gipps, 1994, p. 14)

In addition, a common criticism regarding these standardized, psychometric, English language proficiency tests is the issue of bias in relation to dominating English language norms that constitute proficiency of use (Davies, Hamp-Lyons, Kemp, 2003; Davies, 1999, 2003). This is a particular tension in international education because it is difficult to assert that a particular form of English is correct or incorrect given the multitude of varieties of English both native and non-native, and the role of English as a global language.

To illustrate, learners more accustomed to the speech sounds and patterns of British English may encounter difficulty with the listening component of the North American TOEFL test. Likewise a grammar feature such as use of collective nouns or sequence adverbs is challenging for learners' success in standardized proficiency tests. In UK Standard English (UKSE), it is correct to use a collective nouns (i.e.: committee) in either a singular or plural verb form.

> e.g.: The committee was appointed by the state. (UKSE = correct)
> e.g.: The committee were unable to agree. (UKSE = correct)

However, in North American Standard English (NASE) most collective nouns are treated as singular in relation to verb form.

> e.g.: The committee was unable to agree. (NASE = correct)

In UKSE, sequence adverbs (sometimes referred to as adverbs of frequency) such as *firstly, secondly, thirdly* include the *-ly* ending normal for an adverb form. In NASE, the *-ly* ending is usually omitted and the word usage is *first, second, third,* and so forth. Consequently, the complex question of whether any international, standardized, proficiency test can effectively assess "correct" or "incorrect" English is a tension that exists in international 21st century education. Davidson (1994) states

> Several large English tests hold sway world-wide; tests which are clear agents of the English variety of the nation where they are produced. These tests maintain their agency through statistical epistemology of norm-referenced measurement of language proficiency, [which is] a very difficult beast to assail. (pp. 119–120)

Arguments regarding the privileging of English language norms will likely prevail. Regardless of evidence regarding testing instruments' ability to reliably assess English language proficiency, the fact remains that high-stakes, standardized testing instruments such as IELTS Academic, and the North American equivalent TOEFL (Test of English as a Foreign Language), are internationally recognized, and institutionally accepted measurements of English language proficiency in higher education. Thus, higher education programs that require this form of measurement of English proficiency often incorporate language norms and preparation activities that teach to the testing instrument in the curriculum.

In contrast, the Communicative Language testing (often associated with Performance Assessment) movement rejects prominence of using statistical measures to determine assessment reliability and validity (Fulcher, 2000). Ellis

(2003) asserts the "centrality of the human subject of the test" (p. 282). Communicative language testing assesses by virtue of the ability to perform and complete the target task, rather than discrete emphasis on the specific linguistic elements. In effect, communicative language assessment lays the groundwork for performance assessment of language in practice in that the emphasis rests with communicating the message. However, communicative language assessment has been critiqued for lack of recognition of measures of reliability and validity, other than face validity and lack of recognition of construct validity (Bachman, 1990, 1991, 2000; Bachman & Palmer, 1996). This critique led to Bachman (2000) arguing for both communicative/task centred approaches and construct-centred approaches in relation to effective English language assessment.

Fulcher (2000) asserts that communicative language tests must contain three aspects: performance, authenticity, and scored on real-life outcomes. This means that a communicative test should involve performance of an activity that matches criterion performance as closely as possible, including performance of tasks. Test tasks and target-language use tasks should be aligned. As well, the student taking the test should be able to discern the communicative purpose of the task and be able to respond suitably. The real criterion of successful completion of the test should be whether or not the student was able to complete the task by realizing an acceptable outcome.

Moving from discussions pertaining to ESL assessment toward a discussion of constructivist curriculum and assessment, the literature speaks to tensions for educators. Constructivist curriculum supports the meaning-making processes and encourages collaborative learning, critical thinking, and problem-solving, with the argument being that this approach to curriculum achieves "meaningful" and "relevant" (Drake, 2007; Henderson & Gornik, 2007) learning for the student. However, how can meaningful learning and meaning-making be assessed and effectively accounted for particularly in relation to English language proficiency skills? Stakeholders such as government officials, administrators, and politicians argue for accountability in education (Drake, 2012). According to Henderson and Gornik (2007), standardized test performances in education offer a form of accountability of student learning acceptable to stakeholders because achievement can be assessed quantitatively. However, educators and curriculum developers argue that numbers on a standardized test do not ensure that meaningful, relevant, and transferable learning has been achieved because this form of learning cannot be assessed through standardized test performances (Drake, 2007; Henderson & Gornik, 2007; Robinson, 2000). Hence, tension exists between proponents of curriculum for standardized test performances and curriculum for constructivist learning, which manifests in profound effects on both educators and learners.

According to Drake and Burns (2004), these tensions are between seemingly irreconcilable positions, which they characterize as "accountability [standards] versus relevance [meaningful learning]" (p. 54). This tension results in educators being forced to choose an either/or frame of mind and orientation to teaching practice, which results in educators feeling overwhelmed at the prospect of trying to figure out what to teach or how to teach (Kauffman, Johnson, Kardos, Lui, &

Peske, 2002). Educators who advocate for the curricular emphasis of teaching for standards and accountability argue that this systemizing of curriculum supports and provides guidance to educators by providing them with prescribed lesson objectives, prescribed resources, and prescribed assessment strategies (Schmoker & Marzano, 1999). Educators who disagree with the curricular emphasis of teaching for standards and accountability argue that detailed prescription of curriculum and teaching practice for the objective of high-stakes test achievement, in addition to sustained scrutiny of teaching methods, constrain and handcuff educators who believe they are in the best position to decide and respond to learners' diverse educational needs (McNeil, 2000). This eventually results in "compromising the intrinsic rewards of teaching" (Kauffman et al., 2002, p. 274).

Elmore (1999) observed that the "black box is open and what teachers teach and students learn is increasingly a matter of public scrutiny and debate, subject to direct measurement and inspection" (p. 16). Public pressure exists in many contexts regarding a demand for translating educational practice in a form that the public can understand: grades, statistics, and measurable standards. Educators who desire to create meaningful learning opportunities, which are not necessarily generalizable or quantifiable, may encounter tension as teaching effectiveness is often viewed through accountability standards (Baines & Stanley, 2006; Drake, 2007; Elmore, 1999; Kauffman et al., 2002).

Thus, ontologically, philosophically, and epistemologically, educators encountering this tension between seemingly competing educational objectives may find themselves "lost at sea" (Kauffman et al. 2002, p. 273). These educators may be in flux regarding: priority of educational outcomes of their teaching practices; methods and strategies for use for their teaching practices; considerations regarding what is "correct" and "incorrect" in relation to English proficiencies, and confusion regarding the impact of this tension on their careers. In practice, tension between curriculum emphases of "standards" vs. "relevance" results in learners potentially receiving ineffective teaching strategies such as "teaching to the test" (Drake, 2007, p. 2) which, in the case of DWC, is teaching to the IELTS proficiency assessment which is a mandated requirement for graduation. However, is it possible a balanced approach can be achieved? Can curriculum at DWC support both English language assessment (IELTS preparation) and English language skills for communication and relevant learning in this globalized and rapidly changing country?

English Language in the UAE

Dubai is considered the commercial sector for the UAE and as such the lingua franca in business is primarily English; both North American and UK varieties are standard but many other varieties and mixes of different languages with English are common. DWC, in close contact with the business community, is aware that employers demand that Emirati employees demonstrate proficiency in English according to international standards.

Six educators reported approval of IELTS as a standardized testing measure (Nat, Parker, Cassidy, Corey, Kelsey, Morgan). Nat commented "I love international proficiency standards like TOEFL or IELTS." Parker explained "It is a definite standard that gives an indication of students' level that is understood internationally. That lends external credibility to what we do." All of HD1's English assessments for the listening, reading, and writing assessments mirrored the approach of IELTS, but used different source materials to teach the IELTS test preparation. The reason was "to begin preparing students to pass the IELTS and graduate" (Cassidy). Hence, 70% of the English course grades as outlined and mandated by HCT Academic Services were allocated towards standardized IELTS based English assessment. However, interestingly, Alex pondered:

The real question is why isn't IELTS an entrance requirement rather than an exit requirement? I went to a UN conference in Oman where a local educator was livid, saying everybody in the Middle East is racist against Arabs because we have such low expectations. Very interesting to hear this from an Omani Arab scholar. She believed, if we were a legitimate educational institution, we would have the same English level requirements as other institutions around the world. I have never forgotten that. But, it is our way of accommodating to the context.

All educators questioned the "real" learning achieved from these standardized assessments other than learning how to take a test that would form the learners' graduation requirement. Alex commented on international assessments: "These scores are a convenience factor more than a learning factor, categorization and screening students. They are a necessary evil and they are not going away, they are deeply embedded in academia." Morgan commented on the tension affecting HD1, "English proficiency standards are mismatched with the task-based philosophy. English teaching at DWC is basically all: skills, practices, and assessments." Five other educators believed there was a "wash back" (Jaden) of this graduation requirement (Kelsey, Jaden, Izzy, Corey, & Cassidy). Jaden commented:

Assessment is an issue for English. Here, there is that strong crystallized tradition of standardized testing. There is definitely a tension there. There is the tension between the whole philosophy of our approach – the transformative learning approach and then the tension for these English standards, which is loaded with difficulty for our students. They excel in performance and communicate very well in public – but that does not necessarily manifest when they are working through their English exams which are highly correlated to the IELTS.

HD1 English assessments attempted to address the Dubai workplace societal demand for learners to show English language proficiency to a standard that has international recognition. Thus in addition to teaching the task-based orientation to curriculum, English faculty had to prepare learners for this examination as an institutionally accepted aspect of teaching English in this context. All English

155

assessments and practice activities mirrored the format of the tasks, skills, and questions students will encounter on IELTS.

But, employers also demand a command of English that is inclusive of varieties of Englishes and for communicative competency. In an effort to address this aspect, DWC embraces the need for public communication in English through task achievement. While learners were not formally assessed on English language in terms of specific linguistic components through the tasks, their abilities to communicate with a public audience, express meaning, answer and ask questions and engage in meaningful communication comprised an element of evaluation related to communicative performance in all of the dominating curricular tasks: Company Visit, Bazaar, and Current Issues Forum.

Interestingly, none of the English instructors felt they were satisfied they were providing adequate attention to either the transformative 21st century approach to curriculum through the curricular tasks or the standardized assessment mandates. Cassidy commented "I feel pulled in every direction and I am not sure I am doing justice to anything." Izzy explained: "[In English,] we tried to mix traditional assessment in terms of structure and grading with task-based learning. It comes off in some areas successfully and in some areas not. So we decided we had to be creative and try other ways of managing both emphases in relation to English."

Given the complexity in competing demands, neither of which could be compromised, the educators felt the need to explore ways to meaningfully engage in dealing with English "standards" and "relevance." The IELTS standardized assessment was crystallized in the institution as a graduation requirement, predominantly because the workforce in the UAE demands English proficiency and evidence of success to an international standard. But, the 21st century approach to teaching, learning and curriculum called for more authentic, performance based English assessment. Thus, as Morgan commented "Our English teachers have done innovative things with assessment to address this mismatch in English language emphasis."

Making IELTS Testing Relevant for Emirati Learners

According to English course outlines, 70% of the English grade was generated through a continuous assessment strategy of English skill areas: speaking, reading, listening, grammar and writing in accordance with IELTS testing procedures. In an effort to transform assessment requirements and test practice activities into relevant and authentic opportunities for learner engagement in English, all of the assessments, English content materials, and exam preparation materials are created by the HD1 English team and culled from authentic UAE media sources. They are piloted for accuracy and team graded for consistency. The goal is to address the HCT course outline requirements and provide authentic, contextually relevant learning opportunities. Jaden states "We try and break away from rigid practice. We base our tests that we produce on standardized format but with authentic materials – to make it meaningful." Sam states "It is more than just testing facts. It should be about getting students to analyze their environment." Spencer states

"Practicing test taking skills can be interesting. You can get them to read interesting, relevant passages and analyze them. It takes a lot of creativity, a lot of thought and a lot of time." Ellis states "The benefit is we know the students here and can create activities that they will respond to. The negative is a lot of work that goes into it."

To illustrate, the reading assessment exams are created by a specific team of HD1 English teachers and consist of two readings per two tests, per semester. The readings themselves are chosen from various media outlets in Dubai such as The National, Khaleej Times, Gulf News, Business 24-7, AME Info based on relevance to curricular themes. After appropriate texts are chosen and edited, exam questions are prepared and then the test is piloted by administering it to the rest of the HD1 team. Kelsey states "I can't pick too many holes in the way we do it. It involves many people, we pilot and check and recheck. I would be happy to defend the way we do reading."

The first reading exam is "unseen" meaning that the learners are not provided with the reading script in advance of the test. The second reading exam is "seen" meaning that the last day of the week prior to the exam learners are provided with a copy of both reading scripts to review prior to the exam. The caveat is, the learners may use any strategy they wish to understand the text and vocabulary except communicate in any way about the texts with any teacher. Chronologically the reading exams for semester 1 were: Exam 1 – "How to Communicate across Cultures: Doing Business in Dubai" and "Sheikha Lubna: Dubai's Advocate for Female Emirati Leadership" (unseen); and Exam 2 – "Tall, Blonde and Evil: Barbie Bothers Iran" and "Hosting Effective Multi-Cultural International Business Meetings" (seen). Chronologically, the reading exams for semester 2 were: Exam 1 – "Addressing the Global Crisis: The Impact on Dubai" and "Responding to The Dark Side of Dubai" (unseen); and Exam 2 – "Whatever Their Judgements We Define Who We Are" and "Who Are You" (seen). The scripts for the last two reading exams are appended as Appendix B entitled "Reading Assessment Texts." These last two scripts are important because they also address the issue of Emirati Identity during this time of change.

According to the English language educators (Kelsey, Parker, Jaden, Cassidy, Izzy, Ellis, Corey), the underlying rationale for the "seen" and "unseen" nature of the reading scripts is due to consideration of learners' difficulty with reading. This context is an oral culture traditionally and learners are not motivated to read or to apply effective reading strategies (Kelsey, Parker, Jaden, Ellis, Corey, Izzy, Morgan, Addison, Alex, Cassidy) and this format of assessment allows educators to "see if the reading techniques we teach are being used by students" (Parker). The first reading exam in the semester is unseen and follows a "traditional format. Learners come in, sit down, are given the two reading passages and the question and answer sheets. They have 90 minutes to complete the exam. Izzy believes there is "value in the seen and unseen reading. Reading tends to be something that they do quickly one week before the assessment when they fit in between everything else that they are doing and that is unfortunately their weakest skill." Ellis, Kelsey, Corey, Cassidy, Jaden, Spencer, and Parker agree:

> The English team was thinking about ways we could force them, in a high stakes situation, to use the skills taught. Students take the readings home. We create IELTS type exam questions and get them to think about this by giving them the reading script to study. They know what kind of questions are likely on the test. We give them the text and say "you are going to be tested on this – look at it carefully and come prepared." It turns the assessment into a learning experience. A student shouldn't simply come in, do an assessment, go away and get a mark. It should all be built into the learning process. (Parker)

Teaching English is difficult in this context due to the dual emphasis between mandated achievement of IELTS as a graduation requirement, due in part to the commercial nature of Dubai, and the task-based approach to curriculum. It is further challenged by the oral communicative cultural tradition in this context: Emirati learners generally dislike reading and often it is the weakest English language skill. This tension results in the educators using the IELTS framework to facilitate English with authentic media-based materials relevant to these learners and this context. Educators believe this approach allows learners to practice their exam testing skills, while providing relevance and maintaining a relationship to curricular content and readings with issues meaningful for Emirati learners. Tensions result in the creation of English content and assessments that address the standards mandated by HCT but still provide relevant and meaningful learning. Educators agree that teaching to the test can be relevant, but it takes a great deal of thought, time and creativity.

Standards and Relevance: Examining the Relationship between Teaching for Accountability Standards (IELTS) and Relevance (Integrated Constructivist Curriculum)

Bobbitt (1924) began the discussion of curriculum for achievement on standardized assessments commonly referred to as "accountability" (Drake & Burns, 2004, p. 53; Drake, 2007, pp. 1–2) or "standardized test performances" (Henderson & Gornik, 2007, p. 2). Learners' successfully achieving a score of Band 6 on the IELTS Academic is the accountability standard relevant to this study for two reasons. First, this test is internationally recognized and the employment sector accepts it as a measure of English proficiency. Second, it is a graduate requirement for all learners within the HCT system. DWC supervisors and faculty support an authentic, integrated, experiential, and task-oriented approach to the design and implementation of curriculum, but must also teach to learners' success on the IELTS.

Eleven of the 19 educators discussed tensions in relation to teaching or assessing English. However, their discussions of tensions in their attempts to address all of the seemingly contradictory approaches and outcomes the college defined as required measures of learners' successful completion of their program demonstrated the integrity they bring to their work. They acknowledged that learners' successful achievement on the IELTS examination ultimately leads to learners' success in obtaining employment as this is a market demand in Dubai. The English teachers attempted to support teaching to the test, and supported teaching for relevant learning to allow learners to demonstrate their use of English language skills through performance of their 21st century curricular tasks. Learners' use of communicative strategies during their task performance was evaluated not only by the educators, but also the public attending the open-campus events (formatively), although formal evaluation of English language skills was left to the English language teachers.

Although educators discussed the tension, and identified strategies to attempt to mediate the tension, none of the educators called for an abandonment of the IELTS examination. This was interesting given the fact that every English teacher that participated acknowledged the competing emphases in curriculum and commented on the fact that they felt they were teaching English "to the test." My interpretation of these data is that educators considered a bigger picture in this regard: IELTS Academic success is benchmark to prove to Dubai's employers DWC's learners' English proficiency to a recognizable level, which will help learners be considered employable. The mission of the college is to make learners employable, and the IELTS test provides employers with an English proficiency standard that is internationally recognized and assessed by the British Council, a separate governing body from the HCT system. Learners' success on IELTS Academic is deemed necessary, regardless of personal or professional perspectives teachers hold regarding the demonstration of learning achievable on standardized testing instruments.

The HD1 English teachers must "teach to the test" regardless of some comments about the efficacy of a standardized test as a demonstration of English language proficiency. However, these English teachers identified that their approach to teaching to that test provided learners with authentic, relevant, and meaningful English language learning opportunities to support learners' construction of knowledge. Some of the strategies related to modelling IELTS Academic testing approaches through readings that directly related to the curricular task themes. For example, the writing exam questions focused on the curricular tasks, but followed the IELTS Academic format. The reading exams discussed Dubai-relevant themes, using authentic reading resources, very relevant to these learners, while following the format for reading questions found on IELTS Academic. The listening exam used authentic resources, such as radio programs from Dubai's Business Breakfast and Dubai Eye, while mirroring the format of the listening exam on IELTS Academic. In addition, all English resources including assessments are culled from various media sources in Dubai, and constructed in-house to mirror the IELTS Academic examination. They are also shared throughout the team and piloted for validity and credibility. This is an approach I suggest that other educational facilities may wish to consider if they are in a position to teach to an English language accountability standard and relevance simultaneously. This approach, while it is arguable in terms of real learning that results, mediates between the emphases. Potentially, the authenticity of the media sources and relevance to context may inherently provide an avenue to generate dialogue and thus contribute to meaning-making.

Summary of Standards and Relevance

Thus, perhaps all of the issues surrounding the tension between teaching for relevance or teaching for IELTS testing success may be present and problematic. However, ultimately the findings of this study suggest that these educational issues may be a necessary tension at this moment. Regardless of tension, the educational outcomes related to success on IELTS has a specific purpose for learners that ultimately will contribute to a societal goal of increased presence of Emirati women in the workforce, in leadership positions, and in society. In addition, teaching for relevance, and for communicative competency as is supported through the curricular tasks, which has its own significance in supporting the societal goals of increased presence of Emirati women in the workforce, in leadership positions and in society. The competing demands have a clear purpose and a function for the future of Emirati learners. No educator, at any time, suggested that any of the graduate outcomes or curricular emphases change, including the requirement for IELTS Academic assessment of English. Rather, educators were struggling to address, balance and locate relevance and authenticity through assessment. It is a balancing act that requires great cooperation and a strong team spirit amongst faculty, which all educators identified as present in HD1, at DWC. The balancing act also requires creativity and imagination. I believe that concern about what may appear to be competing educational outcomes can be better understood through a different lens. Perhaps the lens should focus on the following: How can educational facilities foster the team spirit, creativity, and cooperation necessary to allow faculty to facilitate all of the mandated educational outcomes the institution deemed salient to learners' success?

The educators in this study observed that many of the most important elements of the students' learning from HD1's curriculum do not appear on any international standard or accountability measure. All educators identified that learners' experience of all of the aspects of experiencing a task, doing the work for themselves, communicating in the public in English for effective interaction, and being responsible for the success or failure of public tasks including all of the many ways things can go awry were the most important aspects of teaching and learning with this 21st century curriculum. Dewey (1934/1980) believes that life experience provides the basis to understand knowledge and learning. But, what happens when your exposure to life experience is limited or is subject to different life experiences? Higher Diploma Year 1 learners were required, as elements of their learning to delve into all of the traumatizing choices, unavoidable problems, difficult controversies and the general messiness of living a public life as the primary elements of their learning. As well, learners are accomplishing this in English, in a public forum, many of them for the first time in their lives.

DWC learners interviewed a supervisor in a company and presented their work (Company Visit, Task 1). They worked as employees in a public venue business or bank, or ran a non-profit discussion group (Bazaar, Bank and Career Majlis, Task 2). They attended Careers, 2009 and questioned potential employers regarding career opportunities, preferred academic qualifications, salary expectations, and opportunities for advancement. They answered questions from potential employers about themselves and their curriculum vitae. By the end of the academic year, they researched controversial, challenging, and relevant topics, and presented their work in a public venue event (Current Issue Forum, Task 3). They were seen, they asked and answered questions, and they contributed to social interaction. They worked, they evaluated management practices, they presented research, critiqued it, asked and answered questions, and they evaluated and were evaluated on their performances. They completed all of these tasks using the English language as the medium of communication. This is a demonstration of what can be achieved through innovative approaches to curriculum and a balanced approach to the realities of English language needs in an international context.

CONCLUSION

English is a global language. It is the language of international education, international commerce, the Internet, and so forth. As English is the lingua franca for globalized societies, a debate in English language curriculum exists in relation to how you ensure a level of English proficiency. Currently, IELTS and TOEFL international English proficiency tests dominate as academic means of considering proficiency. DWC, in an effort to provide learning that is relevant and meaningful ultimately leading to Emirati successful participation in a globalized environment must integrate English language learning that meets both communicative competency needs for a diverse multinational context, but also address the need of teaching learners for high stakes standardized testing with the IELTS Academic, a graduation requirement. This has led to an approach wherein communicative competency forms an integral component of the evaluation for the curricular tasks, and English testing that mirrors the IELTS Academic test but using authentic resources from various UAE sources. The fact that all English materials are generated by the English team from authentic media sources in the UAE and shared, assists with adding a lens of authenticity to standardized testing preparation, but this takes a great deal of time, effort and creativity from the educators.

CONCLUSION

CHAPTER 11

CAPTURING 21ST CENTURY CURRICULUM DESIGN IN PRACTICE

What Can Be Learned from Higher Education at DWC?

HCT will continue as an institution of world distinction – not only because of the scope and quality of the education it provides, but also because of its service to our society. Our aim is to ensure a clear sense of purpose, to guarantee relevance in our curriculum, excellence in teaching and learning and the graduation of accomplished young men and women who will ensure the highest quality of life for the United Arab Emirates and its people. (H. E. Sheikh Nahayan Mabarak Al Nahayan, as cited in HCT, 2007, p. 14)

INTRODUCTION

This book emanates from a year- long study of the 21st century, trans-disciplinary curriculum designed and implemented at Dubai Women's College in the Higher Diploma Year One (HD1) program. The purpose was to understand the nature of design and implementation of curriculum directed exclusively for Emirati female students in the United Arab Emirates (UAE). I sought to provide a thick description of the 21st century curriculum in this unique context at this particular moment of time. This study focused on the following: the educators' perceptions of the influences of this unique context on the design and implementation of curriculum; the issues and tensions they experienced as teachers and supervisors in the implementation of this curriculum; the connection of 21st century teaching and learning decisions in relation to the religious, social, and cultural needs of context; and the relationship between the twofold mandates of teaching to standards (IELTS) and the 21st century orientation to curriculum.

This chapter provides a summary of the findings of this study. It begins with a discussion of the main finding that contributes to contemporary discussions of educational theory; this primary finding represents a snapshot description of 21st century, transformative and trans-disciplinary curriculum in this Arab, female, higher educational facility, as designed and implemented by this team of international educators. This chapter will then explore 3 primary elements of this curriculum in practice in relation to contemporary scholarly discussions. The chapter will finish with a discussion of implications and final thoughts.

165

Snapshot of 21st Century Curriculum, Teaching and Learning at DWC

The primary finding of this study describes a contextualized, 21st century model of curriculum, in practice, in this Middle Eastern context. Previous discussions of curriculum, teaching, and learning are based predominantly in Western educational contexts, which support learning needs that are different from this Arab context. The findings from this study describe this 21st century curriculum as a highly contextualized construct that embraces 21st century teaching, learning, knowledge and skills while simultaneously embracing complex contextual needs: religious beliefs, culturally responsive teaching, societal responsive teaching and particular political mandates such as Emitarization.

Twenty-first century curriculum is commonly described as constructivist and emphasizing learners' development of conceptual understandings (Vogel-Walcutt, Gebrim, Bowers, Carper, & Nicholson, 2011). The nature of knowledge in a constructivist model is both cognitive and social (Case, Okamoto, Griffin, Keough, Bleiker, & Henderson, 1996). Various scholars have discussed constructivist curriculum in various ways, suggesting a continuum from moderate to radical constructivism (Cronje, 2006; Sánchez & Loredo, 2009; von Glasersfeld, 1996). These models function on this continuum through degrees of objectivity or subjectivity (Sanchez & Laredo, 2009). The basic premise of radical constructivism is that "every reality is unique to the individual" (Karagiorgi & Symeou, 2005, p. 18; see also Cronje, 2006; von Glasersfeld, 1996). Moderate constructivists believe in shared reality with embedded social constraints that affect the constructive process of learning (Cronje, 2006; Karagiorgi & Symeou, 2005).

While the 21st century curriculum that is the focus of this book appears to represent a moderate model of constructivism, I agree with Sánchez and Loredo's (2009) reservations about these dichotomies that may cause "them to loose [sic] the specificity that constructivism has a powerful and original theoretical perspective" (p. 333). Their stance is simply that constructivism is a basis for designing curriculum based on the belief that knowledge is cognitively and socially constructed by the learner as they interact with experiences and ideas. This 21st century curriculum was developed with the grounded understanding that tantamount to learners' construction of knowledge is the recognition that they are "active organisms seeking meaning" (Driscoll, 2005, p. 387), have lived experiences that affect construction of meaning-making, and that curriculum should provide learners with "tool kits" (Jonassen, 1991, p. 6) for mental construction through relevant and experiential learning opportunities.

However, in this meaning-seeking adventure of learning, this study demonstrates that the curriculum design must meet learners where they currently are and recognize the balance of where socially, culturally, and religiously, they are encouraged to go as crucial elements of 21st century international curriculum. This study shows that these factors are entirely dependent on the context. Thus, I believe that curriculum theories and models of learning are context dependent, and must be designed and implemented by those with in-depth knowledge of these specific factors. This study supports my belief that educators outside this context could not have developed this highly contextualized 21st century curriculum as represented in this body of work. To illustrate, three key elements from these data speak to the creation and implementation of this contextually balanced curriculum that is specific for Emirati women at this time, in this changing society. They are discussed as follows:

1. Polarizing Methodologies: The false dichotomy of implementation of "Western" educational theory in an Arab context;
2. Transforming Vision: The use and connection of structural functionalist educational theory and transformative learning theory to empower female Emirati higher education learners as they re/envision their roles as participants in the workforce of Dubai;
3. Postmodern Perspectives: Understanding the impact of specific contextual factors on the design and implementation of curriculum in this Arab context.

All of these elements had a profound impact on the decisions this team of international educators made in the design and implementation of this contextually relevant 21st century curriculum.

Polarizing Methodologies: The False Dichotomy of Implementing of "Western" Educational Theory in an Eastern Context

With globalization, there has been an increased interest in the literature related to international education, particularly in developing nations. Much of the concern in the literature relates to the notion of "exporting methodologies" (Halbach, 2002, p. 243); the exportation and implementation of a specific method, methodology, or theory from one educational system to another in a different country. Primarily, the literature discusses this concern from the perspective of teaching "Western" theories and embedded values (Bleakley et al., 2008; Garson, 2005; Halbach, 2002; Hoppers, 2009; Richardson, 2004) in "Eastern" or developing countries. This concern is valid. The use of any educational theory should be framed with recognition of the underlying values inherent within the theory in relation to the values related to learning in context. It is crucial to recognize that international education should not involve colonialism of education or the notion of '*bringing education to the other.*' Every educator in this study cautioned against this premise whether it be a part of an educator's thinking when he or she decides to go abroad, or part of institutional decision making in relation to curriculum, policy, or approaches.

However, these findings suggest that there is a false dichotomy presented in the literature of "Western" theories and strategies being implemented in "Eastern" contexts. I believe this binary line of distinction obfuscates the opportunity to think about multiple ways theory can be conceptualized, discussed, envisioned, and re-envisioned, in practice and in different places. There is great opportunity in international education for reciprocity in learning, which all educators in this study lived. The educators in this study came from across the globe and have lived in third space through their international experiences for most of their professional lives. The distinction of educators who come from the 'West' and 'East' did not significantly apply to this group of international educators because of this diversity. In addition, these international educators designed and implemented an orientation to curriculum in a manner highly contextualized to the UAE and female Emirati students and enlightens in regard to concerns noted about "exporting methodologies" (Halbach, 2002, p. 243), particularly in relation to constructivist theory and experiential learning theory.

Constructivist Theory and Experiential Learning Theory. Case (1992) asserts learning is facilitated through social interaction and cognition, and curricular design should consider both in the design process. These are consistent with the findings in this study. The curriculum designed by HD1 educators considers the importance of both cognition and social interaction in learners' meaning-making process and specifically incorporates these in learning opportunities within the framework of the task-based orientation to learning. As well, the curriculum focuses on the importance of experiential learning and reflection (Dewey, 1929) through the curricular tasks during learners' meaning-making process. Dewey (1929) argues that education should provide learners with relevant learning experiences that enable their contribution to society. The real-world curricular tasks and authentic resources designed by HD1 educators and supervisors address this aspect of education. In addition, education in this Arab context views learning as a spiritual quest, and as a "means of giving back to their communities" (Merriam & Muhammad, 2000, p. 60) that educators in this study acknowledge as apparent through learners' respect for education, teachers, and learning.

These philosophical orientations about learning parallel commentary by the prominent, ancient Islamic scholar, Al Ghazzali in *Kitab, Book of Knowledge* (translated by Faris & Ashraf, 2003). Hague (2004) states that Al Ghazzali drew from both the Holy Qur'an and the Hadith for this dialogue on learning, to exemplify the spiritual emphasis in Islam on learning and knowledge: "Arabs are found naturally disposed to honour their teachers because the latter are distinguished by a great deal of knowledge derived from experience" (Ghazzali, as cited in Faris & Ashraf, 2003, p. 76). An entire chapter of the Kitab – the Book of Knowledge is devoted to the excellence of knowledge through applying reasoning and thinking processes on experiences. Kamis and Muhammad (2007) articulated that the Holy Qur'an is replete with verses asking and advising people "to use their intellect, to ponder, to think, to know" (p. 32) and requires humanity to "travel the world so they can better reflect on their actions" (Holy Qur'an, 3:137). A verse from the Holy Qur'an (1413 H.: Sura 10) referred to in Islamic education texts: "never will Allah change the condition of a people until they change what is in themselves." Clearly, reflection, reasoning, thinking and constructing meaning based on experiences are not in contravention with Qur'anic ideals.

According to Henderson and Gornik (2007), 21st century curriculum includes the following aspects: experiential, task-based approaches, critical thinking, problem solving, and reflection. Thus, there is a commonality between what is considered contemporary aspects of 21st century curriculum theory and Islamic discussions of learning as articulated by Islamic scholarship (Hague, 2004).

Current literature about education in various Arab contexts questions the suitability of teaching for reflection and critical thinking in an Arab context. Scholars Richardson (2004) and Garson (2005) related students' difficulty with reflection and critical thinking to culture and religion. Richardson questioned the suitability of requiring these aspects from an Arab community when "Arab-Islamic codes of behaviour ... may pose serious obstacles to the implementation of reflective strategies" (p. 429). Both Garson and Richardson specifically indicate a concern about requiring learners to engage in questioning in a context where learners cannot question their Islamic religion or cultural/social hierarchy, and therefore they claim that requiring learners to embrace a questioning epistemology in other areas privileges "Western" orientations to knowledge, which may be unsuitable.

The findings of this study challenge this generalization. While asking learners to question or critique Islam is not acceptable under any circumstance, this study suggests that learners' initial difficulty with higher order learning concepts such as questioning may be linked to prior learning in elementary and secondary schooling that emphasized the transmission model of education. Learners had rarely been given the opportunity and therefore did not know how to engage with these skills. This study indicates that HD1 learners arrived in higher education having few prior learning experiences that have supported active, meaning-based learning, not because it is unacceptable to their culture or religion, but because the opportunities to learn in this way have not been provided. Additionally, three educators specifically indicated that some learners enter the program after experiencing ridicule or corporal punishment for asking questions in their prior learning experiences. However, all educators indicated that with support and guidance through their learning, Emirati learners had developed strong abilities not only to ask questions but to field questions asked on them during their Current Issues Forum presentations. Questioning itself was not unacceptable or unmanageable; rather it was a teaching and learning strategy for learners that needed to be supported and scaffolded throughout the curriculum.

Why are elementary and secondary schooling considered inadequate? Consider the fact that the UAE is a young, developing nation with a dearth of qualified educators, and few Emirati educators. It is important to note that, according to Ali Majd Al Sweidi (2006), Assistant Undersecretary in the Department of Planning and Human Resources Development at the Ministry of Education, there are over 4,500 teachers in the UAE who are not qualified, lacking even a diploma in education, or any other discipline. Many of them are teaching illegally on tourist visas. Some of these educators are from developed nations; they use their privilege as English speaking native speakers to obtain employment regardless of qualifications to teach. This is an aspect of international education that is not limited to the UAE, but extends to other regions in the Middle East, Asia and Africa. With these factors in mind, it is understandable that learners arrive at higher education facilities unprepared for their learning journey and without a basis for developing higher order skills. Culture and religion are not to blame, necessarily. Educators in this study dedicated a significant amount of time and effort to encouraging learners to ask questions. They also taught learners how to ask questions, think critically, conduct and evaluate research, and reflect on a variety of topics in the accomplishment of curricular tasks, while simultaneously requiring learners to envision their future and their identity in this rapidly changing, globalized society.

The HD1 curriculum supports an experiential approach, which all educators observed as extremely challenging for learners in Semester 1. This is hardly surprising given that the HD1 curriculum is totally different from any form of education learners have ever experienced. But, educators acknowledge that by the end of the academic year, learners are taught and required to perform reflection, critical thinking, evaluation, and problem-solving skills. Learners appeared to have a fairly strong grasp of how to manage these activities. In addition, the end of the academic year culminated in the Current Issues Forum where learners presented all of these skills on controversial topics in a public, 3-day event. In addition, educators specifically indicated that reflection is a very challenging task for anyone. Thus, it appears that these tasks and learning strategies are not unsuitable or inappropriate; they are just difficult for learners due to the preponderance of the transmission model of education dominating previous elementary and secondary schooling experiences. Learners arrived unprepared for higher education. Any learner with a similar educational background would find this 21st century curriculum approach new and confusing.

I argue, if learners receive explicit instruction and constant reinforcement across disciplines, if teachers teach and model critical thinking, reflection, and questioning techniques, and if learners are encouraged to use these strategies with content that is authentic and relevant to the specific context of their learning world, then learners can and will embrace these modes of thinking. If they see that these efforts are valued as integral demonstrations of their learning, Arab higher education learners can and will reflect, think critically, and question almost every topic except Islam. In some cases, they will engage in all of these learning activities with highly controversial and sensitive topics and in public domains. For example, learners during the Current Issues Forum presented in public their research regarding genetic birth disorder due to consanguineous marriage – in a context where cousins marrying first cousins is the preferred marriage choice. Thus, the assertion that culture or religion as the basis for certain learning activities being "unsuitable" represents a superficial understanding of the complexity of the issue. The call for disseminating educational theory as "Eastern" or "Western" binary lines of opposition, is therefore, misleading and reductionist. Research from international educators in third space is able to contribute significantly to knowledge in this respect.

Transforming Vision: The Connection of Sociological Functionalist Theory, Transformative Learning Theory, and Empowerment of Emirati Students

This study revealed that sociological functionalist theory and transformative learning theory can be compatible educational theories. Sociological theory of education emphasizes the role of education as a function of society (Angell, 1928), and its utility is to impart the knowledge and behaviour norms necessary to maintain social order (Parsons, 1937). Socialization processes of education operate to unify groups to work toward common goals, in order to keep society from "disintegrating" (Cookson & Sadovnik, 2002, p. 267). Ballantine and Hammack (2009) ask an important question regarding functionalist theory: "Whose knowledge, for whom" (p. 35), and I ask, "For what purpose?"

Transformative learning theory (Mezirow, 2000) promotes adult education focused on changing core values and habits of mind through critical thinking and reflection. The ultimate goal of transformative learning theory is establishing autonomy in thinking processes from socialized influences. Merriam and Ntseane (2008) argue for a re-examination of transformative learning theory in international contexts in order to learn about "the role of context; the nature of catalysts of transformative learning; the importance of emotion and spirituality, and relationships in the process" (p. 184). In this study, sociological functionalist theory and transformative learning theory coalesced to inform in relation to issues of contextual needs for the HD1 curriculum. The essence of these two theories answers the questions "whose knowledge, for whom" (Ballantine & Hammack, 2009, p. 35) and my concerns regarding "why" and "for what purpose?" The answer to these questions underlying HD1's curriculum design is globalized knowledge, for Emirati women for the purpose of increasing their presence and leadership in the social environment and work force of Dubai, United Arab Emirates in a manner which these learners define on their terms.

In Dubai, 2005 census information[1] indicates the following demographics: foreign population 1,183,880 people (estimated in 2013 by Dubai Statistics to be 2.159 million); Emirati nationals 137,573 people (current numbers for Dubai unavailable, but Emiraties in the UAE are estimated to represent 13%). This means that Emirati nationals in 2005 represent 11% of the population in Dubai. Of this, figure, only 12.4% of Emirati women are employed in the workforce (UAE, Ministry of Economy, 2005, p. 15), a statistic the UAE government wants increased because of the population imbalance. Thus, the UAE government, the Ministry of Higher Education, and HRH Sheikh Nayahan the chancellor of Dubai Women's College mandate that the role of the HCT system is to ensure Emirati learners graduate with employable skills in order to meet the Emiratization mandate. The Higher Colleges of Technology centralized Academic Services office mandates the specific outcomes required for each course taught in the curriculum. Emiratization is the driving force for all Emirati higher educational facilities including HCT, which aligns with a sociological functionalist view of education: DWC is educating learners to take a participatory role in the workforce.

However, Emiratization involves more than merely ensuring learners have employable skills and a diploma. Emiratization is also about transforming habits of mind as Dubai continues to transform and position itself in the 21st century. The following integral features from the data are discussed in relation to both functional theory and transformational learning theory: employable skills for a rapidly changing society; behaviour change and work ethic; and ideological change for public female participation in society.

Employable Skills in a Rapidly Changing Society. Sociological functionalist theory connects curriculum and knowledge to the political face of education as a societal entity. A common critique of functionalist theory is that it does not deal with "content" in the educational system (Karabel & Halsey, 1977, p. 11). Critics of functionalist theory also argue that it supports the interest of the dominant group and assumes that change occurs in a slow and deliberate fashion (Ballantine & Hammack, 2009; Davies & Guppy, 2010; Hurn, 1993). In Dubai, according to this study, none of these assumptions or critiques align:

1. The content in this educational system is highly contextualized to the workforce of Dubai and Emirati women in a globalized employment sector.
2. The interests of the Emirati people are the dominant group and they are a powerful minority in their own country. It is arguable whether or not Emirati women represent a dominant group or a disempowered group.
3. Change is not a slow process in Dubai. Change occurs quickly and has a direct impact on the education system.

Throughout the data, educators disclosed information about Emiratization, which refers to a legal sanction for all businesses in the UAE by 2009 to employ an Emirati citizen, and by 2010 to employ an Emirati citizen in a supervisor position (UAE, Ministry of the Economy, 2010, p. 79). The knowledge or content required for this functional purpose are: English language skills; advanced technology skills; mathematical skills; knowledge of the economy; and principles of business management. In addition, for Emiratization, students need to learn to communicate effectively in a public and non-gender segregated and cross-cultural, globalized domain, work in a collaborative, diverse team, engage problem-solving skills, conceptualize and effectively integrate transdisciplinary knowledge, and complete real-world tasks all of which represent 21st century knowledge and skills. All of this knowledge is taught through the HD1 curriculum designed exclusively for Emirati female learners. In addition these skills are necessary for learners to acquire if Emirati women are to take leadership roles in Dubai's business and information technology sectors, where few businesses are gender segregated (an exception being some women-exclusive banks in operation in the UAE). This content aligns with structural functionalist theory (Ballantine & Hammack, 2009; Davies & Guppy, 2010) as the purpose behind the content taught is Emiratization.

Does this purpose support the interest of the dominant group? In consideration of this critique of functionalist theory, several issues must be considered. Emiraties themselves are a population minority in the United Arab Emirates, although they are a politically and economically privileged minority. The infrastructure of Dubai, including finance, business, construction, stock market, and hotels are largely managed or owned by foreigners. Most of the educators and administration is comprised of foreign faculty, which mirrors the population demographics of Dubai. In this study, the foreign faculty deliver global, real-world, information and tasks, with authentic resource materials contextualized to the locale to Emirati female learners. It is arguable as to whether or not this social group represents the dominant group due to the fact that they are only minimally represented in the workforce and society of Dubai.

The curriculum designed and implemented specifically focuses on Emirati female leadership and entrepreneurship as crucial aspects of Emiratization. Ultimately a goal for the HCT system is for increased public participation of Emirati women, in Business and Information Technology sectors, and for public leadership in UAE society as learners transform their identities and envision leadership roles in accordance with their cultural and religious belief structures. While this is in the interest of the government and the Emirati people, it is also an act of transformation. This represents a cultural and societal change upon which these learners must mediate, reflect, and define on their own terms.

The data also indicate a great emphasis on creating educational moments for students to consider, discuss, and conceptualize their Emirati identity in this changing society where they are a minority in their own country and largely unrepresented in the public sector. The foreign faculty, as international educators in third space, raised the issue of Emirati female identity, provided the opportunities for thoughtful consideration, facilitated the tasks, and asked questions. But it is important to note that all educators also practice self-censorship particularly in relation to discussions of Emirati identity. This is integral as these learners must define their Emirati identity in their own terms, according to their religion and culture, in this changing and rapidly developing global society. As HRH Sheikh Nahayan Mubarak al Nahayan states there is an urgency for us to

> Do our part in preparing a new generation of Emiratis confident in themselves, proud of their culture and language, and able to live and work in a changing and globalized world. Teachers are expected to incorporate the theme of the event [Emirati Identity] in the curriculum and projects of the students. (Jawaher & Al Manar, 2009, p. 16)

Functionalist theory assumes change is a slow and deliberate process over time (Ballantine & Hammack, 2009; Davies & Guppy, 2010). However, change in Dubai is fast and unrelenting. Those who live there adapt, or leave. Educators must be able to work with learners to empower them to conceptualize and consider these changes occurring while formulating their vision of themselves and their roles in their changing society.

Quick response to change is edified through HD1 curriculum, which demonstrates the HD1 team's flexibility and the curricular model's ability to transform itself on demand. For example, a sudden global financial crisis occurred in late September 2008, the beginning of the academic year of data collection for this study. By the beginning of November 2008, it became apparent to the international educators that learners were unaware of, or protected from, any knowledge regarding the effect of the crisis on the UAE. The UAE's currency is pegged to the United States dollar, and businesses failed overnight. There is no concept of bankruptcy in the UAE, so people who could not pay their debt either did a "midnight run"[ii] or faced imprisonment. The stock market crashed and many Emirati families felt the pain of the crisis. But, learners did not seem to know a financial crisis occurred or, if they did, they did not seem to be able to comprehend what had happened or how it affected them. Therefore, a curricular change was warranted in order to engage learners with this global issue and it had to occur during that academic year as the impact of the financial crisis would, and did, have an impact on the planning of the upcoming curricular event, Bazaar. By December of the same year, the entire curriculum for the second semester had changed to create a situation where learners had to think about, research, analyze, and present on the effect of the financial crisis on Dubai. The curricular change was successful in raising learners' awareness of the crisis. Change happens fast in the UAE, and education, educational theory, and educational strategy and educators themselves must be able to respond to change equally as quickly.

Behavioural Change and Work Ethic. According to Parsons (1937), the central function of education is to impart the knowledge and the behavioural norms necessary to maintain order in society. This premise aligns with behaviourism which is based on the principle that desirable human behaviour can be the artifact of the influences emanating in an educational environment (Brown & Ciuffetelli, 2009). According to HRH Sheikh Nahayah (2008), the vision of HCT is to remain as "the number one employment-oriented Higher Educational institution … to adapt to the changing economic, environmental and labour market needs" (p. 7). In order to accomplish this vision, HRH Sheikh Nahayan (2008) emphasizes the need to produce graduates who "are prepared to assume their positions in the workplace … are tolerant, knowledgeable of other peoples and their cultures, and are able to function in a global environment" (p. 4).

However, unrealistic salary, benefits, position title expectations, lack of appropriate work ethic, lack of team and collaborative ethos, and lack of appropriate education has led to high unemployment rates and pervasive negative stereotypes about Emirati employees (Ahli, 2009; Randeree, 2009; Al Fahim, 1995; MacPherson et al., 2007; Al Sweidi, 2006; Godwin, 2006) in the United Arab Emirates. Problems in achieving Emiratization quotas in the workforce (Forstenlechner, 2008; Godwin, 2006), and a preponderance of dependence on comparatively inexpensive expatriates, means that Emiraties are encountering difficulties obtaining and maintaining employment. Regardless of quotas and penalizing levies for companies without Emirati employees, both hiring and retention remains an issue for Emirati presence in the workforce (Forstenlechner, 2008; Godwin, 2006). Employers in the UAE prefer hiring expatriates who are seen as less expensive, better qualified and harder working (Ahli, 2009; Fasano & Goyal, 2004; Forstenlechner, 2008; Godwin, 2006; Bin Zayed, 2009):

> Many Nationals are excellent employees (and managers), but many come from a family where great wealth has been the norm for perhaps two generations. The "work ethic" has therefore not been a prominent Gulf Arab characteristic, nor has "good timekeeping." (Dew & Shoult, 2002, p. 209)

Thus, the goal of Emiratization has been slow to achieve and many businesses choose to pay an imposed levy for not meeting Emirati hiring quotas (Ahli, 2009; Forstenlechner, 2008; Godwin, 2006). This circumstance is complicated by the introduction of a governmental labour law that makes it virtually impossible to dismiss an Emirati regardless of workplace behaviour (UAE Ministerial Decision, 2009, No. 176).

Therefore, much of the HD1 curriculum, and rules governing learners' behaviour, focuses on appropriate work place ethics, working within a multinational, multiethnic, and multiracial society, collaboration, and teamwork. The rationale behind these curricular foci is because currently, "the totality of the UAE's population represents one of the most racially, ethnically, religiously, and socially mixed to be found anywhere" (Heard-Bey, 2005, p. 360) and Emirati graduates, if Emiratization is going to function as intended, must be prepared to work collaboratively in the workplace with non-Emirati people. Upon graduation from DWC, learners will be working with men and women of all races, all cultures, and all religions. Learners must be prepared to effectively participate and collaborate in this environment and thus higher education must prepare female learners. Prior to their education at DWC, in most cases, learners have had little to no exposure to the real world of work in Dubai and therefore behaviourist approaches are appropriate.

In order to achieve the contextualized needs of Emirati women and the goals of the HCT system, the findings indicate that a behaviourist approach can ultimately be transformational. To illustrate, the behaviourist approach is mandated for DWC educators who attempt to socialize learners into the demands of the workplace. The behaviourist approach required is guided by two premises: accommodation to culture, and nurturing appropriate workplace ethics.

In accommodating culture, educators acknowledged the many rules imposed on female learners to monitor their behaviour because this is a protected environment for women. "The United Arab Emirates has a very insular culture that discourages women from interacting with men; families tend to be over protective of their female members" (Ahli, 2009, p. 42). Three educators stated that without the rules governing the behaviour of female learners and restricting movement and contact, the college would not exist. It is important to remember, this is cultural, not religious. "While Islam highly encourages women to seek knowledge and education, culturally conservative families are convinced Islam prohibits a woman from leaving her house without a 'mahram' [a male relative whom a woman is prohibited to marry in Islam – a father, brother or uncle]" (Bin Zayed, 2009, p. 26). This is a legacy of thought that continues to this day.

Educators acknowledged a tension between strict enforcement of the rules governing behaviour and the curriculum designed for promoting empowerment of Emirati women. According to educators, not only do the educators question this apparent contradiction, but learners are beginning to question these rules, and also question the people required to enforce them. Learners themselves are making connections between the constant themes of empowerment and the imposed rules governing their lives in their quest for higher education. For example, educators in this study disclosed learners' challenging teachers policing of certain rules, such as the mobile telephone use rule, attendance, tardiness, and chaperone rules. And, change is happening: in June, 2009 a DWC graduate was named as Ambassador to China. Also in that year a woman was appointed as the first female judiciary in the UAE. In fact, in March 2010, I was invited to present this research on campus and I was shocked to discover the campus is now open to male visitors, security guarded, but open nonetheless.

Thus, sociological functionalist theory of education for women, as an act of transformation, must accept and acknowledge that it is necessary to accommodate cultural mores, in order to expand the radius of opportunities for female learners. This allows women to become erudite in a protected environment and question for themselves the rules governing their lives. The goal is to provide the opportunity for educated and empowered Emirati females to learn, grow, question, decide and make changes regarding their futures, which can be accomplished through the provision of a protected educational environment for this cultural community. This is, indeed, transformational.

The results of this study indicate that these rules, while behaviourist, and arguably necessary in this context, are also aspects of transformation. They are part of the movement of educating Emirati citizens to take their rightful roles as leaders in their society, not through nepotism, but due to their ability, effort, responsibility, and integrity.

Ideological Change for Female Participation. A salient and valid critique of functionalist theory of education, particularly in relation to curriculum, relates to its role in the reproduction of societal hegemony found in workplaces. Giroux (2010), Stevens (2007), Apple (1979, 2004, 2008), Liston (1986), and McLaren (2007) discuss sociological functionalist theory of education in terms of a sieve for employment social class structures. In the workplace, credentials and competencies often learned in higher education ensure promotion and success through perceived merit. It is argued that higher education and sociological functionalist theory stream learners along the same principle. Learners are funnelled into college or secondary schooling designed for teaching employable skills for the workforce. Other students are filtered into universities and professions and eventually leadership positions. Society, the workforce, and the class system of hegemony, reproduces itself through schooling. Schooling, as a function of society, determines who is designated for the workforce and who is designated for leadership positions. I argue that this critique and metaphor may be relevant in some circumstances in some developed countries, but are overgeneralized and unsatisfactory for some international contexts, specifically this Arab context.

The HD1 curriculum, overtly, emphasizes the role of Emirati women as the new female leaders of societal change in the United Arab Emirates, and emphasizes Emiratization and teaching employable skills. This is a departure from traditional roles of females in this society and is indeed transformational. The curriculum is designed to teach learners about the business and information technology sectors in Dubai, ultimately for supervisory and leadership roles. The curriculum is designed to allow learners to hone their skills in practice, through real-life engagement of authentic tasks, including entrepreneurial and management-related tasks. The tasks themselves replicate the roles learners can expect to assume in the workforce in their chosen discipline of Business and Information Technology, which is a new and relevant experience for this generation of female Emiraties.

The HD1 curriculum does not represent an exact reproduction of societal hegemony. In this case study, sociological functionalist theory represents the role of schooling as a space for transformation and ideological change about the roles of women in this society. Sociological functionalist theory as an agent for transformation occurs if modernity, ideological change, empowerment, and identity are envisioned within the curriculum and implementation is focussed on the needs of the learners and their future as they choose to define it.

With the task-based orientation to curriculum, students are empowered with control over much of their learning through their completion of the curricular tasks. According to Gutierrez (1995) empowerment is "the process of increasing personal, interpersonal, or political power so that individuals, families, and communities can take action to improve their situations" (p. 29). Learners many of whom have never had within their personal power the opportunity to perform tasks, particularly in a public domain, are indeed empowered to publically engage with the business world in Dubai through their learning. Through this curriculum, learners are engaged in the performance of authentic tasks (Shor & Freire, 1987), together with learning from authentic resources that reflect the real-world political and business-oriented issues and concerns directly relevant to the lives of Emirati women and the Emirati nation. It also provides learning that empowers learners over their learning, and gives them a forum for their public voices. Through the HD1 curriculum, students are seen, working, leading their groups, questioning and evaluating. Their voices are heard and their voices matter.

Postmodern Perspectives: Understanding the Impact of Contextual Factors

Educators in this study were enthusiastic in their beliefs about their roles in education, and their attempts to create and implement extraordinary learning moments for learners. Constructivist curriculum, experiential learning theory, sociological functionalist theory and transformational learning theory were represented through educators' descriptions of the how's and why's of teaching and learning in this Arab context. All educators in this study had made learning about their context a primary function of their roles as educators. This appears to allow these educators to make informed decisions in a contextually relevant and potentially transformative manner. This knowledge is particularly important in relation to understanding of the roles of Emirati culture, Islam, and society of the UAE in learners' lives. This is representative of a relativistic stance that aligns with postmodern perspectives of education (Slattery, 2006, 2013).

Postmodern emphasis on relativist views of education is frequently criticized (Egbo, 2009). However, Merriam and Ntseane (2008) and Taylor (2003, 2007) ask for relativist views with more contributions from various international contexts, particularly in relation to transformative learning theory. They also argue for better understandings of the impact of culture, spirituality, and emotion as they relate to educational theory in order to have more comprehensive and expansive understandings in our global world. I agree with Merriam and Ntseane (2008) and Taylor (2003, 2007) that more research in diverse contexts is necessary in order to understand the relationship of educational theories, learning strategies, culture, spirituality, emotion, and societal change. This case study recognizes educational theory in practice with awareness of the specific needs and issues pertaining to these learners' lived realities as the core operating principles in the design of this 21st century curriculum. I further argue that close and careful consideration of the educator working within a given context is crucial in order to understand and conceptualize any theory, approach or strategy in practice.

It is significant that educators' comments about curriculum or implementation were prefaced or post-scripted with the word "here" indicating that the comment was relative and relevant to this context, these learners, during this spatial moment. This implies that these international educators have acquired a deeply connected vision of their teaching context in order to make informed decisions regarding their day to day practices. Educators in this study had a cultural, religious or societal rationale guiding the *how* and *why* underlying their teaching practice and curricular decisions; hence, the domination of the word "here" in the data.

This knowledge of context guiding practice explains why I refer to my educators as international educators. They were not teacher tourists or travelling teachers; they are international educators who have a sincere dedication and devotion to learning about the land of their current residence in order to make a lasting educational impact through their teaching practices. They demonstrate "cultural curiosity" not as a brief visitor, but as part of the fabric of society. They immersed themselves in their learning about the way culture, religion and society works on a daily basis and how these factors affect the daily lives and educational lives of their learners. International educators engage in dialogues with colleagues, join local social organizations, read books about the history and people that are written by members of the society. Educators in the study discussed how learners *want* teachers to learn about them and how learners are a great resource for learning. International educators in the context of this study shop at souks, bazaars, and community shops. They talk to people living in the community. They read or learn about the Holy Qur'an. They go to weddings and participate in religious festivals and holidays. Many educators fast during Ramadan regardless of their religious persuasion. They read the regional newspapers and use them as resources in the class. They study Arabic.

Thus, regardless of the theory guiding the design and implementation of curriculum, in our postmodern and globalized world, an educator "here" must with sincerity learn about religious factors, cultural factors and societal factors in order to implement any educational theory or strategy.

Religious Factors. All educators acknowledged that Islam is the single most important factor to understand about life in Dubai and the UAE. Islam is the central and common feature among all learners and many of the faculty at DWC. This awareness provided an underlying rationale behind many of the decisions they made. Islam is not part of life; life is part of Islam. Islam rests at the heart of how learners conceptualize knowledge. This is an epistemological difference that sets learners in DWC apart from other learners elsewhere. Epistemologies are "concerned with knowledge and how people come to have knowledge" (Kamberelis & Dimitriadis, 2005, p. 13). As Islam is the central and fundamental lens governing how learners understand their world, any theory, practice, or strategy must begin with recognition of Islam as providing the epistemological basis for these learners. This must be understood and always respected. The separation of church and state, time-honoured in the West, does not exist in Dubai.

Therefore, educators must be willing to understand how Islam will affect learners' understanding of knowledge and embrace learners' connection of content to Islam. This also means that educators must learn which aspects of content must be edited due to its forbidden nature. In order to do so international educators must learn about Islam. According to educators, decisions related to Islam include: natural connections students make to content, censorship of information, and self-censorship.

Educators discussed, but were divided on, inclusion of religious elements to support learners' learning. Some educators chose to completely avoid all discussion in class of anything related to any form of religion and reported the need to censor all resources for anything that could be seen as contravening Islamic ideals. Other educators reported that learners automatically make natural connections of themes to Islam, and these educators actively encourage those connections. For instance, content issues pertaining to social responsibility, calculating interest obligations in business, ethics, speech competitions, entrepreneurial spirit, and women's leadership roles were discussed as content areas students connect to Islamic principles.

I believe that natural connections to Islam can provide a basis for learners to connect personally and meaningfully to curriculum content, but these connections should emanate from the learners: learner-driven, natural connections of their learning to their belief systems. Teachers can encourage these connections from learners, and teachers can act to elicit these connections through inclusion of materials that have a relationship to Islam. But, in order to do so, these educators must become very knowledgeable about Islam. They must be careful about the content they choose, and they must always prompt discussion from a perspective of seeking information, not questioning or criticizing it. The relations must be easily recognizable for learners, which allow the teachers to maintain a position of asking questions to elicit information of learners' connections of the content to their belief systems. However, I also assert that educators must be aware of the boundaries that they must honour because of the centrality of Islam to learners lives and epistemology.

In addition, educators related that there are certain aspects of life that cannot be discussed and must be censored out of any resources including textbooks, websites, newspapers, or anything that is presented or approached in relation to learners' religious beliefs. Censorship must be employed in relation to anything related to sexual relations, dating relationships, sexual diseases, and/or anything related to homosexuality or transgendered issues. This may also include visual images depicting men or women in close proximity, and how they may or may not be fully attired (bare arms, legs, visible flesh). Anything that is *haram* (forbidden) in Islam must be censored, such as anything related to alcohol or the consumption of certain foods. Content that features any form of criticism of Islam must be edited out of curricular content, and even reference or commentary related to other religious beliefs. While these are not negotiable elements, it is important to recognize that this censorship is a changing feature in this educational context. In 2013, I delivered a workshop on 21st century curriculum design in Dubai and many participants indicated that today it is acceptable to include visual representations of men and women together (but not necessarily touching).

Ostensibly, it seems that these content restrictions can be easily accomplished; however, most textbooks are written for a large general population (Pinar, Reynolds, Slattery, & Taubman, 2004) and are not necessarily written for a specific context or an Islamic context. Several educators specifically stated the difficulty of locating a Business or Health and well-being textbook that does not include the above issues, pictures, or elements. Several educators observed that even Arab ESL texts often include pictures of women with bare legs and arms. All of the materials used in HD1 are generated and created by HD1 faculty either organically or they are culled from UAE's media and governmental sources, which assists in the editing and censorship process. Thus, a great deal of time and energy is devoted among the HD1 team to ensuring that content, while still authentic in terms of being culled from public UAE relevant sources, meets this religious requirement for learners.

Educators also discussed the need for heightened self-censorship, particularly in relation to their own religious beliefs. This is a more complex discussion as the Holy Qur'an discusses tolerance for all religions (Ayoub, 2004) and several educators disclosed that learners want to know about the beliefs of foreigners as part of their experience with a person from a different part of the world. However, regardless of learners' interest, educators identified that discussion of individual beliefs may be seen as proselytizing and must be avoided because it is a legal issue. According to the Report on International Religious Freedom, United Arab Emirates:

Non-Muslims in the country are free to practice their religion but may not proselytize publicly or distribute religious literature. The Government follows a policy of tolerance towards non-Muslim religions and, in practice, interferes very little in the religious activities of non-Muslims. (United States Department of State, 2010, p. 241)

Proselytizing, or attempting to convert a person away from Islam is a criminal offence. This recognition must guide educators' behaviours, even when asked questions prompted by students about individual or divergent belief systems.

A question remains about whether all of this editing and censorship is actually harmful for students. When students enter the workforce, they will encounter a diverse multinational society who may or may not be required to self-censor to the degree these international educators normalize as part of their existence. Several educators disclosed that they felt the degree of censorship required from them is overemphasized and detracts from some of the authenticity of their attempts to socialize students into a multinational, multicultural environment. Be this as it may, at this stage, a heightened degree of censorship is necessary in order to allow students to gently experience people who are not from an Emirati culture. Many students have had little or no exposure to the multinational, multireligious population of Dubai and thus a degree of censorship may be what is necessary for these students, at this stage in their education. As they continue in their studies into Year 2 and beyond, they will go on workplace visits (Year 2), have workplace internships (Year 3), and have various international exchanges throughout the following years. Some Year-3 students are granted permission to go on international visits to another country. Because of the gentle exposure students receive in HD1, they may be better prepared for the diversity they will encounter during the rest of their education, and later when they enter the workforce. In essence, this can be considered a first, gradual step.

Cultural Factors. The long arms of tradition and culture adhere and impact on the learning environment, regardless of the economic change and development of the last 20 years in the UAE. Educators acknowledged that the impact of cultural factors is not immediately obvious. "Face," clan, group interaction, family name, leadership, and in-culture intervention were factors identified by educators as necessary cultural knowledge they must have in order to make informed decisions in their professional roles. All educators observed that the nuances of how these cultural factors affect curriculum may not be immediately recognizable to foreigners, even ones who are very knowledgeable about the community. Educators cautioned that educators must be very good observers of the dynamics that occur in any educational event or social event.

"Face" is a prominent factor in relation to the public image of the educational institution. DWC is a governmental institution that regularly pushes cultural boundaries. Often, there is a media backlash against DWC, its educators, and its students. For example, due to the public nature of two campus open events, Bazaar and Current Issues Forum, and the potential that exists for the local media to sensationalize reports, a campus-wide assembly is an annual event before these events. This assembly is to remind learners of rules governing appropriate public behaviour (no dancing, music, games) and attire (proper fastening of *abbayahs* and *shaylahs*, minimal cosmetics, appropriate within gender and across gender behaviour, appropriate height of high-heeled shoes and height of hair), and how their image will be publically presented and reported in the media. This may seem extraordinary elsewhere, but it is necessary in the UAE given the high-profile nature of the college, the restrictions on women, the public nature of these events, and the learning potential these curricular events hold for students.

Faculty, in addition to their roles as assessors and facilitators at these events, are also expected to serve as on-campus security of female behaviour in order to guard the honour the public "face" of the institution against embarrassment. For the duration of the public event, faculty act as security and must ensure that all Emirati females, whether they are students or not, exhibit culturally appropriate behaviour and attire, and guard against any circumstance that has the potential to be perceived negatively. Faculty assume this role in relation to both learners and Emirati female visitors because the press will attribute any behaviour they perceive as negative to the Emirati learners, which dishonours the public "face" of DWC.

"Face" has a positive impact on the willingness of learners to employ extra effort in their tasks. Six educators specifically identified that learners thrive when they need to represent their work and their college in a public domain and will do whatever it takes to ensure success. These educators acknowledged "face" as a motivating element for learners and four educators observed that learners demonstrated leadership and resourcefulness during chaotic moments of task achievement. Perhaps, given the public nature of events, and given the rapid and extreme change that has occurred in Dubai, learners are highly capable of responding to unanticipated circumstances as this represents a common circumstance of life in Dubai. As educators acknowledged, dramatic change happens overnight in Dubai and learners are adept at pooling whatever resources they have to in order to respond. In conversations with Emirati female friends regarding this finding, I was referred back to the life of Emirati women 20 years ago when many lived a Bedouin lifestyle and had to respond circumstances that suddenly presented themselves. Merriam (2007) describes indigenous knowledge as "organic in the sense that it is generated within the daily lives of people in local context. ... This knowledge is typically passed on from one generate to the next in oral, rather than written form" (p. 11). Perhaps, this ability to respond to crisis represents an aspect of indigenous knowledge passed down from grandmothers to mothers to daughters and represents an exciting area of future research.

In addition, the issue of "face" surfaced during the Virtual International Exchanges required for each class in HD1. One educator detailed observations during a virtual international exchange with Canadian learners and the mutual sharing of posters learners in each country created to represent themselves pictographically. The Emirati learners created a poster with a large pictographic representation of a woman wearing an *abbayah, shaylah* and reading a large representation of the Holy Qur'an. This was highly unconventional and subject to great debate among learners for its potential religious and cultural transgression. Emirati students were aware that the poster was for a Western audience and they placed a "Western face" on it out of respect for the Canadian learners and to create a comprehensible poster. It is very likely this act of "face" for a Western audience was not recognized by the Canadian learners or the educator in Canada, but these international educators recognized the role of "face" in relation to this action by Emirati learners. This act of creation of a "Western face" on a poster so that Canadian learners could understand the salience of Islam in their lives provided Emirati learners with an opportunity to engage in a great debate about their role in defining themselves for a different audience who may or may not share the same values. They wanted to create a poster that reflected the importance of Islam to them, and in order to do so, broke a cultural and religious boundary to represent a "Western face" for the Canadian learners.

The issue of "face" also surfaced in relation to resources gathered by educators. Given the emphasis on the use of relevant authentic materials endorsed by educators, "face" in relation to negative elements existing in Dubai must be handled carefully. The use of UAE media sources and governmental websites provide potential resources, as all local media is censored. These resource sites mention issues such as human trafficking, human rights issues, domestic servants and labourer abuse issues. Foreign educators must be careful with materials that criticize any element of life in Dubai as this can be seen as a guest (the international educator) criticizing the host (the Emirati people) and a serious "face" infraction. This does not mean that these issues should be avoided. However, educators must self-censor their responses to ask questions and encourage a dialogue free from their own opinions or conclusions. Educators can raise the issue and ask questions, but it is wise to include a counter-argument from a prominent Emirati perhaps culled from the local media. They must allow the learners to explore the issue free from foreigner judgement and criticism in order to allow learners to maintain "face."

Another aspect of Emirati context discussed in the data related to the curricular emphasis on group work and tensions with tribe and family affiliation. As a group, a collectivist orientation to life is embedded in Emirati culture, particularly with its tribal legacy (Ahli, 2009; Al Fahim, 1995; Christie, 2010; Findlow, 2008; Kazim, 2000; Rabi, 2006). Emirati society has many complex layers (Ahli, 2009; Al Fahim, 1995), which impact educational practice (Godwin, 2006). These layers may not be easily discernable for international educators in their observations of the group work dynamic, and learners may be quite reluctant to speak to the issue with a foreign teacher when difficulties arise. Several educators discussed the role of Student Affairs, a college department employed mainly by Emirati women who provide knowledge through the lens of being within the culture and if need be, provide group work intervention in a culturally acceptable manner. This allows the collaborative effort to continue, but also ensures it is dealt with in a manner within the Emirati community.

Collaborative learning does unfold however through curricular tasks and provides Emiraties with a scaffolded experience of collaboration. All curricular tasks require Emirati learners to be randomly assigned to work in groups with Emirati learners who may be from a different clan. While this had the potential to erupt, and in fact did for some groups, into a form of group conflict unique to this context, this was still a learning experience that many educators described as necessary. Thus, while the collaboration component of the curriculum caused contention and conflict for some learners, which the foreign educators had to address, educators maintained that it is an essential part of the curriculum. However, a crucial aspect from the data was that educators were aware that problems with the group work tasks may have had nothing whatsoever to do with the task itself. Rather the family names and attributed hierarchy within the group could have been the cause of conflict. Thus, educators must be aware of this potential for group breakdown emanating from culturally embedded values. Educators must be prepared to teach collaboration skills, observe group dynamics carefully, and arm themselves with strategies to address these issues in a culturally appropriate manner. In addition, educators must leave this element in the curriculum as a form of scaffolding of learning because when learners leave DWC, they may well be working with Emiraties from other tribes in addition to people from across the globe.

Therefore, "face" is a crucial factor in any educational event for Emirati learners. "Face" is a factor educators consider in relation to the public image of DWC and its students, but can also be a strong motivating factor for learners. "Face" impacts group work and virtual international exchanges between DWC and other institutions. As well, group work can be impacted by tribe, clan, or family affiliation, which may be difficult for foreign educators to discern in periods of group conflict. DWC has a Student Affairs department primarily staffed with Emirati educated women who intervene when issues arise that emanate from cultural tensions.

Societal Factors. There is a direct and essential relationship between schooling and society. Emirati women are redefining their roles and their lives in their society, which means that higher education for Emirati women, should support this endeavour. The Emirates is very demographically diverse but learners in actuality have limited exposure to that diversity. HD1 responds to this through the creation and incorporation of themes and issues exposing learners to this diversity, through tasks and the use of authentic resources. For instance, some of the readings during the 2008–2009 academic year relate to: discussions of labour regulation differences between Emiraties and foreigners in the UAE; International Business Etiquette in Dubai and Multiculturalism; The Dark Side of Dubai's Construction Industry; Emirati Identity and Multiculturalism. This practice of inclusion of local media sources engages learners in the issues, but also honours their culture as the indigenous people of the social reality of the UAE. However, a valid question is how educators can support integration of Emirati women into the workplace and social realm of the UAE, while simultaneously honouring learners' culture and identity.

The government of the UAE declared 2008 as the Year of National Identity. This is a national concern and therefore it is an educational concern for female Emirati learners. With exposure of learners to the multinational, multicultural, and multireligious world of Dubai, it is equally important to include opportunities for them to consider their own Emirati identity in this diverse nation. Their world is vastly different from the one their mothers, sisters, and aunts knew and they need the chance to consider it and define it for themselves.

Therefore, the inclusion of many opportunities for learners to ponder their own identity, and the inclusion of themes pertaining to Emiratization are crucial for Emirati learners (Ahli, 2009). The fact that learners are encouraged to explore these issues with their international educators is important. This provides learners with opportunities to take risks with their thinking regarding these issues, with a diverse audience that is well-versed in maintaining decorum and self-censorship. The key issue is to allow Emirati learners to explore these thoughts with freedom and security, and use their voices to define their identities within the backdrop of globalization and change.

In addition, the use of Virtual International Exchanges that are a required element for each HD1 class offer learners the chance to exchange real information in a protected manner, with people around the globe. This reinforces the notion that learners, as part of their vision for the future, will have to learn how to communicate with people and communities that do not follow or maintain the specific cultural or linguistic codes that Emirati women expect in their homeland. It is an opportunity to share. Perhaps, considering that this element is still in its infancy as this was the first year for this endeavour, the opportunities for cross-global communication remain limited and guarded. In the future, possibilities for multinational educational affiliations, virtual world interactions, and cross-global friendships are potentially achievable and may provide more opportunities for reciprocity in learning trans-globally.

Thus, the HD1 curriculum is responsive to the diversity represented in Dubai, and to the fact that learners, initially, are quite isolated from the issues that arise in relation to this diversity. The HD1 curriculum has direct inclusion of curricular content pertaining to themes of Emirati identity, Emiratization, and the diverse population of foreigners in the UAE. As well, the faculty create opportunities for learners to engage in virtual international exchanges, albeit in a protected fashion. This opens a dialogue for learners to consider their changing roles in the global marketplace. Their learning can feature the premise that global interaction including cross gender interaction does not necessarily involve contravention of cultural or religious mores.

Summary of Postmodern Perspectives. Postmodern perspectives assume a relativist stance (Slattery, 2006, 2013), which is a feature prominent in these data. Significantly, all educators directed their comments specifically to this context. The commentary from these international educators presents a cogent discourse of the salience of factors pertaining to the Islamic faith, Emirati culture, and UAE society in the design and implementation of curriculum. The impact of Islamic faith rests with understanding the epistemological difference for Emirati learners as they understand knowledge through Islam. This inherently involves: learners' natural connections of content to tenets of Islam, censorship of information, and self-censorship. The impact of Emirati culture can take the form of issues pertaining to "face," clan/tribe, group interaction, family name, leadership, and in-culture intervention. The impact of the UAE society rests with acknowledgement that although the UAE is a demographically diverse nation, learners generally have limited exposure to that diversity. HD1 curriculum offers learners an important and gradual step toward the diversity they will encounter in the workforce.

Creating a Contextually Relevant International Curriculum

I believe that higher education facilities must consider the approach through which curricular decisions are made from a new frame of reference: contextualized design-based, 21st century, international curriculum. Given our globalized world, I assert that curriculum should begin with consideration of educational theory through an international lens and that implementation be contextualized to address the lived reality and the complex needs of the regional community as the guiding frame of reference.

First, a contextually relevant 21st century, international curriculum begins with the educators and curriculum designers thinking about educational theory from an international perspective. This means, regardless of the theory chosen to provide an epistemological basis for the educational event, curriculum designers must think about the theory through an international lens, potentially a third space lens. They must look for commonalities and detractions among religious ideals, philosophy, and social movements internationally and consider their relationship with the chosen theoretical basis. This means, perhaps re-conceptualizing educational theory relational to the specific context. For example, Constructivist theory in this context must be re-conceptualized to acknowledge the role of Islam as the epistemological basis for students' construction of knowledge – in education in Dubai, this is not negotiable. Transformative learning theory in Western contexts seeks autonomy in thinking from the influences of socialized beliefs. In this context, this idea is impossible. Transformative learning theory can be better understood, as recognition of the embedded nature of culture and religion on thinking process and understanding the opportunities for transformation within this nature.

The purpose is to locate common ground and areas of potential tension between educational theories and the belief structures and traditions that form societal norms. This process will aid the educator and curriculum designer in making connections between educational theory to be applied and the specific context to the benefit of learners. Looking for commonalities will also ease the tendency of labelling educational theories and strategies as "Eastern" or "Western" and therefore unacceptable because of geographical polarities. Polarization may result in denying learners optimal learning experiences. This polarization may further result in loss of potential opportunities for reciprocity in learning across the global community.

Second, once educational theories are determined, a sincere and in-depth consideration of context is required. This means focusing specifically on one's learners and their purpose for education, which will be different depending on the context. Educators and curriculum designers in international contexts must delve into the intricacies of the specific context of implementation of curriculum. In order to begin this process, the educators must gather information from those already teaching and learning in the specific context: learners' voices and teachers' voices. Thus, I endorse a bottom-up approach to information gathering.

Third, upon understanding the learners and educators in the educational event, in-depth consideration must be attributed to the factors affecting the learning context: learners' religion, learners' culture, and the society of which these learners are a part. This part is not without challenge, as recognizing the impact of religious, cultural and social factors on curriculum and implementation may be difficult to ascertain if you are not part of that particular community. Potentially issues pertaining to tribe, censorship, conceptions of leadership, and "face" are only some of the factors that affect curriculum design and implementation. The educators in this study respected the learners' faith in Islam and acknowledged that implementation of curriculum was affected by this fact. In this study, DWC had several Emirati women, many of whom were former DWC learners, working in the Students Affairs department and several educators attributed their roles as integral to a successful educational event. In addition, at least one Emirati supervisor, who also participated in this study, provided religious and cultural knowledge from within the faith and culture. I believe access to this knowledge is part of the reason DWC was able to innovate and push educational boundaries as it did.

Implications for Education in the 21st Century

As our world becomes more globalized, we need a greater recognition of the potential contribution that can emanate from international educational contexts. We must be willing to reinterpret theory through different lenses including an international lens. We must break down the barriers of understanding theory or strategies from the reductionist view of a "Western" or "Eastern" frame of reference and instead consider educational theories and strategies from an international and contextual frame of reference. We must discover and explore parallels among international philosophies, international religions, and international knowledges courageously and with an open mind. We must discover and explore some of the contentious issues that may relate to international philosophies, international religions, and international knowledge specific to diverse contexts and develop strategies to engage in open dialogue. And further, we must be sensitive to the boundaries of exploration. We must be sincere in this quest and not shy away from the tensions that may surface. In essence, we must embrace a balanced worldview of education from across the globe. There is much to learn from the how's and why's of diverse educational contexts. Globalization ensures that our global interactions and affiliations are part of the future of education.

FINAL REMARKS

The United Arab Emirates is a fascinating and inspirational country. I respect the Emirati people, their devotion to development and change, and their welcoming and gracious nature to guests in their country. I admire their adherence to their religious beliefs. This is an aspect of life in the Emirates that can never be forgotten: above all else, Islam guides all aspects of life. I enjoyed my international experiences, felt welcomed, learned, lived and thrived in this peaceful society in the Middle East. Emirati people are gracious, warm-hearted, and sincere. They want to get to know you, and they want you to get to know them.

As an international educator, I believe that this study is salient for the any educational community to consider. I believe the appropriate lens for international education and research is one of international third space. I believe that this lens allows for understanding and interpreting that belies oppositional forces that can be expected with international migration. I believe this lens offers freedom to think, acknowledges influences on thinking, and provides the mechanism to accommodate those influences.

Our world has changed dramatically and nowhere is that more apparent than in the UAE. The UAE is a global society, complex, changing, and remarkably resilient. Higher education in the UAE strives to move with this change, while maintaining a respect for tradition, culture, and religion. This is honourable. Education, educational theory, and educational andragogy must also move with change as they address the learning needs of learners, society, and our global community.

Curriculum and implementation in our world must embrace both a globalized stance and a relativist stance. It is important for learners to have, as aspects of their learning, opportunities to engage with differences. This representation may emanate from foreign faculty working closely with Emirati nationals, inclusion of international exchanges, resources that represent global issues and concerns, and/or from cross-national higher education affiliations. But, curriculum and implementation must also sincerely understand the needs of context and the contextual factors that affect education. This is a complex balancing act that is crucial in this time of internationalizing efforts among many higher education facilities across the globe.

I argue that it is imperative to learn more from international educators. These educators embrace with sincerity their roles as they live, teach, innovate, and interact in new landscapes as "the other." They have knowledge to share about the boundaries of culture and religious impact on educational theories, curriculum and implementation. They also have knowledge regarding how and when these boundaries can be explored. This knowledge represents significant contributions to both our conceptions of educational theory and our understandings of the implementation of educational theory and practice across the globe, across disciplines, and across educational mandates. I agree with Gee (1994) who believes that English teachers stand at the heart of some of the most complex educational, cultural, and political movements of contemporary society. However, I extend Gee's statement to international educators and supervisors across disciplines as they stand at this forefront of all the complicated conversations (Pinar, et al., 2004) of curriculum affected by our globalized world. These educators recognize and embody the Balancing Act of international higher education.

NOTES

[i] The last full census was completed in 2005.
[ii] A sudden, departure from the country without resigning from work employment, notice to housing of closing bank accounts.

CURRENT ISSUES FORUM: BOOTH ALLOCATIONS

Booth #	Broad Topic	Judge 1	Judge 2
1	Impact of the economic crisis on the GCC.		
2	Impact of the economic crisis on Dubai banking, automobiles, tourism and supporting sectors and how they adjust(banking,real estate)		
3	Black Points and new road radar systems: a control system that works / doesn't work Why?		
4	Blood Screening before marriage: planning, control, decision making system		
5	Banks caused the World Financial / Economic crisis? Bank credit issues and ethics.		
6	Government failure to monitor, regulate and deregulation, caused the World Financial / Economic crisis? Research and discuss – Also consider the ethical issues relating to this crisis.		
7	The banking credit squeeze and economic implications for business		
8	Oil price and implications of the decrease in oil price across the globe		
9	China – GDP decline and the banks, Government reaction and new policies and the impact on companies and the individual and how they adjust		
10	How are Global corporate trying to solve the impact of the economic crisis on their corporation e.g. rising unemployment, bailouts by Governments		
11	Credit card culture e.g. easy to use card technology to purchase goods and services rather than using the cash consumer has saved.		
12	The financial crisis and its impact on companies and investors in Dubai.		
13	Technological allowing easy and fast access to finance – lack of controls		
14	UAE Women – Emirati Identity, Entrepreneurship and Innovation		
15	Unfair Labor market practices in the GCC or UAE: Racism, Hiring practices, United Nations		
16	How should UAE reduce dependence on domestic workers?		

17	Emirati Identity, Change and the Financial Crisis		
18	UAE corporate solutions to the economic crisis		
19	Impact of the economic crisis on Dubai – banks, automobiles, housing, real estate, tourism, construction and supporting sectors and how they adjust		
20	The economic crisis and increases in crime and war		
21	How is the current global financial and economic crisis effecting your company's factors of production and its economic financial environment?		
22	USA – GDP and the banks decline, Government reaction and new policies and the impact on companies and the individual and how they adjust		
23	UAE Government solutions to the economic crisis		
24	Unemployment implications in the UAE from the economic crisis		
25	The economic crisis, impact on increasing bankruptcy and its impact on companies, the economy and investors		
26	Eurozone e.g. Germany, France and the UK – GDP decline and the banks massive loss of profits and assets and in some cases bank collapses. Government reaction and new policies. How do these new policies impact on banks and the individual and how they adjust.		
27	Asia - GDP decline and the banks, Government reaction and new policies and the impact on companies and the individual and how they adjust		
28	Global comparison of government response to financial crisis		
29	Government solutions to the economic crisis		
30	UAE – Dubai – comparison of GDP Q1,2,3 2008 with Q4 2008 by sectors		
31	Technology - media (ethical use / abuse) impact on crisis before, during and after.		
32	The economic crisis and wealth distribution.		
33	The economic histories of recessions and financing		
34	Islamic finance compared to Western banks style financing. Are Islamic banks affected and to what degree? Would Islamic banking controls have prevented the crisis?		
35	USA – Housing and automobile decline, Government reaction and new policies and the impact on companies and the individual and how they adjust		
36	Europe / UK – Housing and automobile decline, Government reaction and new policies and the impact on companies and the individual and how they adjust		

37	Unemployment implications globally from the economic crisis		
38	Economic impact and comparison to prior development of Dubai as cosmopolitan Emirate		
39	Impact of the economic crisis on the UAE - banks, automobiles, tourism, construction and supporting sectors and how they adjust		
40	Impact of the economic crisis on Emirate families		
41	Dubai Government solutions to the economic crisis		
42	UAE budget implications of the economic crisis		
43	The impact of the economic/financial crisis on employment issues re Emiratization and women must use Arab Human Development Study and Tanmai publications on women's issues as part of research		
44	Emirati expectations at work: realistic or not? Issues for working Emiratis: "no bonus and increments, boring job, 4 years working in the same grade and no promotion, parking, bad environment in dept, bad food, difficult to fire, high salaries"		
45	IMF World bank position and action on the economic crisis		
46	Environmental implication of the economic crisis		
47	Real Estate changes in UAE – RERA and new legislation		
48	Monetary Policy and the UAE		
49	The Dubai Executive Council approves part-time work system at governmental departments. Discuss the implications of this decision.		
50	Emiratization: Barriers to women from taking summer or part time employment?		
51	Managing the implementation of UAE Identity Cards by the Identity Authority – issues in technology, control and planning		
52	Motivating Emirati employees "our work is too much boring and I will not get benefit from this experience in future work" "always late" "no parking" "playing Internet" "chatting" "selfish" "untidy" "absenteeism" "customers wait long time for help" PM students only		
53	Domestic Help – Foreign Labour Rights and Abuse		
54	The Impact of Expats purchasing real estate		
55	Impact of Dubai's development on the environment		

56	Impact of new labour laws affecting Emiraties (cannot dismiss ineffective employees)		
57	Emirati identity and a new labour marketplace		
58	The Impact of the financial crisis and UAE's reliance on Domestic Workers		
59	Genetic abnormalities and consanguineous marriage		
60	Implication of the financial crisis on charity and non-profit organizations		
61	UAE Reliance on Domestic Workers		
62	Impact of Financial Crisis on Health Care		

READING ASSESSMENT TEXTS

READING 1: WHATEVER THEIR JUDGEMENTS, WE DEFINE WHO WE ARE

A. Women of the "Orient" are perceived as abaya-covered victims who are suppressed by culture, religion and politics, and are in need of being saved. Or they are viewed as being dangerous and cunning, in need of being watched.

B. I find myself in situations where I have to explain, justify and defend my way of life to outsiders. But at the same time I have to fight, rebel and demand change from my own society.

> "Are you forced to wear your abbaya?"
> "Do you think it's constraining of your movement?"
> "Do you drive in Arabia?"
> "Are your eyebrows real?"

C. I used to answer these questions very patiently, because I couldn't blame people for their ignorance. I sought to deconstruct the "otherness" that has been created by endless stereotypical images. But I have come to realise that my answers will never change others' preconceived ideas, because every time I manage to convince Westerners that I was not as exotic as they had first assumed they would simply come to the conclusion that I was an exception to their preconceived ideas. "You are different, you seem very independent," I have been told.

D. The stereotypical images of Oriental women have pressured developing societies to adopt a "modern" image of women to signify that change has occurred. Women of the "Orient" have been pressured to adopt modernity in order to break from the stereotype of the downtrodden woman of the harem. On the other hand, women are a symbol of the family and the nation's honour. On a personal level they have to be traditional to avoid social ostracism, and on the national level they have to be traditional to emphasise the authenticity of the culture and the nation.

E. The supposed "authentic" image of an Arab Muslim woman has limited their choice of how they present themselves publicly; their choice becomes shaped by how others will perceive them. Women are expected to be both modern and traditional and they are pulled between those two sometimes conflicting notions.

F. Personally, I have been moved back and forth from the modern to the traditional box without my consent. My identity has been defined, dissected and shaped by "others".

G. In school and later at university, many Emirati students feel stereotyped as rich, suppressed, and lacking in intellectual abilities. We have to dissolve this perception by being modern, yet the traditional aspects of our life could not be erased.

H. I remember an incident in a class when after I pointed out that my family wouldn't allow me to go to a certain public event, my lecturer commented, "Come on, you are not really one of them, are you?" I realised that certain assumptions had been made given my appearing to be modern to others. I was not comfortable with others shaping my identity. I switched the way I interacted with that specific lecturer; I limited my conversations with him, cut the jokes short and glued my shaila to my head. I opted to be more reserved because I didn't want to fit into his modern box. Now I realise that I not only allowed him to judge me, but I gave him the power to change me.

I. Similarly, another student at university who usually wore her shaila around her shoulders one day decided that she would wear it on her head. Her lecturer noticed and commented: "So you decided to be a Muslim today?" The way this student chose to dress was not seen as a personal choice but rather as a symbol to define her religious identity.

J. There is a certain expectation of consistency when it comes to the way a Muslim woman dresses. Western women can wear a short skirt one day and long pants the next, and their identity would not be questioned. They would not be faced with answering ridiculous questions like: "So you decided to be conservative today?"

K. In particular there is an obsession with the authenticity of our clothing. I have to constantly answer questions like "Why do you have pink crystals on your abaya?" We are accused of losing the authenticity of the abaya, and that those pink crystals are a sign of "modernity" and women breaking free from tradition. However, who is it who decides what is authentic and what is not? How does one decide if a person is modern or traditional? More importantly, why do we need to fit people into these predefined boxes?

L. Arab and Muslim women's personal identity is far from personal. A woman attempting to define her identity is placed under pressure because she cannot avoid being judged. She has to be traditional yet modern, a rebel and yet a conformist. On top of all of that she has to be consistent, otherwise, she would be guilty of being "inauthentic".

M. The moment we give the "other" the power to judge "us", they are automatically placed in a powerful hierarchal position. It gives the "other" the power to shape who we are.

Hissa al Dhaheri is a sociologist and researcher in cultural studies and holds an MA in Gulf Studies

Al Dhaheri, Hissa. "Whatever their judgements, we define who we are." *The National*, 19 April 2009. 30 April 2009, http://www.thenational.ae/article/20090419/OPINION/386544329

This article has been modified for the purposes of the assessment.

READING 2: WHO ARE YOU?

Emirati students join experts in calling for preservation of the UAE's history, religion, language and culture as essential elements in promoting national identity. Rania Moussly reports from a conference at Sharjah Women's College.

A. Shaikh Nahyan Bin Mubarak Al Nahyan, Minister of Higher Education and Scientific Research and Chancellor of the Higher Colleges of Technology, inaugurated the Mosaic International Conference 2009 at Sharjah Women's College (SWC) last week. The two-day conference titled "Who am I? Who are you? A Dialogue on National Identity" was the final section of the college's annual Mosaic event.

B. Mosaic 2009 was based on a theme of 'Proudly Emirati'. It aimed to inspire in students a sense of wonder and curiosity about the world they live in and have them appreciate the richness of their nation's past and the potential of its future. Throughout the academic year students participated in various activities, consisting of a six-day camel expedition, art exhibits, poetry readings, a video/film festival, educational competitions, international educational trips and visits to significant locations around the nation. The activities concluded with the conference.

C. Dr Fareed Ohan, Director of the Sharjah Higher Colleges of Technology, said: "I am most delighted with the choice of this theme. It is inspired by the vision of our Chancellor Shaikh Nahyan Bin Mubarak Al Nahyan, who urges us to do our part in preparing a new generation of Emiratis, confident in themselves, proud of their culture and language and able to live and work in a changing and globalising world."

D. The opening panel discussion of the conference saw Emirati students from both SWC and Sharjah Men's College (SMC) fill the auditorium in a sea of white and black ready for the debate. It brought together eight national and international academics and professors. Through a series of discussions and lectures, the aim was to spark a dialogue about Emirati identity. The opening session on "national identity in an age of diversity" was moderated by the good-humoured Saudi Arabian journalist Turki Al Dakhil.

E. Speakers stressed the need for personal freedom and equal rights as an essential part of an individual's national identity. UAE national Dr Abdul Khaleq Abdullah, professor of political science at UAE University, stressed the need for individuals to live free of the fear of self-expression. "If these elements are available, then it is impossible for anyone to be anxious about their national identity."

F. Professor Mohammad Arkoun addressed the need for education which allows a person to assimilate with their identity. "We need to teach human science. There is a difference between technological teaching and the education of human needs," he said. He added that the youth today are unaware of their own history, stressing the need to spread knowledge of Islamic history. "This subject is the first condition we need to teach," said Arkoun. He used an example a book written by a German author to illustrate his point that Western scholars are better educated about Arabic and Islamic history than Arabs and Muslims.

G. The debate went on to the definition of Emirati identity and identity as a whole. "Identity is the responsibility of individuals … everyone is a decision-maker [of their own actions]. Identity expresses itself in the form of many factors and the Arabic language comes first. It is important not to change our identity into a group of rituals," said Professor Yasir Sulaiman. He said the way to preserve one's language and religion is to pass it down to one's children.

H. The topic of demographics was raised. The fact that Emiratis are a minority in their own country was addressed by Dr Abdullah who said: "If you are a partner in your country's affairs and know your rights and responsibilities [as a citizen] then you will never feel threatened."

I. He said today the country is facing an identity problem. The Arabic language and Islam are being eroded as a result of the demographic imbalance. He said the UAE is globalising and because of this, it is losing touch with its local identity. However, he added, there are no feelings of xenophobia towards the dominant expatriate population in the UAE.

Who is an Emirati?

J. Notes spoke to Emirati students at the Mosaic International Conference 2009 to grasp their thoughts on the conference and what it means to be an Emirati. Manar Al Majedi, 18, is a media student at Sharjah Women's College. She is also part of the new Shoumoukh leadership advancement programme organised by the college's Career Centre. Manar volunteered to help out at the conference. "It is important for us because as they said there are not many locals here in the UAE so our identity is affected by others. For example, there are some girls who don't talk in Arabic at all.

K. They only speak in English so they should listen to these talks and learn about their identity," she said. Media student Nouf Ali, 21, was displaying books about the UAE outside the conference hall. She expressed her dissatisfaction with the fact that a majority of the speakers were not even UAE nationals.

L. "If they'd brought locals [to speak] it would have been better ... they are all foreigners ... I am disappointed," said Nouf. When asked what it means to be an Emirati Nouf said: "To be what the late Shaikh Zayed Bin Sultan Al Nahyan used to be. A person who doesn't want to lose his identity ... we should go on and do what he used to do. He was a kind person who loved his culture, his sons and his daughters. He used to treat everybody like he was the father of the Emirates," she said. Student Council President Alya Rasheed, 19, said her identity is not defined by the national identity card now mandatory for all residents. "It means my language, my religion, my tradition, my culture, my country, my home, my family – everything ... so it is very important for us to talk about this [topic]," she said.

M. Engineering student Abdul Rahman Bukhalaf, 20, from SMC, said to be Emirati means everything. "The Emirates has offered us many things ... the most important thing is that we give back to the nation ... The nation has done everything for us, given us everything. We've taken and taken but not given back. There comes a time when we have to give the nation as much as we can to help it prosper," said Bukhalaf.

N. "This country has given us things other countries did not give its nationals. Now is the time we give back. The national identity is not just to preserve history; we must develop our culture but at the same time hold on to our history," said Marwan Al Ali, 21, from Dubai Men's College.

Moussly, Rania. "Who are you?" *Gulf News*, 25 April 2009. 3 May 2009 http://archive.gulfnews.com/articles/09/04/24/10307071.html

The text has been modified for the purposes of this assessment.

REFERENCES

Adams M., & Marchesani, L. (1997). Multiple issues course overview. In M. Adams, L. A. Bell, & P. Griffin (Eds.), *Teaching for diversity and social justice education* (pp. 3–17). New York, NY: Routledge.

Ahli, A. (2009). Leading together. *Desert Dawn, 21*(1), 6–9.

Ahmad, B. E., & Majid, F. A. (2010). Cultural influence on SDL among Malay adult learners. *European Journal of Social Sciences, 16*(2), 254–263.

Albertini, T. (2003). The seductiveness of certainty: The destruction of Islam's intellectual legacy by the fundamentalists. *Philosophy East & West, 53*(4), 455–470.

Albertini, T. (2005). Crisis and certainty of knowledge in Al-Ghazzali (1058–1111) and Decartes (1596–1650). *Philosophy East & West, 55*(1), 1–14.

Al Fahim, M. (1995). *From rags to riches.* Dubai, UAE: London Centre of Arab Studies.

Alfred, M. (2003). Sociocultural contexts and learning: Anglophone Caribbean immigrant women in U.S. postsecondary education. *Adult Education Quarterly, 53*(4), 242–260.

Al Sweidi, A. M. (2006). *The time for educational reform.* Ministry of Education, Department of Planning and Human Resources. Retrieved from http://www.government.ae/gov/en/gov/index.jsp

Altun, S., & Büyükduman, F. İ. (2007). Teacher and student beliefs on constructivist instructional design: A case study. *Educational Sciences: Theory & Practice, 7*(1), 30–39.

Ames, R. (2003). Confucianism and Deweyan pragmatism: A dialogue. *Journal of Chinese Philosophy, 30*(3/4), 403–417.

Angell, R. (1928). Science, sociology and education. *Journal of Educational Sociology, 1*(1), 407–413.

Antikainen, A., & Kauppila, J. (2002). Educational generations and the futures of adult education: A Nordic experience. *International Journal of Lifelong Education, 21*(3), 209–219.

Apple, M. (1979). Curriculum and reproduction. *Curriculum Inquiry, 9*(3), 231–252.

Apple, M. (2004) *Ideology and Curriculum; 25th Anniversary* (3rd ed.). New York: Routledge Falmer.

Apple, M. (2008). Can schooling contribute to a more just society? *Education, Citizenship and Social Justice, 3*(3), 239–261. doi: 10.1177/1746197908095134.

Asgharzadeh, A. (2008). The return of the subaltern: International education and politics of voice. *Journal of Studies in International Education, 12*(4), 334–363.

Association of College and Research Libraries. (December, 2014). *Information literacy competency standards for higher education.* Retrieved on December, 2014 from http://www.ala.org/acrl/standards/informationliteracycompetency

Austin, Z., Gregory, P., & Martin, C. (2007). Geographical migration, psychological adjustment, and re-formation of professional identity: The double-culture shock experience of international pharmacy graduates in Ontario (Canada). *Globalisation, Societies & Education, 5*(2), 239–255. doi: 10.1080/14767720701427145

Ayoub, M. (2004). *Islam, faith and history.* Oxford, UK: One World Oxford.

Bachman, L. (1990). *Fundamental consideration in language testing.* Oxford: Oxford University Press.

Bachman, L. (1991). What does language testing have to offer? *TESOL Quarterly, 25,* 671–704 doi: 10.2307/3587082

Bachman, L. (2000). Modern language testing at the turn of the century: Assuring that what we count counts. *Language Testing, 17*(1), 1–42.

Bachman, L., & A. Palmer. (1996). *Language testing in practice.* Oxford: Oxford University Press.

Baines, L., & Stanley, G. (2006). The iatrogenic consequences of standards-based education. *The Clearing House, 79*(3), 119–123.

Ballantine, J., & Hammack, F. (2009). *The sociology of education: A systematic analysis* (6th ed.). Upper Saddle River, NJ: Prentice Hall.

Bednar, A. K., Cunningham, D., Duffy, T. M., & Perry, J. D. (1992). Theory into practice: How do we link? In T. M. Duffy & D. H. Jonassen (Eds.), *Constructivism and the technology of instruction* (pp. 17–34). Hillsdale, NJ: Lawrence Erlbaum Associates.

REFERENCES

Bell, L. (1997). Theoretical foundations for social justice education. In M. Adams, L. A. Bell, & P. Griffin (Eds.), *Teaching for diversity and social justice education* (pp. 3–17). New York, NY: Routledge.

Bergsteiner, H., Avery, G. C., & Neumann, R. (2010). Kolb's experiential learning model: Critique from a modelling perspective. *Studies in Continuing Education, 32*(1), 29–46.

Bhabha, H. (1990). The third space: Interview with Homi Bhabha. In J. Rutherford (Ed.), *Identity: Community, culture, difference* (pp. 207–221). London, UK: Lawrence & Wishart.

Bhabha, H. (1994). *The location of culture.* New York, NY: Routledge.

Big Six. *Big Six skills overview.* Retrieved on November, 2008 from http://big6.com/pages/about/big6-skills-overview.php

Bin Zayed, A. (2009). A woman's education – Her life. *Desert Dawn, 21*(1), 25–27.

Bleakley, A., Brice, J., & Bligh, J. (2008). Thinking the post-colonial in medical education. *Medical Education, 42*(3), 266–270. doi: 10.1111/j.1365-2923.2007.02991.x

Bourdieu, P. (1974). The school as a conservative force. In T. Eggleston (Ed.), *Contemporary research in the sociology of education.* London: Methuen.

Bourdieu, P. (1977). Cultural reproduction and social reproduction. In J. Karabel & A. H. Halsey (Eds.), *Power and ideology in education* (pp. 487–511). New York, NY: Oxford University Press.

Bourdieu, P. (1986). The forms of capital. In J. G. Richardson (Ed.), *Handbook of theory and research for the sociology of education* (pp. 241–258). New York: Greenwood Press.

Bourdieu, P. & Passeron, J. C. (1977). *Reproduction in education, society and culture.* Beverly Hills: Sage.

Brettingham, M. (2007a). Left in the dark about schools in the sun. *Times Educational Supplement, 4734,* 18–19.

Brettingham, M. (2007b). Teaching takes a hit on front line. *Times Educational Supplement, 4729,* 19–19.

Brettingham, M. (2007c). Your ticket to ride. *Times Educational Supplement, 4759,* 26–28.

Brinton, M., &Yamamoto, Y. (2005). *Cultural capital in East Asian educational systems.* UK: Harvard University Press.

The British Council. (2005). *Australia and University of Cambridge ESOL examinations: IELTS handbook.* Cambridge, UK: Cambridge University Press.

Brookfield, S. (1995). *Becoming a critically reflective teacher.* San Francisco, CA: Jossey-Bass.

Brookfield, S. (2006). *The skillful teacher: On technique, trust, and responsiveness in the classroom* (2nd ed.). San Francisco: Jossey Bass/Wiley.

Brookfield, S. (2008). Radical questioning on the long walk to freedom: Nelson Mandela and the practice of critical reflection. *Adult Education Quarterly, 58*(2), 95–109.

Brown, H., & Ciuffetelli Parker, D. (2009). *Foundational methods: Understanding teaching and learning* (3rd ed.). Toronto, Ontario: Pearson Custom Publishing.

Brown, K. (2006). Leadership for social justice and equity: Evaluating a transformative framework and andragogy. *Educational Administration Quarterly, 42*(5), 700–745.

Brown-Jeffy, S., & Cooper, J. E. (2011). Toward a conceptual framework of culturally relevant pedagogy: An overview of the conceptual and theoretical literature. *Teacher Education Quarterly, 38*(1), 65–84. Retrieved from http://www.eric.ed.gov/PDFS/EJ914924.pdf

Burden-Leahy, S. (2005). Addressing the tensions in a process-based quality assurance model through the introduction of graduate outcomes: A case study of the change process in a vocational higher education institution in the United Arab Emirates. *Quality in higher education, 11*(2), 129–136.

Burkhardt, M. (1989). Spirituality: An Analysis of the Concept, *Holistic Nursing Practice, 3*(3), 69-77.

Case, R. (1992). *The mind's staircase: Exploring the conceptual underpinnings of children's thought and knowledge.* Hillsdale, NJ: Lawrence Erlbaum Associates.

Case, R., Okamoto, Y., Griffin, S., McKeough, A., Bleiker, C., & Henderson, B. (1996). The role of central conceptual structures in the development of children's thought. *Monographs of the Society for Research in Child Development, 61*(1/2), 1–266.

Cheng, C. (2005). Confucian ren & Deweyan experience: A review essay on John Grange's Dewey, Confucius & the global philosophy. *Journal of Chinese Philosophy, 32*(4), 641–648.

Chinn, E. (2006). John Dewey and the Buddhist philosophy of the middle way. *Asian Philosophy, 16*(2), 87–98.

Christie, K. (2010). Globalisation, religion and state formation in the United Arab Emirates and Pakistan. *Totalitarian Movements & Political Religions, 11*(2), 203–212. doi: 10.1080/14690764.2010.511460

Clarke, M., & Otaky, D. (2006). Reflection 'on' and 'in' teacher education in the United Arab Emirates. *International Journal of Educational Development, 26*(1), 111–122.

Cohen, R. (2001). Living and teaching across cultures. *International Studies Perspectives, 2*(2), 151.

Cook, B. (1999). Islam versus western conception of education: Reflections on Egypt. *International Review of Education, 45* (3/4), 339–357.

Cook, D. A. (1993). Behaviorism evolves. *Educational Technology, 33*(10), 62–77.

Cookson, P., & Sadovnik, A. (2002). Functionalist theories of education. In D. Levinson, P. Cookson, Jr., & A. Sadovnik (Eds.), *Education and society: An encyclopedia* (pp. 267–271). New York, NY: Routledge.

Cronje, J. (2006). Paradigms regained: Toward integrating objectivism and constructivism in instructional design and the learning sciences. *ETR & D, 54*(4), 387–416.

Cranton, P. (1994). *Understanding and promoting transformative learning.* San Francisco, CA: Jossey-Bass.

Cranton, P. (2000). Individual differences and transformative learning. In J. Mezirow & Associates (Eds.), *Learning as transformation: Critical perspectives on a theory in progress* (pp. 181–204). San Francisco, CA: Jossey-Bass.

Cranton, P. (2002). Teaching for transformation. *New Directions for Adult and Continuing Education, 93*(2), 63–71.

Cranton, P. (2005/1994). *Understanding and promoting transformative learning.* San Francisco, CA: Jossey-Bass.

Cranton, P. (2012). Spiraling into transformative learning. In V. Wang (Ed.), *Vocational Education Technologies and Advances in Adult Learning: New Concepts* (pp. 1–10). Hershey, PA: Information Science Reference. doi: 10.4018/978-1-4666-0252-6.ch001

Cranton, P. & Taylor, E. W. (2012). Transformative learning theory: Seeking a more unified theory. In E. W. Taylor & P. Cranton (Eds.), *Handbook of transformative learning: Theory, research, and practice* (pp. 3–20). San Francisco, CA: Jossey-Bass.

Culturally Responsive Pedagogy (2013). Capacity Building Series, Ontario Canada: Ministry of Education for Ontario. Retrieved from http://www.edu.gov.on.ca/eng/literacynumeracy/inspire/research/CBS_ResponsivePedagogy.pdf

Davidson, C. (2008). *Dubai: The vulnerability of success.* Dubai, UAE: Hurst & Company.

Davidson, F. (1994). Comments and replies. *World Englishes, 13*(1), 119–120.

Davies, A. (1999). Standard English: Discordant voices. *World Englishes, 18*(2), 171–186.

Davies, A. (2003). *The native speaker: Myth and reality.* Clevedon, UK: Multilingual Matters.

Davies, A., Hamp-Lyons, L., & Kemp, C. (2003). Forum on norms and testing whose norms? International proficiency tests in English. *World Englishes, 22*(4), 571–584. doi: 10.1111/j.1467-971X.2003.00324.x

Davies, S., & Guppy, N. (2010). *The schooled society: An introduction to the sociology of education* (2nd ed.). Don Mills, ON: Oxford University Press.

DeBono, E. (2009). *CoRT thinking lessons 1: Breadth thinking tools.* Retrieved on December 14, 2014 from http://www.debonoforschools.com/pdfs/80850_cort1_introduction_section.pdf

DeBono, E. (2015). *Six thinking hats.* Retrieved on December 14, 2015 from http://www.debonogroup.com/six_thinking_hats.php

Dew, P., & Shoult, A. (2002). *Doing business with Oman.* London, UK: Kogan Page.

Dewey, J. (1916). *Democracy and education: An introduction to the philosophy of education.* New York, NY: Macmillan.

REFERENCES

Dewey, J. (1929). *Experience and nature* (2nd ed.). Chicago, IL: Open Court.
Dewey, J. (1980). *Art as experience.* New York, NY: Perigee/Putnam. (Original work published 1934.)
Dewey, J. (1997). *Experience and education.* New York, NY: Simon and Schuster. (Original work published 1938.)
Dirkx, J. (1997). Nurturing soul in adult learning. In P. Cranton (Ed.), *Transformative learning in action* (pp. 79–88). San Francisco, CA: Jossey-Bass.
Dirkx, J. (2006). Engaging emotions in adult learning: A Jungian perspective on emotion and transformative learning. *Teaching for Change: New Directions in Adult and Continuing Education,* 109, 15-26. doi: 10.1002/ace.204
Dirkx, J. (2012). Nurturing soul work: A Jungian approach to transformative learning. In E. Taylor & P. Cranton (Eds.), *The handbook of transformative learning: Theory, research, and practice* (pp. 116–130). San Francisco, CA: Jossey-Bass.
Drake, S. (2007). *Creating standards-based integrated curriculum: Aligning curriculum, content, assessment, and instruction* (2nd ed.). Thousand Oaks, CA: Corwin.
Drake, S. (2012). *Creating standards-based integrated curriculum: Common core state standards edition* (3rd ed.). Thousand Oaks, CA: Corwin Press.
Drake, S., & Burns, R. (2004). *Meeting standards through integrated curriculum.* Alexandria, VI: Association for Supervision and Curriculum Development.
Drake, S., Reid, J., Kolohon, W. (2014). *Interweaving curriculum and assessment in the 21st century: Engaging students in 21st century learning.* Toronto, Can: Oxford University Press.
Driscoll, M. P. (2005). *Psychology of learning for instruction.* Toronto, ON: Pearson.
Durkheim, E. (1956). *Education and sociology* (S. Fox, Trans.). Gelncoe, IL: Free Press.
Durkheim, E. (1977). *The evolution of educational thought* (P. Collins, Trans.). London, UK: Routledge.
Egbo, B. (2009). *Teaching for diversity in Canadian schools.* Toronto, ON: Pearson Prentice Hall.
Eldredge, N., & Gould, S. (1972). Punctuated equilibria: An alternative to phyletic gradualism. In T. J. Schopf (Ed.), *Models in paleobiology* (pp. 82–115). San Francisco, CA: Freeman, Cooper & Co.
Ellis, R., (2003). *Task-based language teaching and learning.* Oxford, UK: Oxford University Press.
Ellis, R. (2006). Task-based learning in an Asian context. *Asian EFL Journal,* 8(3), 1–8.
Elmore, R. (1999). *Leadership of large-scale improvement in American education.* Paper prepared for the Albert Shanker Institute, Washington, DC.
English, L. (2003). Identity, hybridity, and third space: Complicating the lives of international adult educators. *Convergence,* 36(2), 67–80.
ESL Glossary. (n.d.). Retrieved on November, 2014 from http://bogglesworldesl.com/glossary.htm
Faris, N., & Ashraf, S. (2003). *The book of knowledge: Being a translation with notes of Kitab al-Ilm of Al Ghazzalis's Ihya Ulum al-Din* (Online version). Retrieved from http://www.ghazali.org/works/bk1-sec-1.htm
Fasano, U., & Goyal, R. (2004). *Emerging strains in GCC labour markets.* IMF Working Paper Series, International Monetary Fund, Washington, DC.
Fernandes, C., & Awamleh, R. (2006). Impact of organizational justice in an expatriate work environment. *Management Research News,* 29(11), 701–712.
Findlow, S. (2008). Islam, modernity and education in the Arab states. *Intercultural Education,* 19(4), 337–352. doi: 10.1080/14675980802376861
Forstenlechner, I. (2008). Workforce nationalization in the UAE: Image versus integration. *Education, Business, and Society: Contemporary Middle Eastern Issues,* 1(2), 82–91.
Foucault, M. (1980). *The history of sexuality.* New York, NY: Vintage Books.
Four Pilars of Mut'a, The. (2014). Retrieved 14 December 2014 from from http://www.al-islam.org/muta-temporary-marriage-in-islamic-law-sachiko-murata/four-pilars-muta
Fox, E., & Riconscente, M. (2008). Metacognition and self-regulation in James, Piaget, and Vygotsky. *Educational Psychology Review,* 20, 373–389.
Fox, R. (2001). Constructivism examined. *Oxford Review of Education,* 27, 33–39.
Freire, P. (1970). *Pedagogy of the oppressed.* New York, NY: Seabury Press.

Freire, P. (1973). *Education as the practice of freedom in education for critical consciousness.* New York, NY: Continuum.

Freire, P. (1994). *Pedagogy of the oppressed* (Rev. ed.). New York, NY: Continuum.

Fulcher, G. (2000). The "communicative" legacy in language testing. *System, 28,* 483–497.

Gardner, W. (1995). Developing a quality teaching force for the United Arab Emirates. *Journal of Education for Teaching, 21*(3), 289–320.

Garson, B. (2005). Teaching abroad: A cross-cultural journey. *Journal of Education for Business, 80*(6), 322–327.

Gay, G. (2010). *Culturally responsive teaching* (2nd ed.). New York, New York: Teachers College Press.

Gee, J. (1994). Orality and literacy: From the savage mind to ways with words. In J. Maybin (Ed.), *Language and literacy in social practice* (pp. 168–192). Clevedon, UK: Multilingual Matters.

Gendlin, E., (1981). *Focusing.* New York, NY: Bantam.

Gersick, C. J. G. (1991). Revolutionary change theories: A multilevel exploration of the punctuated equilibrium paradigm. *Academy of Management Review, 16*(1), 10–36.

Getty, L. J. (2011). False assumptions: The challenges and politics of teaching in China. *Teaching in Higher Education, 16*(3), 347–352. doi: 10.1080/13562517.2011.560058

Ghosh, R. (2009). The short history of women, human rights and global citizenship. In A. Abdi & L. Shultz (Eds.), *Educating for human rights and global citizenship* (pp. 81–96). New York, NY: State University of New York Press.

Gipps, C. (1994). *Beyond testing: Towards a theory of educational assessment.* London, UK: The Falmer Press.

Giroux, H. (1981). Hegemony, resistance, and the paradox of educational reform. *Interchange, 12*(2/3), 3–26.

Giroux, H. (1983). Theories of reproduction and resistance in the new sociology of education: A critical analysis. *Harvard Educational Review, 53*(3), 261–293.

Giroux, H. (2010). Dumbing down teachers: Rethinking the crisis of public education and the demise of the social state. *Review of Education, Pedagogy & Cultural Studies, 32*(4), 339–381. doi: 10.1080/10714413.2010.510346

Grange, J. (2004). *John Dewey, Confucius, and global philosophy.* New York, NY: State University of New York Press.

Godwin, S. M. (2006). Globalization, education and emiratization: A study of the United Arab Emirates. *Electronic Journal on Information Systems in Developing Countries, 27*(1), 1–14.

Government of Dubai, Dubai Statistics Centre. (2014). *Population and vital statistics.* Retrieved from http://www.dsc.gov.ae/En/Pages/Home.aspx

Griffith, S. (2005). *Teaching English abroad.* New York, NY: Globe Pequot Press.

Guisbond, L., & Neill, M. (2004). Failing our children. *Clearing House, 78*(1), 12–16.

Gunnlaugson, O. (2007). Shedding light on the underlying forms of transformative learning theory: Introducing three distinct categories of consciousness. *Journal of Transformative Education, 5*(2), 134–151.

Guth, S., & Helm, F. (2011). Teaching culture through CALL. In N. Arnold & L. Ducate (Eds.), *Present and future promises of CALL: From theory and research to new directions in language teaching* (pp. 211–256). San Marcos, TX: Calico Publications.

Gutierrez, L. M. (1995). Understanding the empowerment process: Does consciousness make a difference? *Social Work Research, 19,* 229–237.

Hague, A. (2004). Psychology from the Islamic perspective: Contributions of early Muslim scholars and the challenges to contemporary Muslim psychologists. *Journal of Religion and Health, 43*(4), 357–377.

Halbach, A. (2002). Exporting methodologies: The reflective approach in teacher training. *Language, Culture and Curriculum, 13*(3), 243–250.

REFERENCES

Hampel, R. (2006). Rethinking task design for the digital age: A framework for language teaching and learning in a synchronous online environment. *ReCALL, 18*(1), 105–121. http://dx.doi.org/10.1017/S0958344006000711

Hampel, R., & Pleines, C. (2013). Fostering student interaction and engagement in a virtual learning environment: An investigation into activity design and implementation, *Calico Journal The Computer Assisted Language Instruction Consortium, 30*(3), 342–370. doi: 10.11139/cj.30.3.342-370.

Harb, N., & El-Shaarawi, A. (2007). Factors affecting business students' performance: The case of students in United Arab Emirates. *Journal of Education for Business, 82*(5), 282–290.

Harden, R. M., & Laidlaw, R. M., (1996). Task-based learning: An educational strategy For undergraduate, postgraduate and continuing medical education. *Medical Teacher, 18*(1), 7–13, & *18*(2), 91–98.

Hazadiah, M., & Majid, F. (2007). *Scaffolding adult education: Narratives of Malaysian practitioners.* UPENA.

Heard-Bey, F. (2005) the United Arab Emirates: Statehood and nation building in a traditional society. *Middle East Journal, 59*(3), 357–375.

Henderson, J., & Gornik, J. (2007). *Transformative curriculum leadership* (3rd ed.). Upper Saddle River, NJ: Prentice Hall.

Higher Colleges of Technology Academic Services. (2006). *HCT learning model.* Dubai, UAE: Higher Colleges of Technology.

Higher Colleges of Technology Academic Services. (2007). *HCT learning model.* Dubai, UAE: Higher Colleges of Technology.

Hofstede, G. (1997). *Cultures and organizations: Software of the mind.* New York, NY: McGraw-Hill.

Hoppers, C. (2009). Education, culture and society in a globalizing world: Implications for comparative and international education. *Compare*, 39(5), 601–614.

HRH Sheikh Zayed. (2007). *20 Years: An anthology celebrating the twentieth anniversary of the Higher Colleges of Technology in the United Arab Emirates.* Abu Dhabi, UAE: HCT Press.

HRH Sheikh Nahayan Mubarak Al Nahayan. (2007). *20 Years: An anthology celebrating the twentieth anniversary of the Higher Colleges of Technology in the United Arab Emirates.* Abu Dhabi, UAE

HRH Sheikh Nahayan. (2008). *Higher Colleges of Technology Strategic Plan for 2008–2010.* Abu Dhabi, UAE: HCT Press.

Higher Colleges of Technology Academic Services. (2002). *HCT learning model.* Dubai, UAE: Higher Colleges of Technology.

Hurn, C. (1993). *The limits and possibilities of schooling: An introduction to sociology of education* (3rd ed.). Boston, MA: Allyn & Bacon.

Ibn-Habaj, Abul-Hussain. Retrieved on November 13, 2013 from http://hadithcollection.com/sahihmuslim/134Sahih%20Muslim%20Book%2006.%20Fasting/10970-sahih-muslim-book-006-hadith-number-2378.html

Illeris, K. (2002). *The three dimensions of learning: Contemporary learning theory in the tension field between the cognitive, the emotional and the social.* Copenhagen, Denmark: Roskilde University Press.

Illeris, K. (2014). Transformative learning and identity. *Journal of Transformative Education, 12*(2), 148–163.

Irigaray, L. (2005). *Between East and West – From singularity to community.* New Delhi: New Age Books.

James, W. (1890). *The principles of psychology.* New York, NY: Holt.

James, W. (1992). *Writings 1878–1899.* New York, NY: The Library of America.

Jarvis, P. (2010). *Adult education and lifelong learning: Theory and practice.* New York, NY: Routledge.

Jarvis, P. (2012). Learning from everyday life. *HSSRP, 1*(1), 1–20.

Jawaher, S., & Al Manar, A. (2009). *Who am I: Who are you? Proudly Emirati.* Sharjah, UAE: Sharjah Women's College.

Jindapitak, N. (2013). The politics of standard English: An exploration of Thai tertiary English learners' perceptions of the notion of standard English. *Asian Social Science, 9*(5), 118–127. doi: 10.5539/ass.v9n5p118

Jonassen, D. H. (1991). Objectivism versus constructivism: Do we need a new philosophical paradigm? *Educational Technology Research and Development, 39*(3), 5–14.

Joplin, L. (1995). On defining experiential education. In K. Warren, M. Sakofs, & J. Hunt, Jr. (Eds.), *The theory of experiential education* (pp. 15–22). Dubuque, IA: Kendall/Hunt.

Kalupahana, D. (1986). The epistemology of William James and early Buddhism. In J. Runzo & C. K. Ihara (Eds.), *Religious experience and religious belief: Essays in the epistemology of religion* (pp. 160–184). Lanham, MD: University Press of America.

Kamberelis, G., & Dimitriadis, G. (2005). *On qualitative inquiry*. New York, NY: Teachers College Press.

Kamis, M., & Muhammad, M. (2007). Islam's lifelong learning mandate. In S. B. Merriam & Associates (Eds.), *Non-western perspectives on learning and knowing* (pp. 21–40). Malabar, FL: Krieger.

Karabel, J., & Halsey, A. (1977). *Power and ideology in education*. New York, NY: Oxford University Press.

Karagiorgi, Y., & Symeou, L. (2005). Translating constructivism into instructional design: Potential and limitations. *Educational Technology & Society, 8*(1), 17–27.

Kauffman, D., Johnson, S., Kardos, S., Liu, E., & Peske, H. (2002). "Lost at Sea": New teachers' experiences with curriculum and assessment. *Teachers College Record, 104*(2), 273–300.

Kazim, A. (2000). *The United Arab Emirates: A socio-discursive transformation in the Arabian Gulf*. Dubai, UAE: Gulf Book Centre.

Kee, Y. (2007). Adult learning from a Confucian way of thinking. In S. B. Merriam & Associates (Eds.), *Non-western perspectives on learning and knowing* (pp. 153–172). Malabar, FL: Krieger.

Kegan, R. (2000). What "form" transforms? A constructive-developmental approach to transformative learning. In J. Mezirow (Ed.), *Learning in transformation: Critical perspectives on a theory in progress* (pp. 35–69). San Francisco, CA: Jossey-Bass.

Kegan, R., & Lahey, L. (2009*). Immunity to change: How to overcome it and unlock the potential in yourself and your organization (leadership for the common good)*. Boston, MA: Harvard Business School Publishing Corporation.

Kelan, E. (2011). Moving bodies and minds – The quest for embodiment in teaching and learning. *Higher Education Research Network Journal, 3*, 39–46.

Kelly, C. (1997). David Kolb, the theory of experiential learning and ESL. *The Internet TESL Journal, 3*(9), 1–5.

Kirkpatrick, A. (2007). *World Englishes: Implications for international communication and English language teaching*. Cambridge, UK: Cambridge University Press.

Knain, E. (2006). Achieving science literacy through transformation of multimodal textual resources. *Science Education, 90* (4), 656–659.

Knowles, M. (1970). *The modern practice of adult education: Andragogy versus pedagogy*. Chicago, IL: Follett.

Knowles, M. (1980). *The modern practice of adult education. Andragogy versus pedagogy* (Rev. ed.). Englewood Cliffs, NJ: Prentice Hall/Cambridge.

Knowles, M. (1984). *The adult learner: a neglected species*. Houston, TX: Gulf.

Kolb, D. (1984). *Experiential learning: Experience as the source of learning and development*. New Jersey, NY: Prentice-Hall.

Kolb, A. Y., & Kolb, D. A. (2007a). *Experiential learning theory bibliography: 1971–2005*. www.learningfromexperience.com

Kolb, A. Y., & Kolb, D. A. (2007b). *Experiential learning theory bibliography: Recent research 2005–2007*. www.learningfromexperience.com

Kreisberg, S. (1992). *Transforming power: Domination, empowerment, and education*. Albany, NY: State University of New York Press.

REFERENCES

Kubota, R. (2004). Critical multiculturalism and second language education. In B. Norton & K. Toohey's (Eds.), *Critical pedagogies and language learning* (pp. 30–52). Cambridge: Cambridge University Press.

Ladson-Billings, G. (1994). *The dreamkeepers: Successful teaching for African-American students*. San Francisco: Jossey-Bass.

Ladson-Billings, G. (1995). Toward a theory of culturally relevant pedagogy. *American Research Journal, 32*(3), 465–491.

Ladson-Billings, G. J. (2001). *Crossing over to Canaan: The journey of new teachers in diverse classrooms*. San Francisco, CA: Jossey-Bass.

Ladson Billings, G. (2011). Boyz to men? Teaching to restore Black boys' childhood, *Race Ethnicity and Education, 14*(1), 7–15.

Lakoff, G., & Johnson, M. (1999). *Philosophy in the flesh: The embodied mind and its challenge to Western thought*, New York, NY: Basic Books.

Lankshear, C., & Knobel, M. (2006). *New literacies: Everyday practices and classroom learning*. Open University Press, Berkshire, UK.

Lankshear, C., & Knobel, M. (2011). *New literacies: Everyday practices and social learning* (3rd ed.). Open University Press, Maidenhead, UK.

Lebow, D. (1993). Constructivist values for instructional systems design: Five principles toward a new mindset. *Educational Technology Research and Development, 41*(3), 4–16.

Levine P. (2012). *We are the ones we have been waiting for: The philosophy and practice of civic renewal*. New York, NY: Oxford University Press.

Lipman, P. (1995). Bringing out the best in them: The contribution of culturally relevant teachers to education reform. *Theory into Practice, 34*(3), 202–208. Retrieved from: http://www.eric.ed.gov/PDFS/ED374173.pdf

Liston, D. (1986). On fact and values: An analysis of radical curriculum studies. *Educational Theory, 36*(2), 137–152.

Littlewood, W. (2000). Do Asian students really want to listen and obey? *ELT Journal, 54*(1), 31–36.

Loehlin, J.C. (2004). *Latent variable models. An introduction to factor, path and structural analysis* (4th ed.). Mahwah, NJ: Lawrence Erlbaum Publishers.

Lovering, M. (2012). *Beyond the veil: A case study of context, culture, curriculum, and constructivism at Dubai Women's College*. Unpublished doctoral dissertation. Brock University, St. Catharines, Ontario, Canada.

Macpherson, R., Kachelhoffer, P., & El Nemr, M. (2007). The radical modernization of school and education system leadership in the United Arab Emirates: Towards indigenized and educative leadership. *International Studies in Educational Administration (Commonwealth Council for Educational Administration & Management (CCEAM), 35*(1), 60–77.

Matthews, J. C. (1998). Somatic Knowing and Education. *The Educational Forum, 62*(3), 236–242.

McKay, S. L. (2002). *Teaching English as an international language: Rethinking goals and approaches*. Oxford: Oxford University Press.

McKay, S. L. (2003). Toward an appropriate EIL pedagogy: Re-examining common ELT assumptions. *International Journal of Applied Linguistics, 13*(1), 1–22. doi: 10.1111/1473-4192.00035

McLaren, P. (1989). *Life in schools: An introduction to critical pedagogy in the foundations of education*. New York, NY: Longman.

McLaren, P. (1994). *Life in schools: An introduction to critical pedagogy in the foundations of education* (2nd ed.). New York, NY: Longman.

McLaren, P. (2007). *Life in schools: An introduction to critical pedagogy in the foundations of education* (5th ed.). Boston, MA: Pearson.

McNeil, L. (2000). *Contradictions of school reform*. New York, NY: Routledge.

Meddings, L., & Thornbury, S. (2009). *Teaching unplugged: Dogma in English language teaching*. Peaslake, UK: Delta.

Merleau-Ponty, M. (1962). *Phenomenology of perception*, New York, NY: Routledge.

Merleau-Ponty, M. (2002). *Phenomenology of perception* (2nd ed.). London: Routledge.

Merriam, S. B. (2001). Andragogy and self-directed learning. *New Directions for Adult and Continuing Education, 89*, 3–14.

Merriam, S. (2007). An introduction to non-western perspectives on learning and knowing. In S. B. Merriam & Associates (Eds.), *Non-Western perspectives on learning and knowing* (pp. 1–20). Malabar, FL: Krieger.

Merriam, S., & Bierema, L. (2013). *Adult learning: Linking theory and practice*. San Francisco, CA: Jossey-Bass/Wiley.

Merriam, S., & Muhammad, M. (2000). How cultural values shape learning in older adulthood: The case of Malaysia. *Adult Education Quarterly, 51*(1), 45–63.

Merriam, S., & Ntseane, G. (2008). Transformational learning in Botswana: How culture shapes the process. *Adult Education Quarterly, 58*(3), 183–197.

Mezirow, J. (1981). A critical theory of adult learning and education. *Adult Education, 32*(1), 123–139.

Mezirow, J. (1998). On critical reflection. *Adult Education Quarterly, 48*(3), 185–198.

Mezirow, J. (2000). *Learning as transformation: Critical perspectives on a theory in progress*. San Francisco, CA: Jossey-Bass.

Mezirow, J. (2003). Transformative learning as discourse. *Journal of Transformative Education, 1*(1), 58–63.

Michelson, E. (1996). Usual suspects: Experience, reflection, and the (en)gendering of knowledge. *International Journal of Lifelong Education, 15*(6), 438–454.

Moorehouse, W. (2008). Dubai: Globalization on steroids. *The American Scholar*. Retrieved from http://theamericanscholar.org/dubai-globalization-on-steroids/

Mustafa, G. (2002). *English language teaching and learning at government schools in the United Arab Emirates*. Unpublished doctoral dissertation. University of Exeter, UK.

Myrberg, E., & Rosén, M. (2006). Reading achievement and social selection into independent schools in Sweden: Results from IEA PIRLS 2001. *Scandinavian Journal of Educational Research, 50*(2), 23–32.

Nashif, T. (2000, April). *Technological education for women as a tool of upward social mobility with reference to the Middle East*. Paper presented at the Technological Education and National Development (TEND) conference, Abu Dhabi, UAE.

Neill, M. (2003a). The dangers of testing. *Educational Leadership, 60*(5), 43.

Neill, S. (2003b). National curriculum tests. *Education Review, 16*(2), 43–48.

Nowais, S. (2004, December 12). Education system to get overhaul. *Gulf News Online*. Retrieved from http://www.gulfnews.com/articles/print2.asp?ArticleID=141170

Nowais, S. (2005). *Few nationals meet criteria*. Abu Dhabi, UAE: Gulf News.

Parsons, T. (1937). *The structure of social action*. New York, NY: McGraw-Hill.

Parsons, T. (2007). The crisis of executive leadership. In G. Sciortino (Ed.), *American society: A theory of the societal community* (pp. 25–35). Boulder, CO: Paradigm.

Parsons, C., & Fidler, B. (2005). A new theory of educational change – Punctuated equilibrium: The case of the internationalisation of higher education institutions. *British Journal of Educational Studies, 53*(4), 447–465.

Patai, R. (2002). *The Arab mind*. New York, NY: Hatherleigh Press.

Petras, J., & Veltmeyer, H. (2001). *Globalization unmasked: Imperialism in the 21st century*. London, UK: Zed Books.

Phillips, D. C. (1995). The good, the bad, and the ugly: The many faces of constructivism. *Educational Researcher, 24*(7), 5–12.

Piaget, J. (1952). *The origins of intelligence in children*. New York, NY: International Universities Press.

Pinar, W., Reynolds, W., Slattery, P., & Taubman, P. (2004). Understanding curriculum: An introduction to the study of historical and contemporary curriculum discourses. New York, NY: Peter Lang.

Proudly Emirati. (2009). *Mosiac, 2009: Know your world*. Sharjah, UAE: Sharjah Higher Colleges of Technology.

REFERENCES

Pruyn, P.W. (June 9, 2010). An overview of constructive developmental theory (CDT). *Developmental Observer.* http://developmentalobserver.blog.com/2010/06/09/an-overview-of-constructive-developmental-theory-cdt/

Rabi, U. (2006). Oil politics and tribal rulers in eastern Arabia: The reign of Shakhbut (1928–1966). *British Journal of Middle Eastern Studies, 33*(1), 37–50. doi: 10.1080/13530190600603832

Randeree, K. (2009). Strategy, policy and practice in the nationalisation of human capital: 'Project emiratisation', *Research and Practice in Human Resource Management, 17*(1), 71–91.

Reeves, T. C., & Harmon, W. (1994). Systematic evaluation procedures for interactive multimedia for education and training. In S. Reisman (Ed.), *Multimedia computing: Preparing for the 21st century.* Harrisburg, PA: Ida Group.

Rethinking Classroom Assessment with Purpose in Mind. (2006). *Manitoba education, citizenship & youth.* Manitoba, Canada: Government of Manitoba retrieved on November 12, 2014 from http://www.edu.gov.mb.ca/k12/assess/wncp/full_doc.pdf

Richardson, P. (2004). Possible influences of Arabic-Islamic culture on the reflective practices proposed for an education degree at the Higher Colleges of Technology in the United Arab Emirates. *International Journal of Educational Development, 24*(4), 429–436.

Robbins, C. G. (2009). Searching for politics with Henry Giroux: Through cultural studies to public pedagogy and the "terror of neoliberalism." *Review of Education, Pedagogy & Cultural Studies, 31*(5), 428–478. doi: 10.1080/10714410903344361

Robinson, S. (2000). "Miles to go …": Assessment and secondary English. In B. Barrell & R. Hammett (Eds.), *Advocating change: Contemporary issues in subject English* (pp. 254–280). Toronto, ON: Irwin.

Rogers, A. (1996). *Teaching adults* (2nd ed.). Buckingham: Open University Press.

Rogoff, B. (1998). Cognition as a collaborative process. In W. Damon (Ed.), *Handbook of child psychology, Vol. 2: Cognition, perception and language* (5th ed., pp. 679–744). New York, NY: John Wiley and Sons.

Rogoff, B. (2003). *The cultural nature of development.* Oxford, UK: Oxford University Press.

Saavedra, A. R., & Opfer, V. D. (2012). Learning 21st-century skills requires 21st-century teaching. *Phi Delta Kappan, 92*(2), 8–13. Available at http://www.kappanmagazine.org/content/94/2/8.full.pdf

Salloum, H. (2003). Women in the United Arab Emirates. *Contemporary Review, 283,* 101–104.

Sánchez, J. C., & Loredo, J. C. (2009). Constructivisms from a genetic point of view: A critical classification of current tendencies. *Integrative Psychological & Behavioral Science, 43*(4), 332–349. doi: 10.1007/s12124-009-9091-1

Santrock, J., Woloshyn, V., Gallagher, T., Di Petta, T., & Marini, Z. (2007). *Educational psychology* (2nd Canadian ed.). Toronto, ON: McGraw-Hill Ryerson.

Saudelli, M.G. (2012). Unveiling third space: A case study of international educators in Dubai, United Arab Emirates. *Canadian Journal of Education, 35*(3), 85–100.

Saudelli, M. (2014). Making it real: The role of authenticity in interdisciplinary curriculum. *International Journal of Interdisciplinary Education, 2*(2), 20–37.

Schmeichel, Mardi. (2012). Good teaching? An examination of culturally relevant pedagogy as an equity practice. *Journal of Curriculum Studies, 44*(2), 211–231.

Schmoker, M., & Marzano, R. (1999). Realizing the promise of standards-based education. *Educational Leadership, 56*(6), 17–21.

Scott, J., & Marshall, G. (2009). *Oxford dictionary of sociology.* Oxford, UK: Oxford University Press.

Seaman, J. (2008). Experience, reflect, critique: The end of the "learning cycles" era. *Journal of Experiential Education, 31*(1), 3–18. doi: 10.1177/105382590803100103

Sellers-Young, B. (1998). Somatic processes: Convergence of theory & practice. *Theatre Topics, 8*(2), 173–187.

Shor, I., & Freire, P. (1987). What is the "dialogical" method of teaching? *Journal of Education, 169*(3), 11–31.

Sim, M. (2009). Dewey and Confucius: On moral education. *Journal of Chinese Philosophy, 36*(1), 85–105.

Simon, B. (1998). *Is separation of church and state a myth?* Institute for First Amendment Studies Inc. Retrieved on December 14, 2015 from http://www.publiceye.org/ifas/fw/9406/separation.html

Slattery, P. (2006). *Curriculum development in the postmodern era* (2nd ed.). New York, NY: Routledge.

Slattery, P. (2013). *Curriculum development in the postmodern era* (3rd ed.). New York, NY: Routledge.

Smith, M. K. (2001, 2010). David A. Kolb on experiential learning. *The encyclopedia of informal education.* http://infed.org/mobi/david-a-kolb-on-experiential-learning

Spring, J. (2007). *A new paradigm for global school systems: Education for a long and happy life.* Mahwah, NJ: Lawrence Erlbaum Associates.

Stake, R. (Ed.). (2005). *The Sage handbook of qualitative research* (3rd ed.). Thousand Oaks, CA: Sage.

Stapleton, P. (2002). Critical thinking in Japanese L2 writing: Rethinking tired constructs. *ELT Journal, 56*(3), 250–257.

Sternberg, R. J., & Williams, W. M. (2010). *Educational psychology* (2nd ed.). Upper Saddle River, NJ: Pearson.

Stevens, M. L. (2007). *Creating a class: College admissions and the education of elites.* Cambridge, MA: Harvard University Press.

Stevens, M. L., Armstrong, E. A., & Arum, R. (2008). Sieve, incubator, temple, hub: Empirical and theoretical advances in the sociology of higher education. *Annual Review of Sociology, 34*, 127–151.

Stuber, J. (2009). Class, culture, and participation in the collegiate extra-curriculum. *Sociological Forum, 24*(4), 877–900.

Sun, Q. (2008). Confucian educational philosophy and its implication for lifelong learning and lifelong education. *Lifelong Education, 27*(5), 559–578.

Taylor, E. (2003). Looking back five years: A critical review of transformative learning theory. In C. A. Wiessner, S. R. Meyer, N. L. Pfhal, & P. G. Neaman (Eds.), *Proceedings of the fifth international conference on transformative learning* (pp. 396–402). New York, NY: Teachers College Press.

Taylor, E. (2007). An update of transformative learning theory: A critical review of the empirical research. *International Journal of Lifelong education, 26*(2), 173–191.

Taylor, E. (2009). Fostering transformative learning. In J. Mezirow, E. W. Taylor, & Associates (Eds.), *Transformative learning in practice: Insights from community, workplace and higher education.* San Francisco, CA: Jossey-Bass.

Tennant, M. (2009). Lifelong learning as a technology of the self. In K. Illeris (Ed.), *Contemporary theories of learning* (pp. 147–158). London, UK: Routledge.

Tennant, M. (2012). *The learning self: Understanding the potential for transformation.* San Francisco, CA: Jossey-Bass.

Terhart, E. (2003). Constructivism and teaching: A new paradigm in general didactics? *Journal of Curriculum Studies, 35*(1), 24–36.

Torney-Purta, J., & Wilkenfeld, B. S. (2009). *Paths to 21st century competencies through civic education classrooms: An analysis of survey results from ninth-graders.* Washington, DC: Campaign for the Civic Mission of Schools and American Bar Association Division for Public Education. Accessed from http://www.civicyouth.org/?p=360

Tushman, M. L., & Romanelli, E. (1985) Organizational evolution: A metamorphosis model of convergence and reorientation. *Research in Organizational Behaviour, 7*, 171–222.

Tzanakis, M. (2011). Bourdieu's social reproduction thesis and the role of cultural capital in educational attainment: A critical review of key empirical studies. *Educate, 11*(1), 76–90.

Unal, G., & Akpinar, E. (2006). To what extent science teachers are constructivist in their classrooms? *Journal of Baltic Science Education, 10*(2) 40–50.

UNESCO-Beirut, Regional Office for Education in the Arab States. (2003). *Literacy and adult education in the Arab world.* Retrieved from http://www.unesco.org/education/uie/pdf/country/arab_world.pdf

United Nations Department of Economic and Social Affairs, Population Division. (2006). *Trends in total migrant stock: The 2005 revision.* New York, NY: Author.

REFERENCES

UAE Ministerial Decision No. 176. (February, 2009). Regulating the Termination of UAE Nationals Working in the Private Sector. *Emiratisation*. Retrieved from http://emiratisation.org/ index.php?option=com_content&view=article&id=125%3Aunder-what-conditions-can-an-emirate-employee-be-dismissed-&catid=65%3Ajobseekers-faqs&Itemid=98&lang=en

UAE, Ministry of the Economy. (2005). *UAE in numbers 2005*. Retrieved from http://www.economy.ae/English/EconomicAndStatisticReports/StatisticReports/Pages/ UAEinNumbers.aspx

UAE, Ministry of the Economy. (2010, March). *Tanmia (UAE National Human Resource Development and Employment Authority) Emiratization and leadership report*. Dubai, UAE: Author.

Understanding Islam. (2010). Doha, Qatar: Fanfar Qatar Islamic Cultural Center.

United States Department of State. (2010). *Report on international religious freedom in the United Arab Emirates*. Washington, DC: Author.

Vadeboncoeur, J., Hirst, E., & Kostogriz, A. (2006). Spacializing sociocultural research: A reading of mediation and meaning as third spaces. *Mind, culture & activity, 13*(3), 163–175.

Van den Branden, K. (2006). *Task-based language education: From theory to practice*. London, UK: Cambridge University Press.

Vogel-Walcutt, J., Gebrim, J. B., Bowers, C., Carper, T. M., & Nicholson, D. (2011). Cognitive load theory vs. constructivist approaches: Which best leads to efficient, deep learning? *Journal of Computer Assisted Learning, 27*(2), 133–145. doi: 10.1111/j.1365-2729.2010.00381.x

von Glasersfeld, E. (1990). An exposition of constructivism: Why some like it radical. In R. B. Davis, C. A. Maher, & N. Noddings (Eds.), *Constructivist views on the teaching and learning of mathematics* (pp. 19–29). Reston, VA: National Council of Teachers of Mathematics.

von Glasersfeld, E. (1996). Footnotes to "The many faces of constructivism". *Educational Researcher, 25*(6), 19.

Vygotsky, L. S. (1978). *Mind in society: The development of higher psychological processes*. Cambridge, MA: Harvard University Press.

Vygotsky, L. S. (1986). *Thought and language*. Cambridge, MA: MIT Press.

Wagner, T. (2008). *The global achievement gap: Why even our best schools don't teach the new survival skills our children need – And what we can do about it*. New York, NY: Basic Books.

Wang, H. (2007). Self-formation in a creative third space. *Studies in Philosophy & Education, 26*(4), 389–393.

Whiteoak, J., Crawford, N., & Mapstone, R. (2006). Impact of gender and generational differences in work values and attitudes in an Arab culture. *Thunderbird International Business Review, 48*(1), 77–91. doi:10.1002/tie.20086

Yorks, L., & Kasl, E. (2002). Toward a theory and practice for whole-person learning: Reconceptualizing experience and the role of affect. *Adult Education Quarterly, 52*(3), 176.

Zane, T. W. (2009). Performance assessment design principles gleaned from constructivist learning theory (Part 1). *TechTrends: Linking Research & Practice to Improve Learning, 53*(1), 81–90. doi: 10.1007/s11528-009-0242-5

Zhenhuan, Z. (2010). The "Dewey fever" in Jiangsu and Zhejiang during the May fourth movement and its relation to the cultural tradition in Jiangnan. *Chinese Studies in History, 43*(4), 43–62.

Zimmerman, M. A. (1995). Psychological empowerment: Issues and illustrations. *American Journal of Community Psychology, 23*, 581–599.